CU01302447

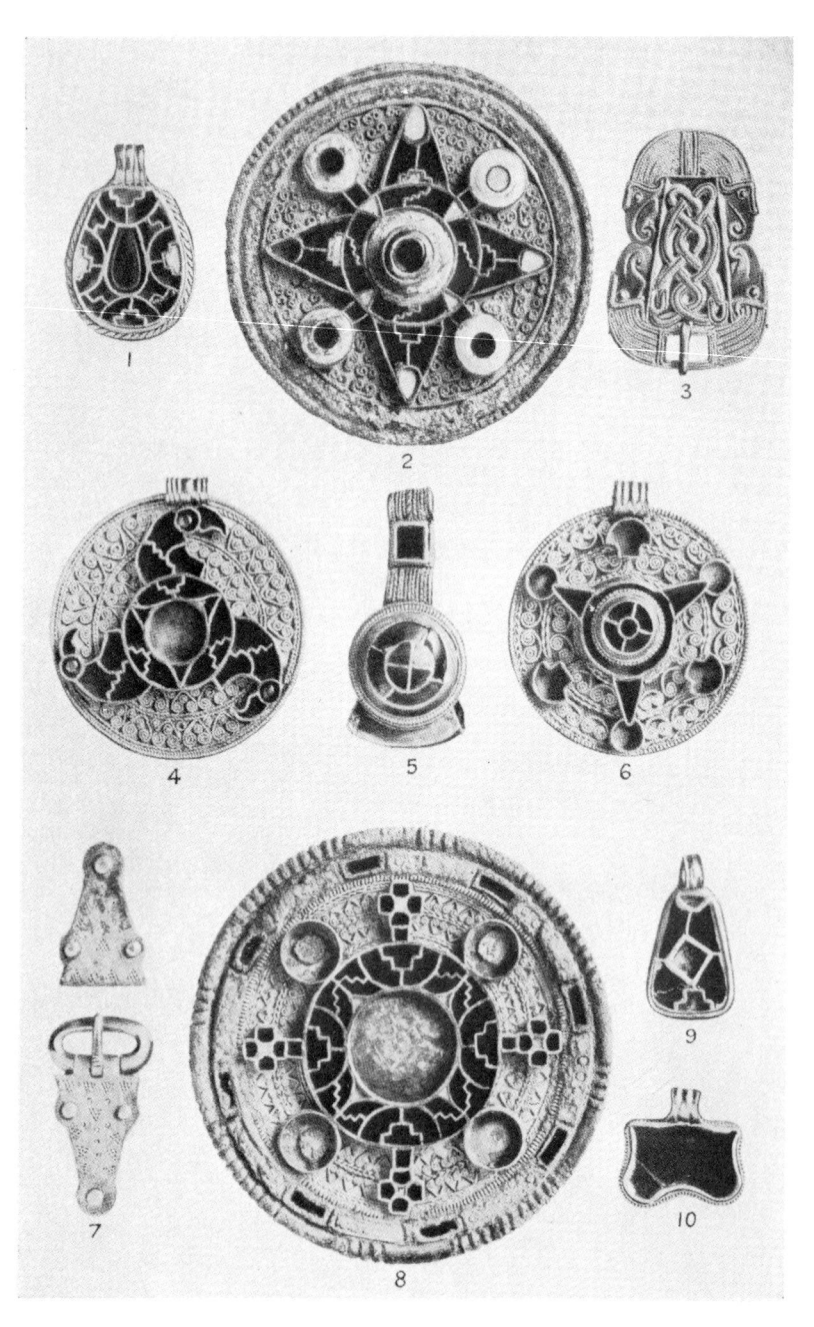

PLATE I. KENTISH JEWELLERY FROM FAVERSHAM AND WINGHAM (no. 2) (¼)
(Case D 5, see pp. 40, 57)

British Museum Guide to Anglo-Saxon Antiquities 1923

R. A. Smith

Anglia Publishing
Watts House
Capel St Mary, Ipswich
Suffolk, IP9 2JB

First published in Great Britain by order of the Trustees of the British Museum, 1923.

This edition published by Anglia Publishing, Ipswich, 1993.

Copyright in this typographic arrangement
© Anglia Publishing 1993.

Printed in Great Britain by The Ipswich Book Company.

ISBN 1-897874-03-0

Also in this series:
London Museum Medieval Catalogue 1940. ISBN 1-897874-01-4
Victoria and Albert Museum Catalogue of Rings 1930. ISBN 1-897874-02-2

Cover
An early Anglo-Saxon bronze-gilt square-headed brooch from Chessel Down, Isle of Wight.

FOREWORD

This is the third book in a series of facsimile reprints of classic guides to antiquities. *London Museum Medieval Catalogue 1940*, the first in the series, was written in the late 1930s. *Victoria and Albert Museum Catalogue of Rings 1930*, the second, was compiled between 1924 and 1929. *British Museum Guide to Anglo-Saxon Antiquities 1923* is a trifle earlier still and has never before been reprinted. It would be surprising if books more than 50 years old wholly represented present day thinking. Most do not and this book is no exception to the general rule. But no library would be complete without the classic reference works of previous generations. They laid the foundations upon which later scholars built. This new series from 'Anglia Publishing' serves to fill important gaps on the bookshelves of anyone involved in the study of archaeology or antiquities. It is my pleasure to introduce a further volume.

Essentially this is a catalogue of the Anglo-Saxon and foreign-related collections which were on display at the British Musum in 1923. Many of the objects were chance finds and many others emanated from excavations carried out between the mid-nineteenth century and 1914. The text of this book is based upon the scholarship of that period. It must not be forgotten that this book was first published 16 years before Basil Brown's excavations at Sutton Hoo. The evidence from this site, and many others discovered since, combined with the re-evaluation of a great many older ones, in Britain and Europe, using advanced techniques and new technology has done much to change theories and alter dates. The mass of information now available on pottery renders the section herein obsolete. The debate on the dating and classification of brooches continues, but there is no doubt that several cited here date from half a century or so later than indicated. Some other conclusions are in need of modification, but as so much has been written in recent years, it is unthinkable that any reader would use this text in isolation and, therefore, my general caution should suffice.

The foundations of the scholarship of the Anglo-Saxon subject were laid down by E.T. Leeds, G. Baldwin Brown and various other pre-war European archaeologists and historians. Their work still underpins much present thinking in this field. The contribution made by certain of these pioneers is acknowledged by Ormande M. Dalton, Keeper of the Department of British and Mediaeval Antiquities, in his original preface to this guide, which was written by his Deputy, Reginald A. Smith. Smith gives an overview of the history of the period from late Roman times through to the Norman Conquest. Although perhaps he takes some aspects of early literary sources too much at face value, he does state his awareness of the unreliability of many early dates in the *Anglo-Saxon Chronicle,* whilst not dismissing Bede's description of the coming of the Saxons to Britain. There is little that has been learned since that need fundamentally alter his account. Smith goes on to describe the development of art into the later Saxon period, drawing on a number of European parallels. Significantly, he reminds his readers that early English art and history must be viewed in a Continental context.

The remainder of the guide is a description of the exhibits, case by case, as they were displayed in 1923. The items are categorised by both function and cultural origin and, despite the passage of time, the guide still provides the reader with a well-illustrated and comprehensive catalogue of antiquities from Dark-Age and early mediaeval Europe. This comparative European material is particularly useful. Outside of specialist publications, there have been few similar selections compiled since. The glossy exhibition catalogues of more recent years show some of these items, but omit much more that is contained in this compact, but well-illustrated, volume. The arrangement of the display of the British Museum collection has, of course, altered radically since 1923. It has been relocated within the building in order to accommodate the many new additions, but significantly, many of the older items referred to herein can no longer be viewed in the public galleries.

When readers can turn to recent catalogues such as *The Golden Age of Anglo-Saxon Art 966-1066*, Backhouse, Turner and Webster (editors), 1984 and *The Making of England. Anglo-Saxon Art and Culture AD 600-900,* Webster and Backhouse (editors), 1992, wherein may be found the most comprehensive and up-to-date lists of further books, papers and articles, it would have been superfluous to provide a bibliography here.

Michael J. Cuddeford
Chelmsford
October, 1993

PREFACE

THE Collections described in Guides previously issued by the Department—those of the Stone Age, the Bronze Age, the Early Iron Age, and of Roman Britain—all comprise objects produced by different races inhabiting these islands at various times; but the present volume, which completes the series, will make a special appeal to the English people, as illustrating what is largely the handiwork of their own forefathers. It is hoped that with the help of these five Guides the visitor may now be able more easily to follow the development of the arts in Britain from the beginning down to the Norman Conquest, so far as the story can be illustrated within the walls of a museum.

The Anglo-Saxon and Foreign Teutonic collections are mainly exhibited on the South side of the Iron Age Gallery, but a certain number are for various reasons shown elsewhere. Heavy stone monuments will be found in the Roman Gallery on the ground floor. Works of art belonging to the Carolingian period, notably ivory carvings and crystal intaglios, are included in the Mediaeval collection at the West end of the King Edward VII Gallery; their characteristic figure-subjects connect them more nearly with the religious art of the advanced Middle Ages than with that of the centuries before Charles the Great, the essential feature of which is formal ornament of pagan origin. Charters and illuminated books of later Anglo-Saxon times take their place in the great series preserved in the Department of Manuscripts, and fine miniatures in books of the Winchester School are exhibited in the Grenville Library opening out of the Entrance Hall.

The task of describing the Collection has been rendered easier by the publication of Vols. III–V of Prof. Baldwin

PREFACE

Brown's *The Arts in Early England,* and by the opportune publication of works on the subject by Haakon Shetelig of Bergen, J. Brøndsted of Copenhagen, Nils Åberg of Upsala, and Prof. Rostovtzeff, late of Petrograd. Detailed references would be out of place in a Guide like the present, where the available space barely suffices for a description of the objects, and the general survey of the period given in the Introduction has been compressed within the narrowest possible limits.

The Trustees are indebted to the Council of the Society of Antiquaries for permission to use figs. 51-3, 69, 70, 116, 120, 138, 141, 160, 161, and 163; and to the Syndics of the Cambridge University Press for the map (fig. 1) from Prof. Chadwick's *The Origin of the English Nation.* Many of the illustrations are published for the first time, and all except those marked with an asterisk * are of objects in the collection. Those marked ($\frac{1}{1}$) are natural size. Any reduction is generally indicated by means of a fraction in brackets: thus ($\frac{1}{2}$) means that the original has twice the length and breadth, but four times the area, of the illustration. Further photographic reproductions in postcard form are to be obtained at the Sale counters in the Museum.

The Guide has been written by Mr. Reginald A. Smith, B.A., F.S.A., Deputy Keeper of the Department, and I have carefully read through the proofs.

O. M. DALTON, *Keeper.*

DEPARTMENT OF BRITISH AND
MEDIAEVAL ANTIQUITIES,
March 1923.

CONTENTS

	PAGE
List of Plates	vi
List of Illustrations	vii
Map of Anglo-Saxon settlements	xii
Introduction	1
Description of Exhibits :—	
Cases 43–5: pottery	20, 52
Evolution of brooches	23
Cases D 5, 48, 49 : Faversham (Gibbs collection) . . .	39
,, D 2, D 4 : other Kentish sites	52
,, D 2, D 1 : jewellery in Kentish style	60, 75
,, 46, 50 : Broomfield and Taplow burials . . .	63
,, 39, 40 : Chessel Down, I. W.	65
,, 37, 38 : Long Wittenham, Berks.	68
,, D 1 : East Shefford, Berks.	71
,, 42, 43 : Kempston, Beds.	72
,, D 1, D 2 : Leagrave and Desborough	75
,, 41 : bronze bowls	76
,, 45–7 : Wheathampstead, Croydon, Harnham Hill	80
,, 51, C : Anglian sites	82
,, 52, A 3, A 4, D 6 : tools, weapons, stirrups . . .	90
Central pedestal : Franks casket	96
Cases 52, D 3, D 2 : silver, enamel, seals . . .	98, 110
,, 52, A 5 : silver hoards	99, 107
,, D 2 : finger-rings and runes	114
,, 34, 35, ground-floor : Ogham and other gravestones	119
,, 53, 54, A 2 : Scotland and Ireland	127
,, A 1, B, 59, A 6, 57, 58 : France	142
,, B : Spain and Algeria	152
,, 60, 61 : Italy	153
,, 62, 63 : Germany and Hungary	156
,, 55, 56 : Scandinavia	158
,, 60, 64–6 : Balkans, S. Russia, Siberia	168
Index	175

LIST OF PLATES

I. Kentish jewellery, from Faversham and Wingham *Frontispiece*
(no. 2)
(Case D 5, see pp. 40, 57)   FACING PAGE

II. Cinerary urns found in England 20
(Cases 43, 44, see p. 21)

III. Anglo-Saxon and Viking jewellery from England . . . 42
(Cases D and A 5, see pp. 42, 57, 62, 117)

IV. Pendants with garnets, and gold necklace 62
(Case D 2, see pp. 61, 75)

V. Jewellery and bronze bowl from grave at Taplow . . . 63
(Case 50, see p. 64)

VI. Typical iron weapons, English and foreign 92
(Cases A 3, D 6, 57, 45, see pp. 65, 81, 92, 148)

VII. Horn sword-handle with gold filigree and garnets, Cumberland 93
(Case D 2, see p. 92)

VIII. The Franks casket of whale's bone, Northumbrian work . 98
(Central pedestal, see p. 96)

IX. Set of silver pins from the Witham, Lincoln . . . 100
(Case D 3, see p. 98)

X. Enamelled brooches, from Scotland and Italy . . . 101
(Cases D 2, 61, see pp. 101, 155)

XI. Gilt penannular brooches, eighth century 134
(Case A 2, see pp. 134, 136)

XII. The Breadalbane brooch, with disks on back . . . 135
(Case A 2, see p. 135)

XIII. Bell of St. Cuilleann in its shrine 142
(Case 53, see p. 141)

XIV. Jewellery from Herpes, Charente, France 143
(Case B, see p. 144)

XV. Foreign jewellery set with garnets 152
(Cases A 6, B, 61, 63, see pp. 150-2, 155)

XVI. Box-brooches of bronze from Gotland, ... 166
(Case 56, see p. 166)

XVII. Group of Livonian ornaments 167
(Case 64, see p. 174)

LIST OF ILLUSTRATIONS

FIG.		PAGE
1.	Map of Anglo-Saxon Settlements (after Chadwick) . . .	xii
2.	Bronze casting with development, Anán'ino, Vyatka, S. Russia	8
3.	Bronze plate with lions and 'chip-carving'	9
4.	Buckle with 'chip-carving' pattern, Smithfield . . .	9
5.	Terminals of drinking-horns, Taplow	10
6.	Sword-pommel, Crundale Down, Kent	11
7.	David and Goliath (Cotton MS. Tib. C. vi)	16
*8	Figure with Sword (Benedictional of St. Æthelwold) . .	16
9.	Engraved bronze-gilt plate, Berkshire	18
10.	Openwork bronze from Norway	18
11.	Stamped patterns on Anglo-Saxon pottery	21
12.	Bone comb and iron knife from urn, Eye	22
*13.	Bronze brooch with returned foot, Sweden	23
*14.	Primitive 'long' brooch, with back of head, Sweden . .	24
15.	Bronze 'long' brooch (front and side views)	24
16.	Long brooch, with side view, Malton, Cambs	26
17.	Bronze 'long' brooch, Kenninghall, Norfolk	27
18.	Bronze brooch with swastika, Sleaford, Lincs.	28
19.	Bronze cruciform brooch, Sleaford, Lincs.	28
*20.	Silver square-headed brooch, Denmark	29
21.	Square-headed brooch, Kenninghall	29
22.	Bronze-gilt square-headed brooch, Chessel Down, I. W. .	30
23.	Bronze round-headed brooch (front and back), Crimea . .	31
*24.	Bronze round-headed brooch (front and back), Crimea . .	32
25.	Bronze radiated brooch, Crimea	33
26.	Silver-gilt radiated brooch, Suffolk	33
27.	Bronze 'applied' brooch, Fairford	34
28.	Bronze-gilt saucer-brooch, Leighton Buzzard	34
29.	Bronze-gilt saucer-brooch, Oxfordshire	35
30.	Bronze-gilt saucer-brooch, found in England	35
31.	Bronze 'applied' brooch, Kempston	36
32.	Engraved disk-brooches, Long Wittenham, Berks. . . .	37
33.	Silver keystone brooch, Faversham	38
34.	Silver 'strap-end', with garnets, Faversham	40
35.	Buckle, with shoe-shaped rivets, Aisne, France . . .	40
36.	Iron buckle-plate, inlaid with silver, Faversham . . .	41
37.	Bronze plate engraved on both sides, Faversham . . .	42
38.	Engraved bronze disk, Faversham	42
39.	Silver buckle-plate, with side view, Faversham . . .	43
40.	Bronze-gilt pin, Faversham	43
41.	Bronze-gilt pin, Faversham	43
42.	Bronze-gilt buckle, Faversham	44
43.	Mount of drinking-cup, Faversham	44
44.	Bronze pyramid, with side and base, Faversham . . .	44

LIST OF ILLUSTRATIONS

FIG.		PAGE
45.	Silver finger-rings, Faversham	45
46.	Silver armlet, Faversham	45
47.	Bronze toilet implement, Faversham	46
48.	Bronze 'girdle-hanger', Faversham	46
49.	Ring-brooches, East Shefford and Faversham	48
50.	Draughtsmen, Taplow and Faversham	48
51.	Openwork escutcheon of a bowl, with side view, Faversham	49
52.	Enamelled escutcheon of bowl, with side view	50
53.	Enamelled escutcheons of bowls, Faversham	50
54.	Specimens of Anglo-Saxon glass	51
55.	Pottery bottles of Jutish type	52
56.	Jewelled square-headed brooch, Milton-next-Sittingbourne	53
57.	Jewelled square-headed brooch with disk on bow, Howletts	53
58.	Details of silver quoit-brooch, Howletts	54
59.	Details of silver quoit-brooch, Sarre	55
60.	Jewelled brooch and necklace of coins, Sarre	56
61.	Iron weaving-implement, Chessel Down, I. W.	56
62.	Bronze strap-end, Sarre	57
63.	Jewelled pin, Wingham	58
64.	Cruciform pendant, Wingham	58
65.	Bronze pin with cross, Breach Down	58
66.	Bronze buckles and counter-plate, Kent	60
67.	Bronze buckle-plate from Barn Elms	61
68.	Jewelled S-brooch, Iffley	62
69.	Openwork jewel with garnets, Twickenham	62
70.	Iron shield-boss, Twickenham	62
71.	Bronze-gilt mount of drinking-horn, Taplow	64
72.	Mount of drinking-cup, Taplow	65
73.	Crystal sphere with mounting, Chessel Down	66
74.	Sword-hilt with runes, Chessel Down	66
75.	Gilt pendant from bucket, Leagrave	67
*76.	Bucket with pendants (Maidstone Museum)	67
77.	Bronze bowl with iron handle, Long Wittenham	68
78.	Stoup and details, Long Wittenham	69
79.	Small square-headed brooches, Long Wittenham	71
80.	Bronze brooch, with side view, Kempston	72
81.	Equal-armed bronze brooch, Kempston	72
82.	Small bow-brooches, Kempston	73
83.	Bronze work-box, Kirby Underdale	74
84.	Meerschaum buckle, Kempston	74
85.	Badge in form of fish, Kempston	74
86.	Openwork bronze ring, Kempston	75
87.	Bronze pin with spangles, Leagrave	75
88.	Spoon, with side view, Desborough	76
89.	Hinged clasp, Desborough	76
90.	Bronze bowl, Faversham	77
91.	Bronze bowl with escutcheons, Ewelme	77
92.	Bronze hanging-bowl, Hawnby	78
93.	Enamelled escutcheon of bowl	79
94.	Bronze ewer, Wheathampstead	79
95.	Bronze-gilt head of pin, Harnham Hill	82
96.	Bone draughtsman and section, Pensthorpe	82
97.	Clasp of spiral wire, Kenninghall, Norfolk	83

LIST OF ILLUSTRATIONS

FIG.		PAGE
98.	Horned brooch, Farndish, Beds.	84
99.	Bronze-gilt clasp, Cambridgeshire	84
100.	Silver-gilt sleeve ornament	84
101.	Gold bracteate, Longbridge, Warwick	86
102.	Embossed silver disk, Caenby, Lincs.	86
*103.	Frieze of animals, Book of Durrow	86
104.	Bronze-gilt mounts, Caenby, Lincs.	87
105.	Openwork brooch with swastika, Sleaford	88
106.	Silver disk with triskele, Sleaford	88
107.	Girdle-hangers, with side view, Searby	89
108.	Bronze buckle with peacocks	90
*109.	Figure with axe. St. Gall MS.	90
110.	Inlaid stirrup, with side view, Thames at Battersea	91
111.	Shield-boss, section and handle	92
112.	Silver sword-handle (restored), Fetter Lane	93
113.	Sword from Thames, off the Temple	94
114.	King Canute (Stowe MS. 944)	94
115.	Bronze sword-guard, Exeter	95
116.	Scramasax with inscription, Sittingbourne	95
117.	Scramasax from the Thames, with Runes	96
118.	Silver chalice, Trewhiddle	99
119.	Silver scourge, Trewhiddle	100
120.	Ornaments from Trewhiddle hoard	100
121.	Enamelled brooch, Cambois, Bedlington, Northumberland	101
122.	Silver trefoil brooch, Kirkoswald	102
123.	Pendant cross of silver, Gravesend	103
124.	Silver brooch of Aelfgivu, Cuxton	103
125.	Bronze brooch, City of London	103
126.	Bronze book-clasp with design, Lincoln	104
127.	Bronze bucket with details, Hexham	105
128.	Embossed silver plate with bust, Hexham	106
129.	Part of leather sheath, Hexham	106
130.	Silver spoon and fork, Sevington	107
131.	Ornamental strap-ends	107
132.	Selection from silver hoard, Cuerdale	108
133.	Silver brooches and fragments from hoard, Goldsborough, W. R. Yorks	109
134.	Silver-gilt cup, Halton Moor, Lancs.	109
135.	Seal of Ethilwald, Eye	110
136.	Impression of King Coenwulf's seal	111
137.	Ivory seal of Godwin with impression and reverse	111
138.	Bone writing-tablet (inside and out), Blythburgh	112
139.	Bone carving (front and back) from the Thames	113
140	Bone pin from the Thames	113
141.	Bronze model of gravestone, Thames at Hammersmith	114
142.	Bone trial-piece from London	115
143.	Design on Ethelwulf's ring	115
144.	Gold ring of Ethelswith, with interior inscription, W. R. Yorks.	115
145.	Inscription on gold ring of Aethred, Lancashire	115
146.	Inscription on gold ring of Buredruth, near Swindon	116
147.	Gold ring with engraved bezels, near Peterborough	116
148.	Gold ring with runes, Kingmoor, Cumberland	116
149.	Agate ring with runic inscription	117

LIST OF ILLUSTRATIONS

FIG.		PAGE
150.	Bone comb-case with runes, Lincoln	117
151.	Runic inscription on bone, Derbyshire	118
152.	Terminal of bronze fitting, Thames	118
153.	Ogham characters	119
154.	Llywel stone showing Ogham inscription	120
155.	Small gravestones, Hartlepool	122
156.	Gravestone, Billingham, co. Durham	123
157.	Stone cross with runes, Lancaster	124
158.	Inscribed fragment of cross, Dewsbury	124
159.	Gravestone from City of London	125
160.	Design on gravestone, Bibury, Gloucs.	126
161.	Design on faces of gravestone, Bibury	127
162.	Stone slab with bull, Burghead	127
163.	Engraved stone with details, Portsoy, Banffshire	128
164.	Tortoise brooch, with side view, Barra, Hebrides	129
165.	Pin, Keady Mountain, co. Derry, Ireland	130
166.	Ornamented pin, Ireland	130
167.	Pin, Craigywarren Bog, co. Antrim, Ireland	131
168.	Pin, Clogher, co. Tyrone, Ireland	131
169.	Silver pin, with detail, Ireland	131
170.	Bronze latchet, Ireland	132
171.	Bronze latchet, Newry	132
172.	Enamelled bronze latchet, Dowris, King's co.	133
173.	Penannular brooch, Porth Dafarch, Holyhead	133
174.	Penannular brooch with birds' heads, Antrim	133
175.	Penannular brooch of silver	134
176.	Back of pin-head of brooches	134
177.	Detail from Londesborough brooch	135
178.	Silver penannular brooch (back)	135
179.	Silver penannular brooch (back), with design on edge, Donegal	135
180.	Bronze brooch, Killucan, co. Westmeath	136
181.	Part of penannular brooch, co. Westmeath	136
182.	Silver penannular brooch, Ireland	137
183.	Various pins from Ireland	138
184.	Bronze-gilt boss, Steeple Bumpstead, Essex	138
185.	Detail of Steeple Bumpstead boss	139
186.	Whorls on Steeple Bumpstead boss	139
187.	Bronze-gilt mount, Phoenix Park, Dublin	140
188.	Stone trial-piece, Killaloe, co. Clare	140
189.	Openwork bronze ornament, Ireland	141
190.	Bowl with pearled border, Herpes	145
191.	Frankish pottery	146
192.	Foreign Teutonic glass	146
193.	Frankish buckles from Charente and Marne	147
194.	Purse-guard set with garnets, Herpes	147
195.	Toilet implements from cemetery, Herpes	147
196.	Bronze clasp with hooks, Herpes	148
197.	Bone die, Herpes	148
198.	Bronze buckle from grave, Gourgançon	148
199.	Openwork bronze with Daniel and the lions, Amiens	149
200.	Enamelled brooch, with cross, France	150
201.	Bronze brooch, Moncetz, Marne	150
202.	Buckle-plates with cross, France	151

LIST OF ILLUSTRATIONS xi

FIG. PAGE
203. Silver-gilt finger-ring (developed) 151
204. Brooch in form of horse, with side view, France . . . 151
205. Pommel of sword with filigree, Seine 152
206. Bronze-gilt buckle with engraving, Algeria 152
207. Jewelled brooch with side view, Algeria 153
208. Radiated brooch, probably from Italy 154
209. Jewelled sword pommel, probably from Italy 155
210. Cruciform brooch, with side view, Hardanger, Norway . . 159
211. Bronze tortoise-brooch, with design, Bergen, Norway . . 160
212. Trefoil brooch, with detail, Roskilde, Denmark . . . 160
213. Gold bracteate, probably from Denmark 161
214. Folding scales and case, Gotland 162
215. Tracked stone (quartz), with side view, Upland, Sweden . . 162
216. Whale's bone plaque with horses' heads, Namdalen, Norway . 163
217. Iron-mounted pottery bucket, near Bergen, Norway . . 164
218. Bronze key of padlock, Denmark 164
219. Brooches with disk on bow, Gotland 165
220. Scandinavian box-brooch (side, bottom, and top views) . . 166
221. Evolution of boar's head brooch 167
222. Bronze chape of scabbard, Gotland 168
223. Silver-gilt belt with garnet cell-work, Sofia 169
224. Brooch with side and back views, and buckle, Kerch . . 171
225. Iron bridle-bit with bridle-spurs, Kerch 171
226. Silver figures of lions, Kanef, Kiev 172
227. Engraved silver brooch, near Kanef 172
228. Buckle with openwork plate, Kanef 173
229. Ornaments from Govt. Kiev 173
230. Radiated brooch, Govt. Kiev 173
231. Brooch with returned foot, Kiev 173
232. Silver bracelet with engraved panels, Govt. Kiev . . . 174

Fig. 1. Map of Anglo-Saxon Settlements (after Chadwick).

(By permission of Cambridge University Press)

INTRODUCTION

THE first mention of Saxons in British history occurs in the time of Carausius (A. D. 286), when the Roman province was suffering from piratical raids, not only by these barbarians from beyond the North Sea, but by Picts and Scots nearer home; and in spite of a period of peace and prosperity under Constantine the Great, it was this pressure from without that put an end not merely to Roman rule in Britain but also to the civilization which had resulted from four centuries of association in the Empire. In 364, during the reign of Valentinian I, the Saxons made another assault on Britain; and although the record is imperfect, it may be inferred that descents on the coast and raids inland became more common as the Roman power declined. Once imperial protection was withdrawn in 410, the end cannot have been far off; and when the curtain is raised again in the sixth century, a large part of the province is in the occupation of Saxons and their kinsmen from beyond the seas. To them the Britons were Welsh or foreigners; and the representatives of the race that had subdued the country in the Early Iron Age and absorbed a full share of Roman civilization, were gradually relegated to the mountains of the west, the Welsh principality of our own day, where the Keltic tongue still bears witness to their foreign connexions. The explicit statement of the Venerable Bede as to the original homes of the Teutonic invaders seems to embody the national tradition, and the main facts may well have been transmitted to him intact, as the interval was little more than two hundred years. The immigrants, he says, belonged to three of the leading nations of Germany—the Saxons, Angles, and Jutes. Those who settled in Kent and the Isle of Wight were Jutes, and even in his day there was a Jutish settlement in West Saxon territory opposite the Isle of Wight. The East, South, and West Saxons were an offshoot of the Old Saxons, as they were called when he wrote; and from the district called in Latin *Angulus*, situated between the Jutes and Saxons, and left uninhabited down to his own time, came the Angles, who settled in East and Middle Anglia, in Mercia and Northumbria (the district beyond the Humber), and elsewhere (fig. 1).

Archaeology confirms this connexion between Kent and Wight (p. 66), but the Cantwaras (in Latin, *Cantuarii*) are not elsewhere described as Jutes, and like the other early settlers are called

Saxons or Angles indifferently. The Romans, Welsh, and Irish generally spoke of these Teutonic invaders as Saxons, but they themselves preferred the English name, e.g. *Angelcyn* (the English nation) and *Angelcynnes lond* (the land of the English nation); and Bede himself in more than one passage uses the terms Saxon and Angle as almost synonymous and not exclusive of the Jutes. The relics, however, endorse this triple division, and throw some light on the source and progress of the various invasions that carved England out of Britain.

From 286 onwards the Latin historians used Saxon as a general term to denote the pirates who infested the North Sea and compelled the imperial government to fortify the south-east coast, their contemporaries the Picts and Scots coming respectively from Scotland and the north of Ireland. But there is geographical (if not ethnological) warrant for Bede's classification, and the 'Saxon Shore' (from Southampton Water to the Wash) subsequently formed part of Saxon, Kentish, and East Anglian kingdoms. The geographer Ptolemy in the second century placed the Saxons north of the Elbe, 'on the neck of the Cimbric peninsula' (the modern Holstein), with access to the North Sea. In the third century they coalesced with the Chauci and occupied together the province of Hanover, between the Elbe and the Ems. Early in the sixth century the Old Saxons are found bordering on the Frisians, who held the Dutch coast, and spoke a language more closely related than any other to English. Both Tacitus and Ptolemy are vague as to the territory of the Angli; but if Bede's version is correct, they were a Baltic people from what is now called Slesvig (more precisely from Angel, between the Sle and the Flensborg Fiord); and a plausible inference is that the Saxons were their neighbours originally on the west and the Jutes originally inhabited Jutland, in spite of some linguistic difficulties in this identification. According to Prof. Chadwick, the evidence of the social systems (such as the *wergeld* or price of a life) confirms in a striking manner Bede's statement that the inhabitants of Kent were of a different nationality from those of the surrounding kingdoms. It is, however, difficult to reconcile the archaeological evidence with this hypothesis. As Mr. Leeds has pointed out, the characteristic Kentish jewellery and pottery point unmistakably to the Rhine about Bonn and Cologne, certainly not to Jutland, unless indeed the gold bracteates can be traced to Danish originals. At a time when many tribes were seeking new territory, it is possible that a number of Jutes moved 350 miles south by west to the lower Rhine and thence to Britain, after absorbing the Frankish culture; or the Jutish royal house may have led a Frankish host across the Channel late in the fifth century, as there are a few examples in Kent of early Frankish workmanship (p. 40). The Saxons in any case had reached the Rhine about the middle of the fourth century.

The break with Rome in A.D. 410 (or some thirty years later, according to Prof. Bury) was probably regretted on both sides and was certainly not the fault of the Romanized Britons who, when left to their own resources, offered a prolonged resistance to desperate enemies attacking them on every side. For how long and to what extent the civilization of Rome survived in Britain cannot now be accurately estimated. By some writers the Britons are said to have saved the elements of culture, including the Christian religion, which they had openly professed since 323; but another opinion, for which there is only too much evidence, is that religion, government, the arts, and the amenities of life all disappeared in the pagan deluge, and life in Britain sank to a level lower than Julius Caesar found it five centuries before. The Welsh monk Gildas was in a sense the mouthpiece of the unfortunate natives, but his testimony is vitiated by sectarian bias and a limited outlook; and the only hope of filling in the outlines lies in further archaeological discoveries.

That Vortigern invited Hengist and Horsa to defend Britain from the Picts, and that successive arrivals of Jutes enabled the brothers to become masters of Kent, is not unlikely; but the date of their arrival is uncertain, the year 428 for this event being derived from Welsh sources and 449 from Saxon records. Perhaps different stages of the Jutish conquest are marked by these dates, but the area conquered is beyond all doubt. The same cannot be said of the West Saxon invasion, which is dated half a century later. The manner in which the campaigns are recorded inspires little confidence; and if, as Bede mentions, Jutes occupied the Isle of Wight and the adjoining district of Hampshire, it is unlikely that Southampton Water gave the West Saxons access to the interior. On the other hand there is strong archaeological evidence, as Sir Henry Howorth has contended, for an original advance up the Thames, and an early settlement of West Saxons in the upper valley of that river (Berkshire, Oxfordshire, Gloucestershire, and N. Wilts.). This would bring them into line with the East and Middle Saxons, though Middlesex was not one of the early political divisions. Sixth-century remains of the West Saxons are extremely rare in Hampshire (which is usually regarded as their head-quarters at the time), and seem to be unknown in Dorset. If Gen. Pitt-Rivers's theory of the Wansdyke is accepted, it was in the south-west that the Romanized Britons were secluded and protected by the great earthwork that seems to have run, with its ditch on the north, from Portbury on the Bristol Channel, south of Bristol and Bath and through Savernake to Inkpen; and Bokerly Dyke and other earthworks within the area may mark the gradual shrinkage of the

British holding before the advancing Saxons. As the territorial names north of Essex indicate, all the east coast of what subsequently became England, was seized by Angles, who gradually penetrated inland and broke up into several petty kingdoms. It was only in the reign of Offa (777) that the Thames became the southern frontier of the Mercians, and Wessex was confined between that river and the south coast.

History and archaeology alike support the view that Essex never formed part of East Anglia; and the conclusion is that the Stour separated Saxon and East Anglian from the first. As a defence against invasion on the land side it was of little value, and its estuary would only invite settlers from beyond the sea to occupy territory north or south of the river. Perhaps this frontier was agreed upon by two kindred peoples, or one people later provided with local designations; but the foundation of either kingdom is only dated in the vaguest manner. Essex first appears in history as a sub-kingdom included in the dominions of Æthelberht of Kent (560–616), who ruled as far north as the Humber. The absence or extreme rarity of cinerary urns attributable to the pagan invaders of Essex, suggests a difference both in date and nationality between the East Saxon and East Anglian settlers, the latter arriving first, but only coming into prominence under their king Rædwald (593–617) who, according to Bede, superseded Æthelberht as Bretwalda, or paramount chief of Britain. If the genealogies can be trusted, the East Anglian state was founded by Rædwald's grandfather about 520, when a great British victory in the West forced the invaders to consolidate rather than extend their conquests.

North of Essex the east coast was occupied by the Angles, perhaps as far north as the Firth of Forth, for it is held by some that Edinburgh was founded by Edwin of Northumbria (617–33). The country north of the Humber and east of the Pennines consisted of Bernicia, bounded on the south by the Tyne, with Bamborough established as its capital in 547; and Deira, corresponding to Yorkshire, founded by Aella (585–8). With one possible exception from Buchan, Aberdeenshire, no cinerary urns of Anglian type have been found in Scotland; and it may be that cremation had ceased before the middle of the sixth century, though Christianity did not reach these parts till about 635, and communion with Canterbury and Rome was delayed till the synod of Whitby in 664.

Relations between the English and Scandinavian tribes are implied in the Anglo-Saxon poem of *Beowulf*, the only manuscript of which is in the British Museum. It dates about the year 1000, but deals with events of the early sixth century, combined with a large portion of legend. The hero was a prince of the Geatas, a people living near the great lakes of Sweden and in the Baltic island of Gotland. They had friends in Denmark, but to the north of them lay the Swedes (Svear) who were destined to take the lead in Sweden (p. 161). There are Christian traces in the poem, but hardly anything of English history; and its interest here is the evidence it affords of intercourse between Teutonic peoples on both sides of the North Sea at a time when gold was abundant (p. 161), and just before the break in those relations as indicated by the long brooches (p. 27). The lays may have been composed about 550, but were not committed to writing till early in the eighth century, an obvious parallel being the poems of Homer.

Though full of archaeological interest, the Anglo-Saxon epic throws little light on the two centuries of tribal movements and settlement, which are the most obscure in English history; and for this Migration period the sole contemporary authority on the native side is Gildas, the British Jeremiah, who refers to the last appeal to Rome in 446 as the Groans of the Britons. He wrote the *De Excidio*, etc., about 545-6, and though ignorant of the course of events a century before, can be trusted for contemporary events, and puts the battle of Mount Badon, near the mouth of the Severn, in the year of his own birth. This was probably between 500 and 503, though according to a Welsh record the victory took place in 516-17, and so far checked the Anglo-Saxon advance inland that the invaders had to content themselves with isolated settlements on the coast till the West Saxons resumed their conquests under Cuthwulf in 571. A battle at Bedford in that year led to the surrender of the four towns—Aylesbury, Bensington (Benson), Eynsham, and perhaps Lenbury—but it has been suggested, in view of the alleged foundation of the West Saxon kingdom in 519, that these places were captured, not from the Britons, but from some Teutonic tribe that had penetrated beyond the Chilterns.

In any case this campaign must be regarded merely as an attempt to extend the frontier of Wessex north of the Thames, and there is ample archaeological evidence that the Upper Thames basin, as well as certain localities on the south side of the river towards its mouth, had then been in West Saxon occupation perhaps a century. The sequence at Frilford, for instance, four miles west of Abingdon, Berks., can be explained historically, and seems to be complete for the pagan period. Interments in leaden coffins are shown by coins to date from the fourth century; and graverows practically east and west, without coffins, may be referred to the Romanized Britons of the fifth century when their prosperity had waned. The invading Teuton is represented by urns containing cremated bones, and this funeral rite was essentially pagan, though unburnt burials were by no means exclusively Christian, as the fourth series at Frilford consisted of shallow inhumations, without any regular orientation, but provided with the usual grave-furniture of the Anglo-Saxons. Here and again at Mitcham, Surrey, the finds prove Saxon settlement at least as early as A. D. 500. According to the Chronicle, Aella and his three sons established themselves in Sussex in 477, and Cerdic conquered the Isle of Wight in 530; but both the island and the Meon district in south-east Hampshire seem to have been Jutish till 661, when the Mercian king Wulfhere handed them over to Sussex to be a thorn in the side of Wessex. Winchester appears to have become the West Saxon capital about 643.

In 577 Ceawlin advanced into what was undoubtedly British territory, and gained a victory at Deorham (Dyrham) ten miles from Bath, thus driving a wedge into the Welsh position and separating the south-west from the Severn valley. The half century following the battle of Mount Badon is filled with entries in the *Anglo-Saxon Chronicle* of a suspicious character, events and personages being apparently deduced from place-names; and in any case the Chronicle was only compiled under Alfred about 891-2, and for the fifth and sixth centuries was based on Bede's *Ecclesiastical History*, which was written in Latin about 730 and incorporates Anglo-Saxon traditions not always consistent with the Welsh authorities. The *Historia Brittonum*, generally known by the name of Nennius (who edited it about 800) and dating about 680-5, gives the story of Hengist and Horsa, but has not enough independent authority to make King Arthur anything but a legendary character: his reign is given in Keltic authorities as 467-93, by others on the Saxon side as 517-42. It is possible that the Arthurian legend sprang from the exploits of Ambrosius Aurelianus, who seems to have claimed or inherited the imperial purple as independent ruler of Britain, and as leader of the national forces to have resisted the barbarian invaders during the last thirty years of the fifth century, much as Alfred did 400 years later.

Christianity had been the state religion since the days of Constantine, and Gildas the monk naturally emphasizes the paganism of the invaders, though he can hardly be regarded as typical of the British church. The Irish were not entirely strangers to Christianity and had Palladius as their bishop in 431, but owed their conversion mainly to St. Patrick and his followers; and from about 432, when the Saint landed near Wicklow from Gaul, where he had been trained after leaving his home in Britain, the new faith was received with enthusiasm. Missionary zeal was a special feature of the Irish Church; and St. Columba, who crossed from Ulster to Hii (erroneously called Iona, a misreading of Ioua) about 563, found that others had begun the conversion of the Dalriad Scots, who had established the kingdom of Strathclyde in 498. From the same small Scottish island Aidan was sent to the Northumbrian court in 635, and with king Oswald's encouragement brought the Anglian kingdom over to the Irish Church. It is a reflection on the traditional Christianity of Roman Britain that the Welsh king Cadwallon showed more bitterness than his pagan ally Penda of Mercia against Edwin, the Christian king of Northumbria, who was killed in battle against them at Hatfield, near Doncaster, in 633. Nor was this an isolated instance. Two centuries before, St. Patrick's letter of protest showed that Coroticus (Ceretic), the Christian ruler of Strathclyde with Dumbarton as his capital, had led or sent his 'Roman' soldiers in company with the heathen Picts of Galloway to raid the coast of Ireland, probably in Dalriada, where the Christian inhabitants, including some newly baptized still clothed in white, were killed or captured, and their homes despoiled.

The poverty of the British church, its isolation from the continent, and the rare occurrence of ritual objects familiar elsewhere, all tend to minimize the value of archaeological evidence as to the prevalence of Christianity; and even the Long Wittenham stoup (p. 69) from a grave in Wessex is not a native product, but almost certainly came from Gaul with which the converted Britons had been in communication at least till 454. The record of visits paid by Germanus, bishop of Auxerre, first (429) with Lupus of Troyes and later with Severus of Trèves, throws some light on the period, their object being to put an end to the Pelagian heresy.

Little trace of British art and industry can indeed be found anywhere in the country during what is known as the Migration period, the standard of civilization reached by either side being then at its lowest. There is certainly a small class of enamelled bronzes—escutcheons for attaching chains to hanging bowls (p. 79) found in various parts of England and dating probably from the seventh century—which exhibit surprising skill both in the art of enamelling and in design (as in Britain before the Roman conquest), but they are merely exceptions to the rule that art in England was Teutonic, inspired to some extent by classical models, but essentially barbaric and to the British population something new and strange.

The comparative abundance and general uniformity of Anglo-Saxon relics, which are mostly recovered from the graves, might be taken to support the theory that the Britons were exterminated wherever the invaders settled in force; but it must be remembered that even in Devon and Cornwall, Wales and Cumbria, there are practically no relics of this period, except gravestones with epitaphs poorly carved in questionable Latin; so that the comparison fails for want of material. The view now generally taken is that the Romanized Briton, retaining perhaps some scanty relics of his religion, art, and education, was suffered to remain in the occupied regions, but only in a subordinate class. It was against this Teutonic tyranny that Gildas hurled invective from Holy Writ about the middle of the sixth century.

About the same time Teutonic art shook itself free of classical tradition, and reached the stage designated by Dr. Bernhard Salin of Stockholm in 1904 as Style I. With regard to its origin, archaeologists have been at issue for a generation, some regarding the Teutonic animal-ornament as a mere adaptation of classical (provincial Roman) motives, others claiming these grotesque forms as an independent Teutonic invention. A compromise has now been reached, and the Germanic craftsman is found to have trans-

FIG. 2. Bronze casting with development, Anán'ino, Vyatka, S. Russia. ($\frac{2}{3}$)

formed the semi-oriental models as thoroughly, though not so artistically, as the early Briton transformed the European art of La Tène.

Western Asia was the ultimate source of early Teutonic art, and it was from the Scythian culture of South Russia that the Goths acquired the taste for animal ornament, of which a specimen from Anán'ino is illustrated (fig. 2). It shows a quadruped in course of dissolution owing to repeated copying; the hind-leg is twisted over the back in the Scythian manner; and the eye and open jaws, as well as the suppression of two legs, can be matched on many specimens of the sixth century in the West. Contact perhaps with the Sarmatians gave the Germanic immigrants a taste for coloured effects (polychromy), obtained either by fixing precious stones of convex form (*en cabochon*) to flat surfaces by means of collars (as in the famous Szilágy Somlyó hoard, dating just before 400), or by arranging sliced garnets and other stones in a number of adjacent cells (*cloisonné*) to form a pattern (as in the Sofia belt, fig. 223). This oriental love of colour enables us to trace the progress of the Gothic element over most of Europe; and, like the animal motive, it dominated Teutonic art throughout the Migration period.

Apart from the classical revival under the Emperor Charlemagne

(768-814) when acanthus foliage became a dominant feature, Teutonic art mainly consisted of animal ornament applied to flat surfaces. The animal represented is generally a nondescript quadruped, perhaps derived from the lion; but a head somewhat resembling that of a horse is often found in low relief (fig. 14), and the head of a bird or gryphon recalls the early connexion between the Goths while yet in South Russia (p. 170), and the oriental civilization of Iran. A transitional stage is illustrated in a bronze plate obtained in Rome (fig. 3), which can be dated approximately by a series from the Franco-Roman cemetery at Vermand, in the French department of the Aisne, about A.D. 400. It shows a geometrical design executed in the manner of chip-carving in wood, known by the German name of *Keil-* or *Kerbschnitt* owing to the V or wedge-shaped incisions imitated in casting. Running scrolls are often found in this technique (as fig. 4), accompanied by stars or other geometrical patterns, as on certain saucer-brooches (fig. 28), and wood-carving in this style is to this day characteristic of Scandinavia; but the Teutonic element in the Migration period was rather the animal form that at first appears only on the edge, in a complete and intelligible form. In that position it was capable of extension lengthwise; but as it gradually invaded the field, difficulty was experienced in filling angular and irregular spaces with this motive, and recourse was had to multiplication and division. The animal was split up into head, trunk, and

FIG. 3. Bronze plate with lions and 'chip carving'. ($\frac{3}{4}$)

FIG. 4. Buckle with 'chip-carving' pattern, Smithfield. ($\frac{2}{3}$)

limbs, and any one part was repeated in rows without any regard to logic or anatomy.

Teutonic art stands in vivid contrast to the classical, though both derived many of their motives from the animal world. In the early centuries of our era animal designs of Iranian origin served the Germanic purpose, which was to decorate the surface, without symbolism or idealism, and with little fidelity to any animated model. Among Greeks and Romans, on the other hand, the leading idea in art was representation, a rendering more or less idealized of the human form, or familiar plants and animals—a portrait rather than a pattern.

In England the 'chip-carving' style is characteristic of the period A.D. 500-50: and was followed by Style I (about 550 600), in which the Teutonic treatment of the animal motive is practically the same all over the conquered territory of Western Europe except Gaul, the Lombards introducing it into Italy after the invasion of 568. It was more remarkable for its gilding and execution than for design; and when dismemberment and degeneration had ruined the animal motive, a new decorative principle came to restore cohesion and give some meaning to the animal form, grotesquely unnatural as it still remained throughout the Teutonic area. Only in a few cases (as on the gold bracteates) can any symbolism be detected, and the animal motive in Teutonic hands was frankly and fundamentally ornamental, merely a device for filling spaces on the flat.

FIG. 5. Terminals of drinking-horns, Taplow. (⅔)

Teutonic art in Style II belongs to the seventh century and more particularly to Scandinavia and central Europe, owing its inception to influences from eastern Europe. The new feature is interlacing, which, though occasionally found in the late sixth century, now profoundly alters the anatomy and application of the traditional animal. It had a splendid development in Scandinavia (as in the early Vendel finds), but is poorly represented in England and west of the Rhine, except in Burgundy. It is also rare in Italy, the Lombards having been drawn into the Byzantine orbit soon after A.D. 600.

The dismembered animal gives place in Style II to a fantastic creature represented in profile, with an angular band behind the eye, extending above or below it (sometimes in both directions); also double profile-lines to represent the body, but instead of enclosing a space, interlacing with each other in any direction and to any extent. Another characteristic of the seventh century is the angular lower jaw (fig 5, top); but though the head is often carefully executed, the complete animal is even rarer than in Style I, and legs became a superfluity. The transition to interlacing is well represented by the sword pommel from the Isle of Wight (fig. 6), which has a pair of elongated animals confronted, with coherent bodies and elongated heads but without the typical point on the lower jaw. It may be placed early in the seventh century.

To this century as well as to the late sixth and early eighth belong the small Anglo-Saxon coins known as *sceattas* (a word with the same root as the German *Schatz*, treasure), which circulated in the south of England

FIG. 6. Sword-pommel, Crundale Down, Kent. (¹⁄₁)

and represent the earliest mintage on a large scale among the Anglo-Saxons. The art displayed on these coins is in some respects distinct from that of contemporary ornaments from the graves, and has been specially studied by Prof. Baldwin Brown. This form of silver currency was derived from the Frankish *triens*, or third of the Roman *solidus* or *aureus* (a gold coin known later as the bezant, from its connexion with Byzantium, and somewhat larger than an English half-sovereign); but the two series differed in many respects beside the metals employed. The *sceatta* types are surprisingly varied, and include such Roman motives as the female centaur and Romulus and Remus with the Wolf; the Christian emblem possibly copied by a pagan moneyer, various animals and birds, and the vine-scroll which recalls the leading motive of Northumbrian sculpture from about A.D. 670 to 870. The full-face occurs both on the coins and on objects from the graves, but the profile head is confined to the *sceattas*, and is one of many features which distinguish the artistic styles of the two series. It should be noted that *sceattas* are also found in Holland (the ancient Frisia), a country with which England had much intercourse at that time; but it is clear that a large proportion were struck in England, where they are almost the only artistic products in the south between 650 and 750. The *sceatta* currency was in part contemporary with the Northumbrian *styca* (from the German *Stück*, a piece) which was often inscribed. Then in the midlands and south came the penny, first struck by Offa of Mercia (757–796), whose coinage ranks among the most successful of the Charlemagne period. Examples are exhibited in the Coins and Medals Exhibition gallery near the head of the main staircase.

The eighth century was marked by the domination of Mercia, which was originally built up of several Anglian groups with a permanent capital at Tamworth on the border of Staffordshire and Warwickshire. Extension of its limits further south brought most of England under a single rule, and might have resulted in the unification of the country, if Offa's heirs had proved of equal ability. Between 760 and 777 he seems to have conquered all the minor states south of the Humber, and in the latter year, by his victory over Wessex at Bensington, became master of the Chilterns. But these events were too late to affect the archaeology of the grave-finds, and the previous century is more important from that point of view. The original centre of Mercia was the Trent valley near Burton, and the remains support the view that the Mercians were the most westerly body of Angles, their kinsmen the Middle and South Angles having occupied or obtained control of that part of the Midlands lying between Sherwood on the north and Arden and Rockingham Forest on the south. They were thus the neighbours of the West Saxons and the Hwiccas of the Lower Severn, originally allied to Wessex; but as the southern kingdom declined, the Mercians pressed southwards under Wulfhere (657–675), the son of Penda, the last champion of paganism in England. Shifting frontiers may therefore explain a certain mixture of types in the valleys of the Severn and Warwickshire Avon, though these events hardly belonged to the pagan period.

From about 670 dates an artistic phase in the north of England that may be accounted for by historical events. By that time the conversion of the English to Christianity had been almost completed, the last province to renounce the worship of Woden (Odin) being the Isle of Wight, at the instance of Bishop Wilfrid (686). The heathen practice of depositing weapons and ornaments with the dead consequently ceased about the middle of the century; and burials were henceforth confined to the consecrated ground of the churchyard, where the orthodox direction of a grave was east and west, with the head at the west end. In consequence of this change in funeral rites, later relics of Anglo-Saxon art and industry are rare, and have with few exceptions been either preserved by the Church or accidentally discovered in the soil. But though grave-furniture came to an end, Christian graves were often marked by stone crosses, many of which have survived, especially in the north of England, Scotland, Ireland, and the Isle of Man. The earliest of the series (perhaps dating from the Roman period) are slabs carved with a cross or the Christian monogram (the Chi-Rho, or first two Greek letters of the name Christ), with a commemorative inscription below; and in Wales and Cornwall epitaphs in rude Roman capitals and barbarous Latin may be attributed to the British church that survived from the days of Constantine.

It was in Northumbria at this time that sculpture reached its highest development, and its oriental inspiration is no longer questioned. Theodore of Tarsus in Cilicia, 'the last and greatest of the foreign primates', arrived in England in 669 and may have given a new direction to artistic impulse in the north. In any case it was about his time that the Syrian vine-scroll and figure-sculpture were introduced into a district where suitable stone was available for the sculptor. Such masterpieces as the Bewcastle and Ruthwell crosses were not the earliest of their kind, though they date about 670–80, when Northumbria was still the leading power in England; and the Franks casket (pl. VIII) was produced a generation later. A gradual change can be traced for almost two centuries, and the style succumbed to Danish influence about 875. At first the birds and animals that occupied singly the loops of foliage (as on the ivory chair of Maximian at Ravenna in the sixth century) were subordinate features of the design; but from about 750 they became independent of the vine-scroll, and during the ninth century played a dominant rôle on Northumbrian crosses. A precious example of the early style in metal is the Ormside bowl of gilt metal, now in the York Museum.

In the eighth century Teutonic art reached its zenith, and Salin's Style III flourished in Scandinavia, but is not represented in the British Isles though Ireland had a parallel development. Some of the best examples were derived from the later graves at Vendel, Upland (the earlier being in Style II). Essentially it is the decoration of flat surfaces with grotesque animal forms interlaced with amazing dexterity; and the head, limbs, and body can readily be distinguished from those of their predecessors.

Towards the end of the century, panels of animal forms in Style III are often found (as in Gotland) on the same objects (p. 166) as a new style, distinct in origin and character, and due to the renaissance of art under Charlemagne in the West. It can be traced back to classical motives which were then still available in south and south-east Europe; and, apart from a stiff variety of acanthus foliage generally used as a border, consisted for the most part of a quadruped (originally a lion), represented in plastic form and generally connected with others of its kind by biting or gripping of the limbs (fig. 164 and pl. xvi, no. 4). At this period the Teutonic North was evidently in communication with the West, the importation and adoption of the trefoil brooch (fig. 212) being sufficient evidence in itself; and the Scandinavian development of animals in relief is abundantly illustrated in the ship and furniture found at Oseberg on the west side of Christiania Fiord, the work on which covers the period about 800-50. This blend is expressed in the equation Oseberg I = Vendel II with the addition of Carolingian motives, such as the 'grasping' animal.

Contemporary with Style III (and in a sense parallel to it, as an outcome of Style II) was a brilliant development of art in Ireland, resulting in such masterpieces as the Books of Durrow and Kells, the Tara and Hunterston (Scotland) brooches, and the Ardagh chalice, all probably in existence by 750. Some of these are obviously connected with the Christian religion which had been planted in the island four centuries before, but there is a curious paucity of recognized Christian symbols in artistic products of this time, and Irish crosses only become prominent during the Viking period. Irish art in its best phase is represented in the British Museum by the Londesborough silver-gilt brooch (locality unknown) and the Steeple Bumpstead boss (found in Essex); nor can the Lindisfarne Gospels (Gospels of St. Cuthbert or Book of Durham) in the Dept. of MSS. be passed over, though its art is not of purely Irish origin, in spite of the early connexion of Lindisfarne (or Holy Island, off Northumberland) with the Irish community under St. Columba (p. 6), Aidan having fixed his see there in 635. It is generally described as Hiberno-Saxon, and was written and illuminated by Eadfrith, probably before he became bishop of Lindisfarne in 698. Certain liturgical features of the text point to some connexion with Naples; and it is significant that Adrian came to England from an island monastery off Naples in 668-9, and visited Lindisfarne with Theodore, archbishop of Canterbury, who reorganized the English Church (669-90). But above all, Northumbria owed its artistic predominance in the time of Bede to Benedict Biscop who was a great builder (founded Wearmouth 674 and Jarrow 682), and is known to have collected many books, pictures, and vestments on his frequent journeys to Rome. These would serve as models in the *Scriptorium* of the monastery, and counterbalance to some extent the decorative fancies of Irish art at its best. The figure-subjects were certainly taken from imported miniatures, and the St. Matthew in the Lindisfarne Gospels is almost identical with a seated figure (perhaps a South Italian portrait of Cassiodorus in his library) in the first quire of the *Codex Amiatinus*, now at Florence. This manuscript is known to have been in the possession of Ceolfrid of Jarrow, who died at Langres in 716 on his way to Rome with it as a present to the Pope.

In Prof. Baldwin Brown's opinion, a comparison of the weirdly beautiful Irish codex, radiating all the glamour of Keltic romance, with the far plainer and more rigid Northumbrian masterpiece, leads to the conviction that, while the Book of Kells as a human document is far more wonderful, Lindisfarne is more satisfying to the sober aesthetic judgement.

In the absence of grave-furniture, Anglo-Saxon antiquities of the Christian period are comparatively rare, though at this time, to judge by the ninth-century *Liber Pontificalis*, our native craftsmen had a European reputation ; but there are a few more illuminated manuscripts of this period connected with monastic houses in England and no doubt of English craftsmanship. The eighth-century Psalter of St. Augustine's, Canterbury (Vesp. A. i), has initials illuminated in the Irish style, but with much gold-leaf, which is unknown in purely Irish MSS. Its only miniature is of late classical composition, in an arch which combines Irish and Roman details ; but Irish influence is clear in most English MSS. of this century, and another well-known Canterbury MS. is the *Codex aureus* of Stockholm. The eighth and ninth centuries are characterized in Southern England by a blend of Irish, North English, and oriental elements, the last through Merovingian channels. Style II synchronized with the conversion of England, and Style III is unrepresented here, the English now coming into closer contact with their immediate neighbours, and only resuming relations (unwillingly enough) with Scandinavia from the time of King Alfred. At this period a peculiar style of decoration, based on Merovingian models, prevailed in England, the best example in metal-work being the fragmentary silver of the Trewhiddle hoard (p. 100), with grotesque but easily traceable animals arranged singly in angular panels. Less pure is the decoration of the Fetter Lane sword (fig. 112), but specially English is the outline drawing of figure subjects in illuminated MSS. of the Winchester and Canterbury schools from the close of the tenth century ; and the most famous of the group is the Benedictional of St. Æthelwold (made bishop of Winchester in 963). Characteristic, at least of the earlier examples, are the hunched shoulders, the gesticulating limbs and fluttering draperies (as figs. 7, 8) ; and the Museum possesses perhaps the earliest specimen, King Edgar's Charter to New Minster at Winchester, dated 966 (Cotton MS. Vespasian A. viii).

16 INTRODUCTION

York fell to the Danish host in 867, and from that date till about 950 the sepulchral monuments of the north country are executed in a style that is strongly Scandinavian. Irish influence, which is so clear in the stone monuments of Scotland, Wales, and Cornwall, is barely perceptible in Northumbrian work of the Danish period. The animal forms, once subordinated to the oriental vine-scroll, now claim a separate existence; and, as the result of a grosser execution, develop into the 'great beast', which dominates the sepulchral slabs of northern England till the end of the Danish occupation.

In the homeland of the Vikings a phase of art beginning soon after 850 was the result of contact with Ireland for half

FIG. 7. David and Goliath (Cotton MS. Tib. C. VI).

*FIG. 8. Figure with Sword (Benedictional of St. Æthelwold).

a century. The Norwegian freebooters were there known as the white strangers (Finn-Gaill) and seem to have had a monopoly from about 830 till 849, when they were interfered with in Dublin by the Danes or dark strangers (Dubh-Gaill). They regained control in 853 and Dublin remained the Norse head-quarters till the Irish defeated them at Clontarf in 1014. The sea-rovers, who from the eighth to the eleventh century issued from one or another creek (*vik*) in Scandinavia, were on that account called Vikings. Most of those who raided and settled in Ireland were Norwegians, but the Danes were dominant in Cork and Limerick. The loot they carried off was much appreciated in Scandinavia, and the Norwegian museums contain much gilt metal-work that is acknowledged to be of Irish origin. The influence of these models is seen in the Borre style, which succeeded the Oseberg style about the middle of the ninth century; and with the addition of (i) the lappet springing from the back of the head, (ii) the double contour lines, with transverse lines (hatching) on the body, and (iii) the spiral curves on the shoulder, thus merges into the Jellinge style, so called from the famous royal grave found at Jellinge in Jutland and dating about 935-940. The basis of ornament remains an animal form in some respects akin to that of Style III (eighth century), but its execution is more logical, the interlacing of the neck, lappet, body, limbs, and tail being traceable as in Irish work, the head in profile and the body ribbon-like.

Another Jellinge monument, the gravestone erected by Harold Bluetooth to his parents Gorm and Thyra about 980, marks a turning-point in northern art, at least in its monumental aspect, for smaller objects such as bronze brooches were hardly affected. This carving represents a fantastic lion struggling with a serpent, in a style remote from that of Jellinge proper and evidently derived from the 'great beast' of Anglian grave-slabs, England now reacting on Denmark after a century of Danish rule in York. It is a definitely Christian monument, as the other face bears a representation of the Crucifixion in the same style; but now the animal motive recedes into the background for half a century, and there is a curious development of interlaced foliage which is held to be a local adaptation of the acanthus and other conventional plant-forms in the illuminated MSS. of southern England.

Considerable progress had been made in the arts in spite of the insecurity of private and monastic property during the Viking period; and carvings, both in ivory and stone, reached a high level. Mention may be made of a beautiful morse-ivory tau-cross (staff-head) from Alcester, which is regarded by Sir Hercules Read as Anglo-Saxon work of about 1020 (exhibited in King Edward VII Gallery, table case in Bay XXI: *Cat. Ivory Carvings*, no. 32, pl. XIX).

It was late in the tenth century that the Winchester and Canterbury schools of illumination produced manuscripts bordered and otherwise enriched with the stiff acanthus foliage characteristic of the classical renaissance during the reign of Charlemagne (768–814). The introduction of foliage into an art that had hitherto consisted almost exclusively of animal motives was a momentous change that affected Scandinavia as well as England. Late in the tenth century the great beast of the Northumbrian school crossed the North Sea, and appears (as already mentioned) on the great Jellinge stone; but there, too, the accessories tended to oust the animal form; and tight diagonal interlacing of limbs, lappet, and tail becomes an independent form of decoration, its original connexion with the body being more and more obscured. Thus the gravestone from St. Paul's Churchyard (now in the Guildhall Museum) dates from about 1030 and represents an animal with

18   INTRODUCTION

the interlacing exaggerated but still subordinate; whereas a second stone, probably from the same site (fig. 159), has pure interlacing, of the peculiar style named after Ringerike in Buskerud, Norway, where typical examples have been found, all carved on the spot in red sandstone. A bronze-gilt fragment (fig. 9) from Berkshire will serve to illustrate this phase of Northern art. Its duration in Scandinavia was about 1000-50, after which the loosely intertwined animal-patterns of the Jellinge style are revived in a manner best illustrated by the wooden carved doors of Urnes Church in Sogn, Norway, which date from about 1060 to 1080, and mark the close of paganism in Scandinavia. The Urnes style is represented in Case 55 by a Norwegian specimen (fig. 10); but in England the influence

FIG. 9. Engraved bronze-gilt plate, Berkshire. ($\frac{1}{1}$)

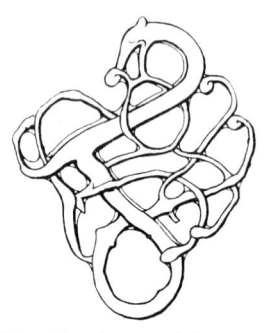

FIG. 10. Openwork bronze from Norway. ($\frac{3}{4}$)

of the Church and close contact with western civilization were all against its adoption.

The winged dragon then makes its appearance in Viking art, heralding the adoption of the Christian Romanesque style (called Norman in England), a Teutonic version of the Roman and Byzantine manner, centred till about 1100 in the Lower Rhine and Lombardy; but the animal motive, for all its pagan associations, survived in Ireland till the English conquest in the latter part of the twelfth century; and the Cross of Cong is extant to show how seven centuries of evolution had transformed a quadruped that Teuton and Roman provincial alike had borrowed from the Orient.

A final verdict on the artistic talent of England before the Norman Conquest can only be given in general terms. The various sources and successive impulses have been already mentioned, and at each stage it may at least be said that native work did not fall below the average level reached on the Continent. In answer to his own question, Was the Anglo-Saxon an artist?

Prof. Baldwin Brown protests against 'the popular prejudice which regards the Anglo-Saxon as a rather clumsy, boorish creature, who had to subsidize the needy foreigner to do his artistic work for him'. As to outstanding productions like the Northumbrian crosses, the sceattas, the Alfred jewel or the Franks casket, he holds 'that archaeological evidence is convincingly in favour of local origin. The fact is that the only possible ground for doubting this local origin is the intrinsic excellence of the products'. The function of the present Guide is to draw attention to other national antiquities not so well known, and to appraise the art of our forefathers by means of foreign parallels.

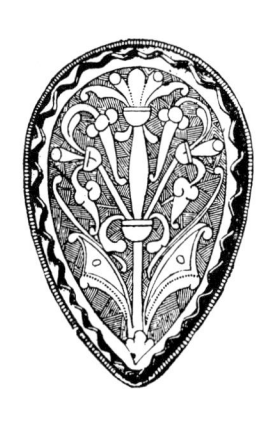

DESCRIPTION OF EXHIBITS

RADICAL changes in the funeral rite have been often noticed in prehistory, one of the most striking being the transition from inhumation to cremation about the middle of the Bronze Age. The reverse seems to have taken place in the Teutonic world; and cinerary urns of post-Roman date are comparatively rare in the South of England, more frequent in the North, but nearly all referable to the early part of the pagan period.

Most of the Anglo-Saxon pottery in the collection is massed in Cases 42–45, and shows many varieties of form and decoration. It is nearly all hand-made (without the use of a potter's wheel), and is of soft ware in various shades of grey and brown, some specimens being black and slightly lustrous. It belongs to two main classes—the larger being cinerary urns to hold the ashes of the dead after cremation, and the smaller being accessory vessels placed with the skeleton for ceremonial reasons, and generally quite plain. The cinerary urns are found more especially in Anglian districts, but occur also in mixed cemeteries all over the eastern half of England, though they are almost unknown in Kent, where inhumation was the rule from the first. They may therefore be due to a difference of race or of period; and if both elements are taken into consideration, it may be said that all the earliest Teutonic invaders of Britain, except the Jutes, burnt their dead, but that this rite gave way to inhumation sooner in the West Saxon and East Anglian areas than in the midlands and northern counties. There are a few cremations of advanced date (perhaps Mercian of Penda's time), but all no doubt precède the conversion of England to Christianity in the first half of the seventh century (p. 6); and in cemeteries where both rites are found, the urns seem to belong to the earliest settlers, datable objects in unburnt burials being sufficient to indicate when burning was abandoned. The rite belongs essentially to peoples resident in woodland districts where fuel was abundant, and Germany seems to be its original home in northern Europe. It was long ago pointed out by J. R. Kemble and Sir Wollaston Franks (the first Keeper of this Department) that there is a close resemblance between Anglo-Saxon urns and those found at Stade on the Elbe; and it is to North Germany rather than to Denmark that one must turn for light on the sepulchral pottery of the earliest invaders.

The relief mouldings are generally formed by pressing out the

PLATE II. CINERARY URNS FOUND IN ENGLAND
(Cases 43, 44, see p. 21)

clay from within, but in some cases the ribs were applied outside. Grooves round the neck and on the shoulder were produced by a pointed tool of wood or bone; and stamps were freely used to ornament spaces so enclosed. The few impressions here illustrated (fig. 11) include two forms of the swastika or fylfot, which is generally considered one of the earliest sun-symbols; but it is doubtful if the others are anything but ornamental.

The pottery jug found at Great Addington, Northamptonshire (pl. II, no. 2), is a rarity of very early date, when the great migrations of the Teutonic peoples were in progress and the English kingdoms had not yet taken shape. It was found 6 ft. deep in blue lias clay on a hill overlooking the river Nene, and differs from the Teutonic cinerary urn in form, decoration, and fabric. The height is 7½ in. and the handle is perforated to serve

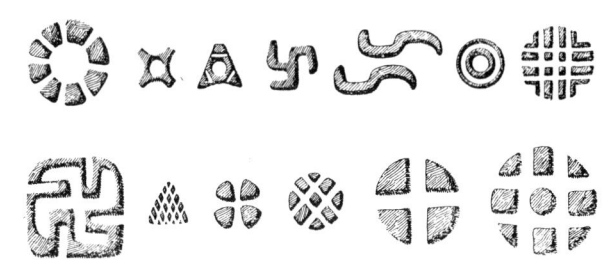

FIG. 11. Stamped patterns on Anglo-Saxon pottery. (⅔)

as a spout. Close parallels have been found near Stade (mouth of the Elbe), in South-west Norway (Stavanger), and in the Danish island of Fyen. Only about half a dozen are known, and all seem to date from the fifth century.

The ordinary type of cinerary urn can be easily traced back to Saxony, where several groups were abundantly represented in the Early Iron Age (Case 4 in this Gallery, and Cases 31-34 in Prehistoric Room). A grave-find at Leuna, near Meiseburg (Case 63), is some evidence that in the Migration period a bold profile and decoration in relief were gradually replaced by a plain contour and incised or stamped decoration; and certain stages of evolution can be traced in England during the cremation period (about A.D. 450-600). Thus the earliest of this type on pl. II appear to be nos. 3 (Kempston) and 6 (Shropham); the first recalling the *Buckelurnen* of N. Germany with bosses under arches round the shoulder, and the other with bold ribbing of corded pattern and stamps (rosette and swastika) in zones between incised lines. With these may be classed two of more oval form with small mouths (Case 44) from Shropham and Croydon, with vertical ribs and arches in relief enclosing bosses. What seems to be a later edition of no. 6 is the urn found between Cavenham and Lackford, in which the profile is simplified and the stamped patterns less striking. Another from Kempston (no. 4) marks the last stage of the arch motive, and the decoration is confined to double or triple incised lines, with chevrons on the shoulder. The next stage would be marked by no. 1 (from the Towneley collection, without locality), with groups of impressions in the chevrons and round the neck; and this arrangement is elaborated in no. 5 (Shropham), which may be compared with the larger specimen from Little Wilbraham. The latter still retains the primitive vertical rib, which is well seen, flanked by double lines, in the urn

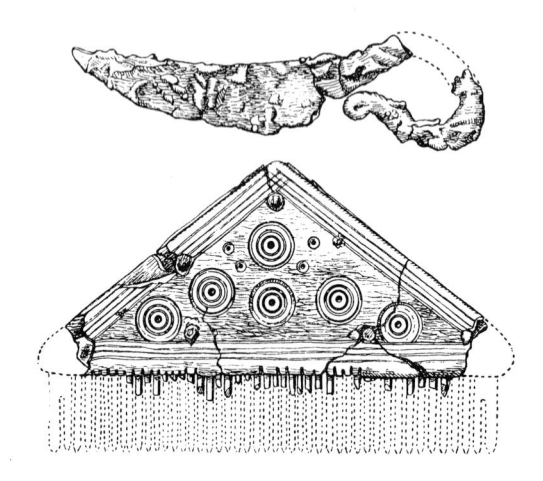

FIG. 12. Bone comb and iron knife from urn, Eye. ($\frac{2}{3}$)

from Eye, that contained among the ashes a curved iron knife and triangular bone comb of late classical type (fig. 12), with iron shears and pair of tweezers.

The extensive series of cinerary and other sepulchral pottery in Case 42 from Barton Seagrave, Northants., shows the variety in shape and ornamentation that was possible in a single locality, and also points the contrast between pottery vessels to contain the ashes and those deposited with the unburnt body; for on this site both rites were practised, and the iron shield-boss with bronze-gilt disk, the glass beads and brooches in Case C evidently came from inhumations.

The practice of placing pottery vessels with the dead body goes back to prehistoric times, and food and drink were perhaps supplied in this way for the journey to the other world. Anglo-

Saxon specimens are almost always of dark brown or black ware and shaped either like a cup (as Brixworth and Quarrington) or a gourd, with globular body, rounded base, and cylindrical neck (as Cransley, Henlow, and Twickenham). This class of pottery, which must be carefully distinguished from the cinerary urns, is generally quite plain; but small vases with angular shoulder often bear ornament, and two in Case 42 (Malton, Cambs., and Sandy, Beds.) have the shoulder scalloped, with stamped patterns round the neck.

Whether ornaments and weapons were included in the funeral pyre, or added intact to the subsequent burial, cinerary urns are rarely found in early England with much in the way of grave-furniture. A comb, a few beads, or draughtsmen do not throw much light on the date or origin of the Teutonic invader; but the absence of antiquities that are known to be later, and the obvious connexion of the urns themselves with continental ware, point to the cremated burials being the earliest of the English series. The interment of human remains unburnt gave fuller scope to the practice of furnishing the grave with objects connected with the dead; and burial groups, sometimes of great variety, form the basis of any classification of pagan antiquities. Association in a single grave is necessarily the most useful from this point of view; but failing this, the collection of objects from a group of burials that belong to a generation or two can often be of considerable service, and several cases will be noticed below; but before such associations can be properly appreciated, it is necessary to sketch the evolution of the leading types. Of these the most useful and the most ornamental are undoubtedly the brooches, sometimes called by the Latin name *fibulae*: their origin and development can in most cases be determined with considerable precision.

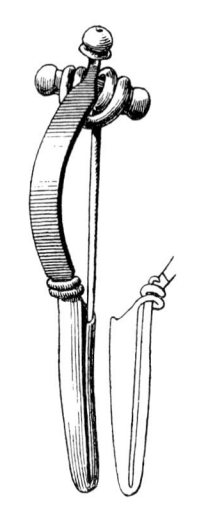

*Fig. 13. Bronze brooch with returned foot, Sweden. ($\frac{2}{3}$)

A brooch as common as any in England is the long or cruciform pattern, the latter term being better reserved for the closing stages of its evolution when the front assumes the form of a cross, though unconnected with Christianity. In the earlier forms the cross is not so striking a feature, especially as the arms are often incomplete; and length is their leading characteristic. Formerly it was believed that it was derived from the Roman provincial cross-bow type (*Guide to Roman Britain*, fig. 69), which certainly influenced a small minority in Scandinavia; but most are descendants of the brooch with returned foot which was invented or adopted by the Goths while they were yet in South Russia. Discoveries at Kerch in the Crimea (p. 170) have illuminated the third century in Europe; and a stream of influence, if not of migration, has now been traced from South Russia (about A.D. 200)

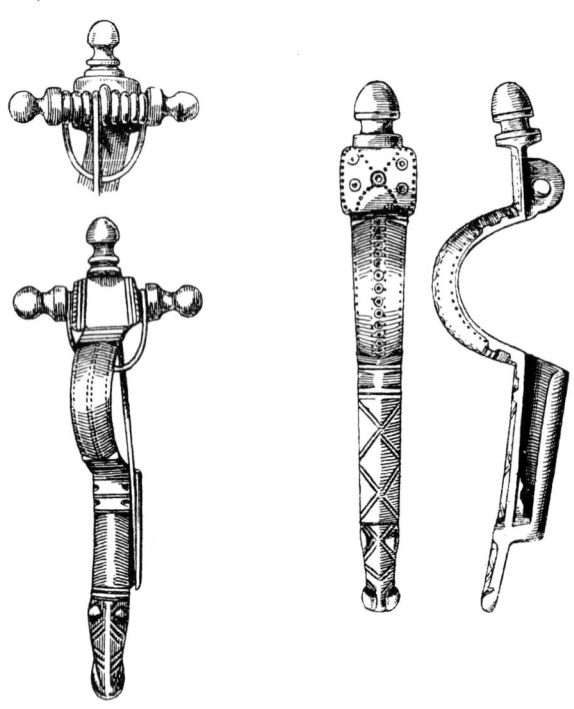

*FIG. 14. Primitive 'long' brooch, with back of head, Sweden. ($\frac{2}{3}$)

FIG. 15. Bronze 'long' brooch (front and side views). ($\frac{2}{3}$)

to East Prussia, viâ the Baltic coast to Denmark, Sweden, and, above all, Norway. In Kerch is found, among other brooches, a type with narrow-arched bow and returned foot (fig. 13), the tendril-like end of which is bound round the lower part of the bow. The end of the foot was fastened to the bow during the transition from La Tène I to II, five centuries before, but was then turned in the opposite direction. The spring is still of La Tène type, with a series of bilateral coils, but passes round a short cross-bar which terminates in knobs; another knob is attached to the extremity of the bow, called the head of the brooch, and the essential features of the Crimean brooch can be traced all through the series (figs. 13-19). The evolution of the long or cruciform brooch in Scandinavia has been fully described by Dr. Haakon Shetelig of Bergen, in connexion with Anglo-Saxon parallels.

The prototype is seen to have a foot almost as long as the bow, and to be provided with a long socket or catch for the pin-head when in use. In the early stages of development this long catch is prominent (fig. 15), but gradually shortens and moves away from the extremity of the foot, fig. 14 in this respect being more advanced than fig. 15, though the former best illustrates the transition from fig. 13, as the head is perfect. Before the brooch-type reached England it underwent changes due to Roman influence in Germany, and the facets so common on metal-work in the late Roman period are shown in fig. 14, representing the coils seen at the junction of bow and foot in fig. 13; while another tendency of the period is visible in the animal-head termination of the foot. This ornament was of North German origin and may be best described as a horse's head seen from the front, the salient points being the eyes and nostrils, and the latter rounding off the foot; while the eyes are separated from the bow by a bevelled surface, sometimes engraved, as in fig. 15. The bow is also bevelled and sometimes ornamented along the central ridges and edges, and the beginnings of the head-plate are well seen in fig. 14. This expansion of the bar that primarily continued the bow and held the central knob and cross-bar for the spring, was perhaps due to a desire to conceal the spring of the pin; but it incidentally gave scope for additional ornamentation, and grew larger and larger. Above is a back view of the head, showing the spring coiled round a bar that passes through an eyelet attached to the head-plate, the chord that provides the tension being still visible from the front. The next specimen (fig. 15) has a somewhat earlier form of catch, but a decorated head-plate and more pronounced knob; and the side view shows the eyelet that once held the cross-bar now missing.

Its original appearance can easily be inferred from fig. 14; and it is quite possible that fig. 15 was found in East Anglia. It was not, however, till the next stage was reached that specimens were at all common in England, and their appearance here in the fifth century points to a Scandinavian invasion long prior to the Viking period. It is, moreover, clear from a comparison of specimens, that during the fifth century the connexion was with Denmark and the mouth of the Elbe, rather than with Norway or Sweden; and the main points of resemblance may here be enumerated. English and Danish cruciform brooches are chiefly distinguished from contemporary specimens in Norway and Sweden by the manner in which the side-knobs are attached to the head-plate. The brooches are not (at least, during the fifth century) cast all in one piece, but at first have the side-knobs quite independent of the head-plate and later have the edges of the head-plate reduced by bevelling so as to fit into notches cut in the knobs that terminate the cross-bar of the spring. The result is that these knobs are generally missing altogether, as the bar was only of wire and peculiarly liable to decay, so that the knobs have generally been lost, as in figs. 15 and 17.

Further, on Danish and English specimens, the nostrils of the horse are a pair of semicircular, slightly convex wings, while the Norwegian brooches have instead two hemispherical knobs in that position. The English, and still more the Danish, examples have a flatter bow than those from the Scandinavian peninsula; and the head-plate is frequently bent concave at the back so as to give more play to the spring-coil.

The next illustration (fig. 16) shows considerable development and the peculiarly English tendency to broad flat forms, which at a later stage afforded space for animal ornament. The bevelled edges of the head-plate already mentioned are now no longer functional, as the side-knobs are not attached to the cross-bar but cast in one piece with the brooch, as commonly in Norway and Sweden; and the raised panel in the centre of the head-plate survives merely as an ornamental feature. This is usually the case with Norwegian specimens, and at this stage the connexion between England and Denmark had evidently been interrupted, and relations established with the western coast of Norway. This

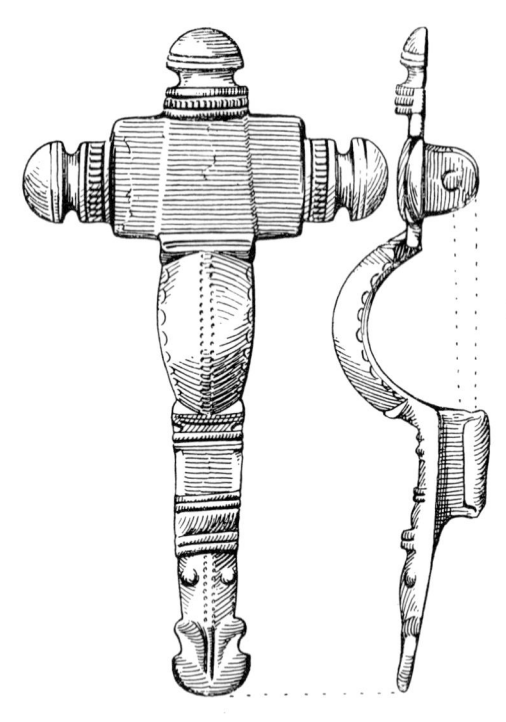

FIG. 16. Long brooch, with side view, Malton, Cambs. (¼)

new connexion dates from the close of the fifth century, and lasted at any rate to the middle of the next, when the cruciform brooches of Norway came to an end, and England was left to continue their development or degradation. An increase of width is seen in the head-plate, the bow, and the nostrils of the horse-head terminal; but the essential features remain the same, and fig. 16 may be regarded as a typical specimen of the early long-brooch in England. During this period a peculiar notch in the moulding next the eyes of the horse, in the line of the main axis, is sometimes noticed. No explanation of this peculiarity is forthcoming, but it is confined to English specimens.

The decoration of the brooch is mainly executed in the casting, and consists of facets and mouldings at intervals along the foot; but simple punched patterns also occur, generally along the edges of the raised panel of the head-plate. The knobs, which have become part of the decoration, are no longer cast complete, but are flat or hollowed out at the back, to economize the metal as well as to have an even surface to rest on the clothing when in use.

The next specimen, illustrated in fig. 17, ushers in the later Anglo-Saxon series, though it happens also to have had the side-knobs attached in the primitive manner. The notches in the head-plate show clearly enough where and how the knobs now lost were originally attached, and recall specimens of the period before 500; but there are other features that show a new departure. The top knob has a projection that becomes more and more conspicuous in England, and there is an analogous extension of the foot, a wedge springing from between the nostrils, which are themselves more prominent than heretofore.

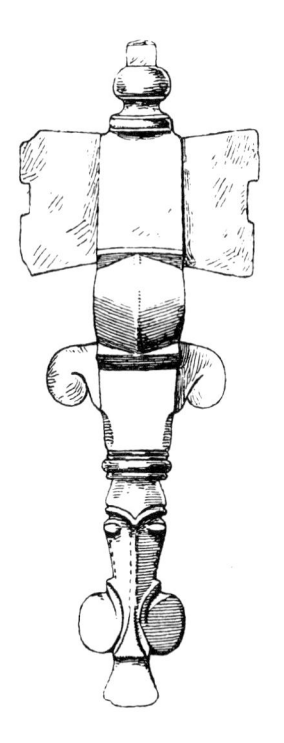

FIG. 17. Bronze 'long' brooch, Kenninghall, Norfolk. ($\frac{2}{3}$)

Above all, there are wings added to the foot just below the bow, a feature that may be conveniently held to mark the later period. These wings are not confined to this country, but occur on late and decadent examples in Norway (A.D. 500–550), where they would no doubt have had a parallel development if the series had not there been brought to an end sooner than on this side of the North Sea.

The Anglo-Saxon preference for broad effects and lavish ornament had now full play, and the somewhat severe forms of the early period were soon elaborated almost beyond recognition. With a view to getting the largest possible surface with a given weight of metal, the brooch was cast thinner and flatter than before, and all extremities extravagantly ornamented. It is at this stage that the term *cruciform* may most fittingly be applied

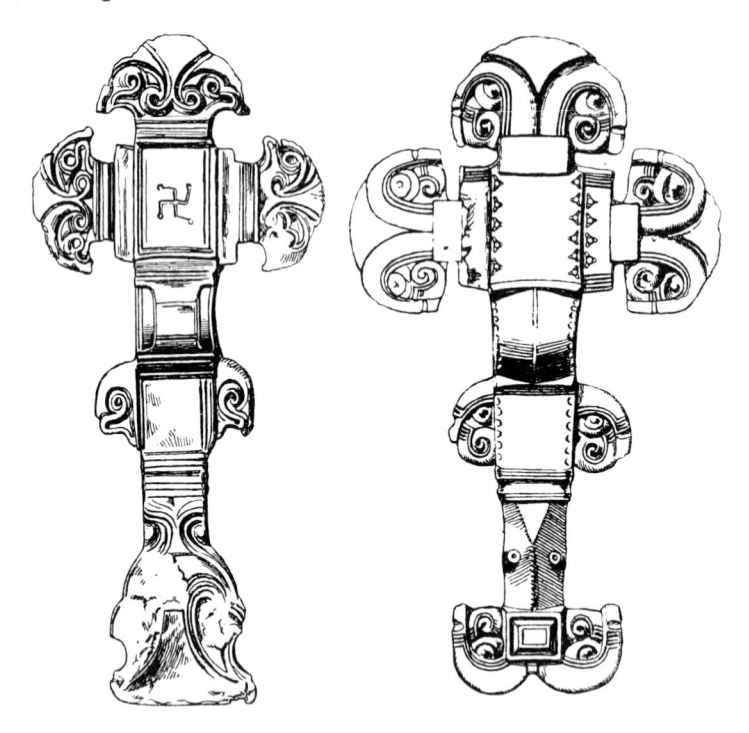

FIG. 18. Bronze brooch with swastika, Sleaford, Lincs. ($\frac{2}{3}$)

FIG. 19. Bronze cruciform brooch, Sleaford, Lincs. ($\frac{2}{3}$)

to English specimens, for the knobs are now a permanent addition to the head-plate and have been flattened out to provide a surface for deep engraving, or rather for designs cast in that style. The wedge or fan-shaped projection from between the nostrils has been exaggerated, and similar forms have been added to the three arms of the head. The plain panel just below the bow certainly survives, but is flanked by engraved wings, and the corresponding space in the centre of the head-plate of fig. 18 bears an engraved swastika (fylfot), while the bow has lost its central ridge and

THE SQUARE-HEADED BROOCH 29

bears a raised panel at the top, which should be compared with that on the end of the foot of fig. 19.

The particular form of animal head occurring in pairs on all the extremities of fig. 19 have been assigned to Salin's Style II (A.D. 600-700), and the specimen illustrated may be considered as one of the latest of its class, though more debased examples

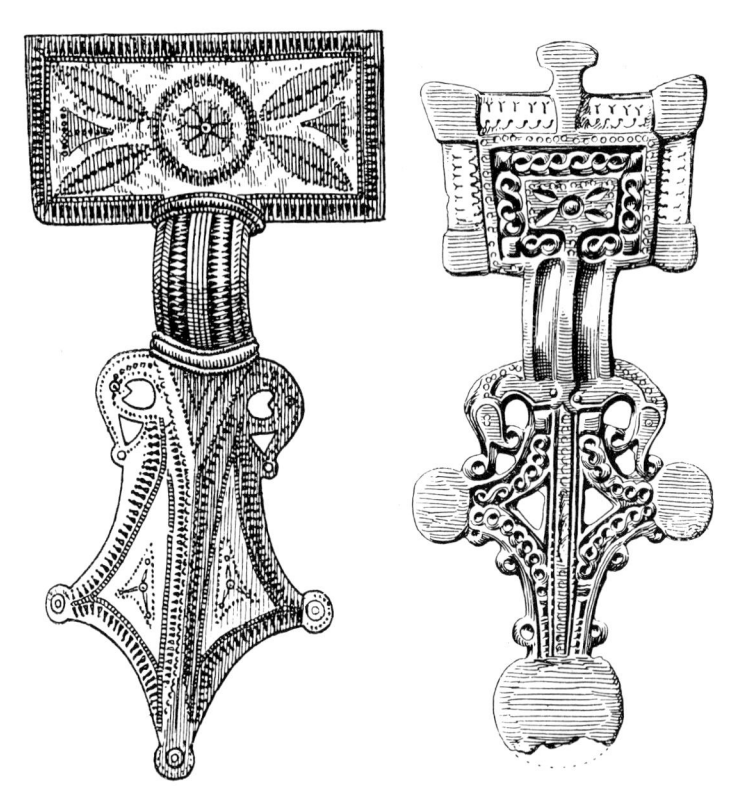

*FIG. 20. Silver square-headed brooch, Denmark. ($\frac{2}{3}$)

FIG. 21. Square-headed brooch, Kenninghall. ($\frac{2}{3}$)

may be seen in Case C. Comparison with fig. 18 will explain its grotesque appearance, and the blend of traditional and novel details is of interest. Stamped patterns, as of old, fringe the central panel of the head-plate, the bow, and the adjoining plate of the foot; while the collars of the knobs are replaced by oblong plates of silver, and an oblong garnet setting occupies the space between the nostrils, these in their turn being entirely metamorphosed. The decoration of this brooch was evidently influenced by the contemporary square-headed type that may conveniently be considered next.

Denmark seems to have become the home of the square-headed brooch; but if a specimen from the Crimea (fig. 224) can be regarded as the prototype, the rectangular head was evolved in some region between the Baltic and the Black Sea, as it was not originally a central European form. The square (or rather oblong) head-plate originally served to connect and screen two, three, or more rods on which were wound spiral coils of wire as though to give tension to the pin, but only one was functional. The unnecessary coils were soon omitted, and the bar that held the spiral spring passed through a single eyelet behind the head-plate, which at this stage is ornamented with semi-classical patterns, soon to be ousted by Teutonic animal motives. The open-jawed heads of monsters make their appearance at this stage immediately below the bow, and remain there throughout, though much conventionalized. Comparison of figs. 20 and 21 is instructive as showing the contrast between the Roman and Teutonic ideas of decoration.

FIG. 22. Bronze-gilt square-headed brooch, Chessel Down, I. W. (⅔)

In the sixth century the triangular spaces in the middle of the foot become crowded with detail and reduced in size; the three round terminals of the foot increase in size and become a leading feature, at least in England. A specimen from Kenninghall, Norfolk (fig. 21), dating about A.D. 500, has an openwork foot, giving greater prominence to the animal heads below the bow; and there is no need to insist on its connexion with the Danish prototype, as even the central panel of the head bears the same design in both. Running scrolls are seen both

THE ROUND-HEADED BROOCH

on the Kenninghall specimen and on a later brooch from Chessel Down, Isle of Wight (fig. 22), but the latter alone has animal ornament applied to the interior panels, and may date from about 550.

Round the head and the disks of the foot is a chevron pattern executed in niello and silver, the contrast of colours being very popular at this time (p. 8); and in the present instance there is no doubt about the human face in the side terminals of the foot. In some specimens these terminals are embellished with thin silver disks, that contrast with the gilt surface of the brooch. At a later stage the animal ornament encroaches on the bow, and the

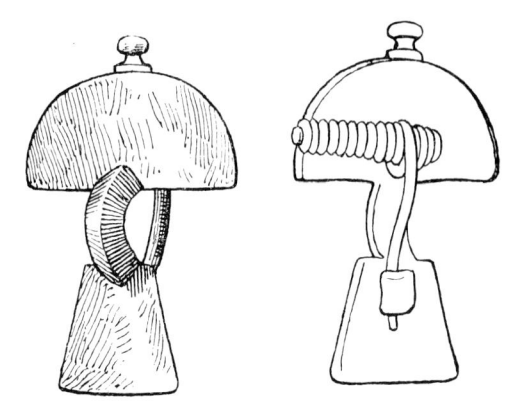

FIG. 23. Bronze round-headed brooch (front and back), Crimea. ($\frac{1}{1}$)

outer rim of the head is filled with repetitions of a spectacle-like pattern, while the panels contain the merest vestiges of the Teutonic animal. The head is no longer straight-sided, and spindle-shaped settings of purple enamel are sometimes found at the angles; while the colour effect is enhanced by garnet settings of various forms.

Several examples of this type can be easily distinguished from the continental (as pl. xiv, no. 11), the latter falling into two main groups which influenced each other to a certain extent but evidently belonged to different schools of art. Communication between the northern and southern streams of influence seems to have been by way of Hanover; and these brooches above all reflect the tribal migrations and affinities of the fifth and sixth centuries.

Parallel in some respects to the square-headed brooch is the radiated type, for which a prototype has again been found in the Crimea. The characteristics of fig. 23 are a semicircular head, an arched bow, and a spreading foot, with a blunt end that persists on certain varieties of this type (fig. 26). As before, the spiral coil, wound on an axis that passes through an eyelet behind the head, gives tension to the pin and is itself subject to extraordinary elaboration. In fig. 23 the knob at the top seems useless, but when associated (as in fig. 24) with the terminals of the spring-axes, it becomes an essential feature of the decoration. The next stage is illustrated by a pair from Kerch, late fourth century (fig. 25): the knobs are no longer functional but cast in one piece with the head, purely as ornament. The foot has become lozenge-

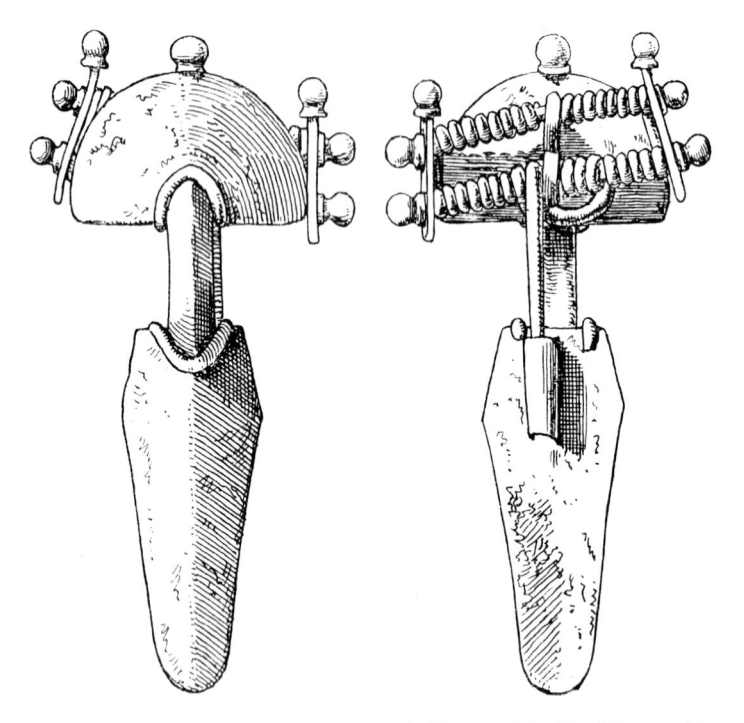

*FIG. 24. Bronze round-headed brooch (front and back), Crimea. ($\frac{1}{1}$)

shaped, and while its terminal takes the form of a knob, the side-angles are furnished with projecting studs, in this case set with cabochon garnets. The ground has simple scrolls and lines parallel to the margins; but further developments took place in the fifth century. The foot, either of lozenge form (as fig. 25) or with parallel sides and blunt end (as fig. 26), is enriched with gilding, garnets, niello, and engraving. The knobs and terminals frequently assume the shape of birds' heads, a bird of prey (perhaps the hawk) being a common motive among the Gothic peoples (p. 43); but apart from this it should be observed that no trace of animal ornament occurs on this type, which hardly survived the fifth century, and just overlaps the square-headed type.

The circular form of brooch was also much affected by the Anglo-Saxons, and two varieties seem to be intimately connected: they occur sometimes in the same cemetery, though the exact

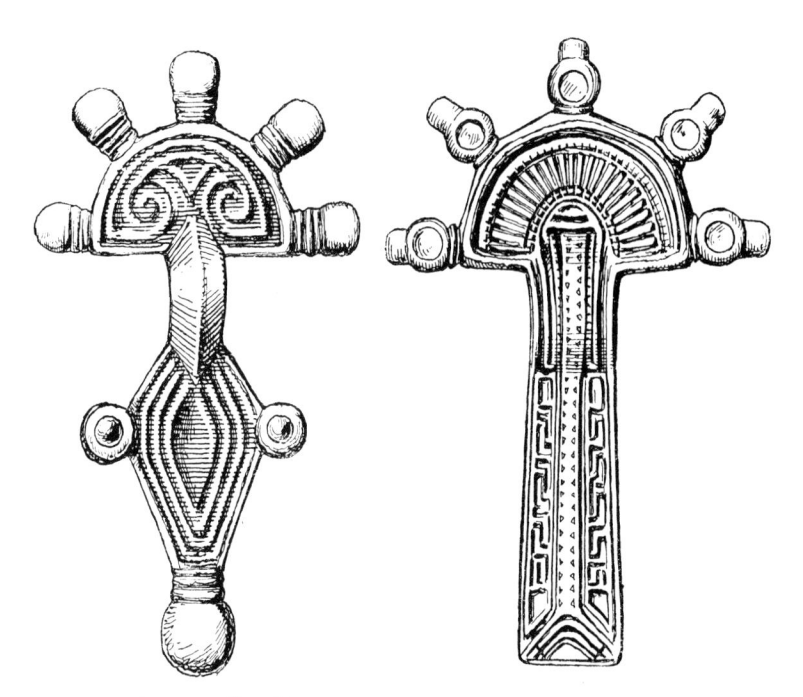

FIG. 25. Bronze radiated brooch, Crimea. ($\frac{1}{1}$)

FIG. 26. Silver-gilt radiated brooch, Suffolk. ($\frac{1}{1}$)

relation between them is at present obscure. The term saucer-brooch is often applied to both, but should be reserved for the solid series (made in one piece), while the brooch with an embossed plate attached to the front may be called the 'applied' brooch for the sake of brevity. The latter is composite, and consists of a bronze disk-base, slightly dished and surrounded by a narrow vertical bronze band affixed at right angles to contain the cement which forms a bed for the embossed front of gilt bronze. A specimen from Fairford, Gloucs. (fig. 27), shows the method of construction, as the applied disk is damaged and reveals the internal arrangements. The design is semi-classical, the plaited border being found on many a Roman pavement, and the zone round the central star being derived probably from the Amazon shield or (as Mr. Leeds suggests) the human face seen in a more recognizable form on fig. 31. This comes from the principal site for this type and has the Teutonic animal motive surrounding an equal-armed cross : other examples retain traces of the classical egg-and-tongue border, which is best illustrated on what must be an early example found at Sigy, Neufchâtel, Seine-Inférieure. Another, probably from Lombardy (Case 61), with an

FIG. 27. Bronze 'applied' brooch, Fairford. ($\frac{1}{1}$)

FIG. 28. Bronze-gilt saucer-brooch, Leighton Buzzard. ($\frac{1}{1}$)

eagle preying on a hare embossed on the front, belongs to the late classical period.

The saucer-brooch, properly so called, exhibits at times some traces of classical design ; and the star (fig. 28) and running scroll (fig. 29) are favourite patterns that are quite independent of Teutonic art and may have been derived from Roman models in England (*Guide to Roman Britain*, p. 74). The construction of the brooch is constant and extremely simple : a stout bronze plate is dished, and ornamented in the flat central space in the chip-carving (*Keilschnitt*) style, the cast design being finished with the graver and the whole of the interior gilt. The pin is attached as usual at the back, and works on a hinge as in the preceding type. The classical feeling of those with geometrical patterns suggests an early date in the Anglo-Saxon period ; but the animal ornament is also frequent on the saucer-brooch (fig. 30), and carries the type from about A.D. 550 to 650, the latest specimens being large and degenerate in design (specimen from Stone, Bucks., in Case D 1).

Some saucer-brooches have in addition a circular stud in the centre, and these are almost confined to the eastern midlands. One from Dover (Case D) has this peculiarity, and it is evidently one of the later examples of its kind, rather out of place in the county. Other Kentish examples that may have been left at Faversham and west of the Medway by West Saxons on their way up the Thames include one (Case 49) with a disk of red enamel at the centre, where a garnet setting is sometimes found, as on a smaller example in the same Case, and on larger ones from Longbridge, Warwickshire, in Case 47 adjoining.

FIG. 29. Bronze-gilt saucer-brooch, Oxfordshire. ($\frac{1}{1}$)

FIG. 30. Bronze-gilt saucer-brooch, found in England. ($\frac{1}{1}$)

The saucer-brooch was certainly West Saxon, but perhaps not exclusively so, as it is found among the Middle Angles and Gyrwas of the Fens as well as in the Hwiccan district (south-east of Warwickshire, Worcestershire, and Gloucestershire). At Longbridge, for instance (Case 47), on the north bank of the Avon about a mile west of Warwick, have been found specimens with star-pattern (as fig. 28) and running scrolls (as fig. 29), characteristic of early Wessex ; yet the Warwickshire Avon was apparently not reached by the West Saxons till after the battle of Deorham in 577 ; and Hwiccia seems to have become part of Mercia under Penda about 628. If these dates can be trusted, they limit the occurrence of West Saxon brooches in these parts to about half a century. The distribution of the type points to an advance up the Thames, though few examples come from the Jutish areas of Kent, Wight, and southern Hampshire (Case D 6). Several are known from Surrey (Mitcham) and Middlesex (Hanwell), and the type abounds in Berkshire, Oxfordshire, north Wiltshire, and Gloucestershire. It is also well represented in Buckinghamshire, and can be traced farther north-east through Bedfordshire, Cambridgeshire, and the surrounding counties to Leicestershire, Lincolnshire, Rutland, and especially Northamptonshire.

In the area that is known to have been West Saxon before the battle of Bedford (571), the solid saucer type prevails, and the decoration is mainly geometrical; whereas in the Bedford and Cambridge area, presumably conquered at that date, the applied

FIG. 31. Bronze 'applied' brooch, Kempston. ($\frac{1}{1}$)

type is more common and the animal ornament predominates. This might be taken to imply the earlier arrival of the type in the upper Thames valley where Roman patterns were still available, and the priority of the solid saucer form; but these minor divergences may only be due to the occupation of the two adjoining areas by different Teutonic tribes. Geometrical patterns occur in both districts, and should indicate occupation by West Saxon kindred considerably before 571; but the records of the time are so imperfect that archaeology can hardly be said to contradict them.

As to the origin of the type, Mr. Thurlow Leeds has observed that 'the evolution of the saucer-brooch was in process of becoming a realized fact at exactly the point at which the migrations to

England were beginning'. He cites a pair, about $\frac{7}{8}$ in. across, found in the province of Hanover west of Hamburg, and suggests that the absence of later forms from Germany was due to the migration hither of the whole population, as intimated by Bede, to whose day the original Anglia remained a desert. It may be added that the German pair referred to are solid saucers, though others consist of two parts, a disk of bronze to which is affixed another embossed disk; but there is no rim as in the English brooches.

Another variety of the round brooch is quite flat, sometimes tinned to give the effect of silver, and poorly ornamented with punched or engraved geometrical designs. Two specimens from Long Wittenham are illustrated (fig. 32); but the type is widely

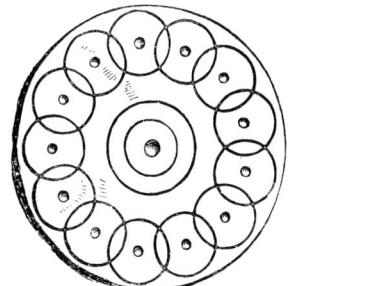

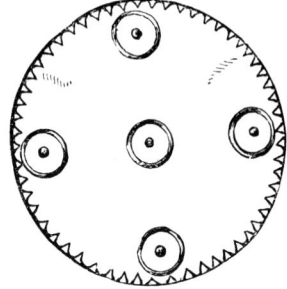

FIG. 32. Engraved disk-brooches, Long Wittenham, Berks. ($\frac{1}{1}$)

dispersed in England, and occurs not only in Saxon but in certain Anglian districts (Cases D 1 and C).

More attractive, and more important from the artistic point of view, are the jewelled circular brooches of Kent, which require coloured illustrations to do them justice. The bulk of these round brooches, made and worn by the Jutes, can be conveniently divided into four classes here illustrated. The commonest may be called the keystone brooch (fig. 33), from the form of the principal garnet settings, which radiate from the centre like the keystone of an arch. The specimen illustrated has secondary garnet inlays of oblong form; and in the band between them semicircles that represent the eye of the Teutonic animal, the rest of the body being crowded out. A constant feature in this and other jewelled Kentish brooches is a central boss of some white substance that may have been ivory, mother-of-pearl, or even meerschaum, analysis having failed to make any distinction in their present state. Garnets are often inlaid in the top of these bosses, and sometimes remain after the material of the boss itself has perished. Another feature common to many Kentish brooches, circular and otherwise, is the zigzag border of silver and niello; and the material of the brooch itself is generally silver more or less pure, but occasionally gold.

Another variety, of much rarer occurrence, has T-shaped garnets set in a band that is otherwise filled with animal patterns, generally of a decadent nature and difficult to recognize as such; and circular settings generally of blue glass imitating lapis lazuli. In the exceptional specimen illustrated (frontisp. no. 8) the T has assumed the form of a Latin cross, which in this case may be of Christian significance, as the conversion of Kent began probably before the brooch was made.

A third variety has a star pattern of inlaid work, with three or four points separated by (and sometimes ending in) white bosses set with garnets on a hatched backing of gold-foil, and sometimes with blue glass in imitation of lapis lazuli. The spaces between the points is generally ornamented with gold filigree in zones of S or C scrolls.

The last series consist of a limited number of larger brooches often combining many forms of decoration; and the finest example is the Kingston brooch, found on Kingston Down south of Canterbury, and now in Liverpool Museum. The illustrated specimen (fig. 60) is roughly dated by the coin pendants found with it on a necklace (p. 55). It has five bosses of white material surmounted by table and cabochon garnets, garnet cell-work on hatched gold-foil with step-pattern partitions, and zones of filigree in rings and S-scrolls. The Berkshire specimen in Case D, one of a pair found at Abingdon, is of this class; and a plainer example in Case 61 (pl. xv, no. 8) is known to have come from Italy, though its likeness to Kentish work is very striking.

FIG. 33. Silver keystone brooch, Faversham. ($\frac{1}{1}$)

Other groups of brooches that can be arranged typologicaly, that is, in the supposed order of evolution, are noticed elsewhere, but enough has been said concerning the leading types to render them useful as indications of date in dealing with series of antiquities from the various burial-grounds of pagan England; and the richest of these have been discovered in Kent. These naturally come first in the series selected to show the antiquities characteristic of the various tribal areas before the conversion of the people to Christianity and the absorption of their petty kingdoms into larger political units.

Kent has been particularly favoured not only in the abundance and quality of its grave-furniture, but also in its archaeologists, who began systematic exploration in this country, and saw to the preservation and publication of the antiquities they found. The Rev. Bryan Faussett's journal of his excavations near Canterbury extends from 1757 to 1773, and was edited, with coloured illustrations, by C. Roach Smith in 1856 ; and in 1793 the Rev. James Douglas published his researches under the title of *Nenia Britannica*, much of the material being derived from Kent (especially on Chatham Lines). The Faussett collection was presented by Mr. Joseph Mayer to Liverpool in 1850 ; and many of Douglas's finds are now in the Ashmolean Museum, Oxford. The richest cemetery, known as the King's Field, was undoubtedly on and near the site of the railway station at Faversham ; and the best of the jewellery in this collection comes from graves disturbed there during the construction of the railway ; but the work was not properly supervised, and the antiquities would have been dispersed but for the zeal of Mr. William Gibbs of that town, who bequeathed his collection to the nation in 1870.

The Gibbs collection is exhibited in Wall-cases 48, 49, and in section 5 of Table-case D. Unhappily no record was kept of the grouping of the objects, and the connexion between various types must be determined on other evidence ; but the series may be dated between the late fifth and early seventh centuries of our era.

Faussett made it clear that most of the Kentish burials were east and west, with the head at the west end. Instances of Anglo-Saxon cremation are extremely rare in the county (p. 20), and many of the skeletons were found in wooden coffins, some of which showed traces of burning, and had probably passed the fire, as a symbolic rite, though Faussett thought the coffin was burnt to make the wood more durable. In digging the graves, earlier cremated burials were sometimes disturbed, and cases are on record of a broken cinerary urn of Roman date being included in the Jutish grave, the burnt bones being readily distinguished from the later interment. In Kent a large number of the burials were below small barrows or grave-mounds of circular outline, but there were also cemeteries with no indication on the surface, the graves being arranged in rows side by side with the same orientation.

Perhaps the most striking relic from Faversham is a large circular brooch of gold (Case D 5), like the Kingston brooch but smaller, with nearly all the garnets and filigree missing from the cells with which the face is covered. The step-pattern is here arranged in zones, and the cruciform knot is also found on many a Roman pavement. It is this type above all that points to the Rhine as the ultimate source of this Kentish industry ;

and between the Rhine and Italy there must have been some connexion in early Teutonic times.

Other jewellery from Faversham is illustrated on the frontispiece (all but no. 2). The decoration consists mainly of garnet cell-work on a filigree ground, but a few blue settings are included in nos. 1, 2, 6, 8, and 9. Cabochon garnets fill the eyes of the birds in triskele form on no. 4, and the animal heads flanking no. 3 have pointed jaws in Style II. The buckle with counter-plate (no. 7) has triangular stamps made up of dots.

A silver strap-end (fig. 34) is set with garnets like a series of weapons and ornaments (Troyes Museum) found at Pouan, Dept.

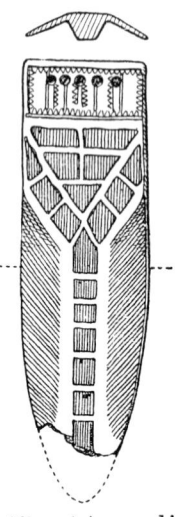

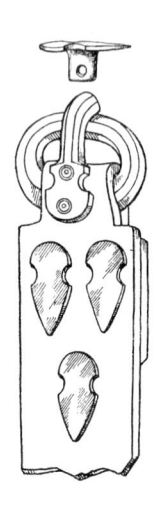

FIG. 34. Silver 'strap-end', with garnets, Faversham. (¾)

FIG. 35. Buckle, with shoe-shaped rivets, Aisne, France. (½)

Aube, France, in 1842 and associated by some authorities with the Visigothic king Theodoric, who was killed at Châlons in the battle against Attila in 451. The tomb of Childeric, king of the Franks, discovered at Tournay, Belgium, is more authentic, and contained garnet cell-work with straight and wavy partitions which shows the style prevalent in the third quarter of the fifth century, as he died in 481. There can be little hesitation, therefore, in assigning the Faversham tab to the fifth century, to which a few small circular brooches of similar technique no doubt belong; but jewellery of that early date is rare in England, even in Kent, where continental influence might be looked for sooner than anywhere else.

Another link between the Jutish areas and the Continent is the use of bronze studs, called for want of a better name 'shoe-shaped', for fastening the buckle to a belt; the accompanying diagram (fig. 35) shows one in profile at the top, and three in position, as found at Caranda, Aisne. Occasionally two such rivets were cast together, side by side, with connecting rods, and the hole in the tang was provided for a wire or bar to secure it on the inner face of the belt. The leather was cut narrow to pass through the hoop of the buckle, and pierced to receive the loop which projected from the broad end of the tongue. The illustration shows a common Frankish type, well represented at Faversham, that has been dated after 600, and called the buckle with shield-shaped tongue; but the description is not a happy one, and as the complete tongue has an outline not unlike the violin, it will be convenient to refer to the series with this common feature as the 'violin' type of buckle. The smaller buckles are often made of white metal (French, *potain*), a hard but brittle alloy of copper, zinc, and tin, with the appearance of nickel; and while these are occasionally found in England, the large engraved or damascened buckles with violin tongues are almost unknown in this country, and belong to a later period in France (fig. 193). Part of a buckle-plate (fig. 36) from Faversham is of iron plated with silver, of the rarest occurrence in England; and though the pattern is early, this technique is usually a sign of the seventh or eighth century. There is another fragment from this site in Case 49.

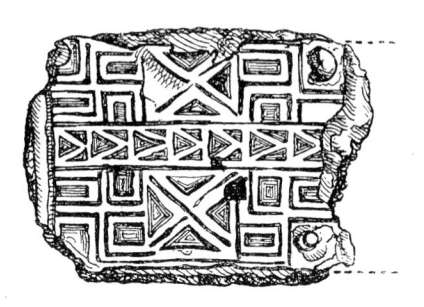

FIG. 36. Iron buckle-plate, inlaid with silver, Faversham. ($\frac{1}{1}$)

The normal type in Kent has a triangular buckle-plate with a large stud at the point and two smaller studs at the sides near the hoop, as in the jewelled specimen from the Taplow barrow (pl. v). The type occurs also in France, where it attained enormous dimensions, but in England may be attributed to the Jutes, even when found in districts occupied by other tribes.

Of unfamiliar appearance is a gilt buckle with tongue of the type shown in pl. xv, no. 7, and a broad oval plate set with glass inlay now much discoloured. The style is coarse and probably primitive, and the Vandal series from Bône, Algeria (Case B), furnishes parallels both for the shape (fig. 206) and the cell-work (fig. 207). A buckle of this shape comes from Herpes, Charente (Case B), where it contrasts with the normal types; and some improvement in the cell-work is seen on the gold jewel (pl. III, no. 3) from Kent, probably in the neighbourhood of Sittingbourne (Case D 2). Most of the cells are still filled with garnets; the central stone is of greenish colour, and flanking it are two cabochon sapphires or imitations in glass. As the back is quite plain, the jewel has never been worn as a brooch.

A bronze plate (fig. 37) is engraved on both faces in a late classical (Romanizing) style quite distinct from the Teutonic, and belongs to a small series found in the south-eastern counties. The design in this case consists of a central panel with saltire, arcading, ring-and-dot pattern, and formal borders; but in another case the outer border has confronted animals in the style of the Sarre brooch (fig. 59). These are hardly realistic, but are evidently nearer the source of the animal ornament than the majority of Teutonic antiquities. The series is not particularly early, and no doubt emanated from some centre where classical tradition had not been entirely abandoned even in the sixth century.

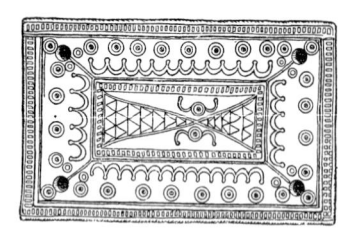

FIG. 37. Bronze plate engraved on both sides, Faversham. (¼)

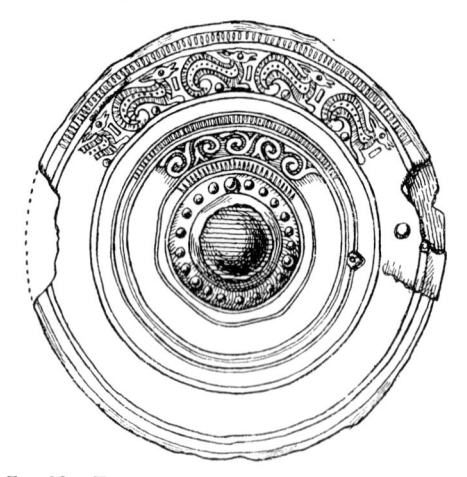

FIG. 38. Engraved bronze disk, Faversham. (¼)

A zone of similar animals is seen on the bronze disk from Faversham (fig. 38), which has a boss of blue glass at the centre, surrounded by disconnected scrolls, a somewhat unusual variety.

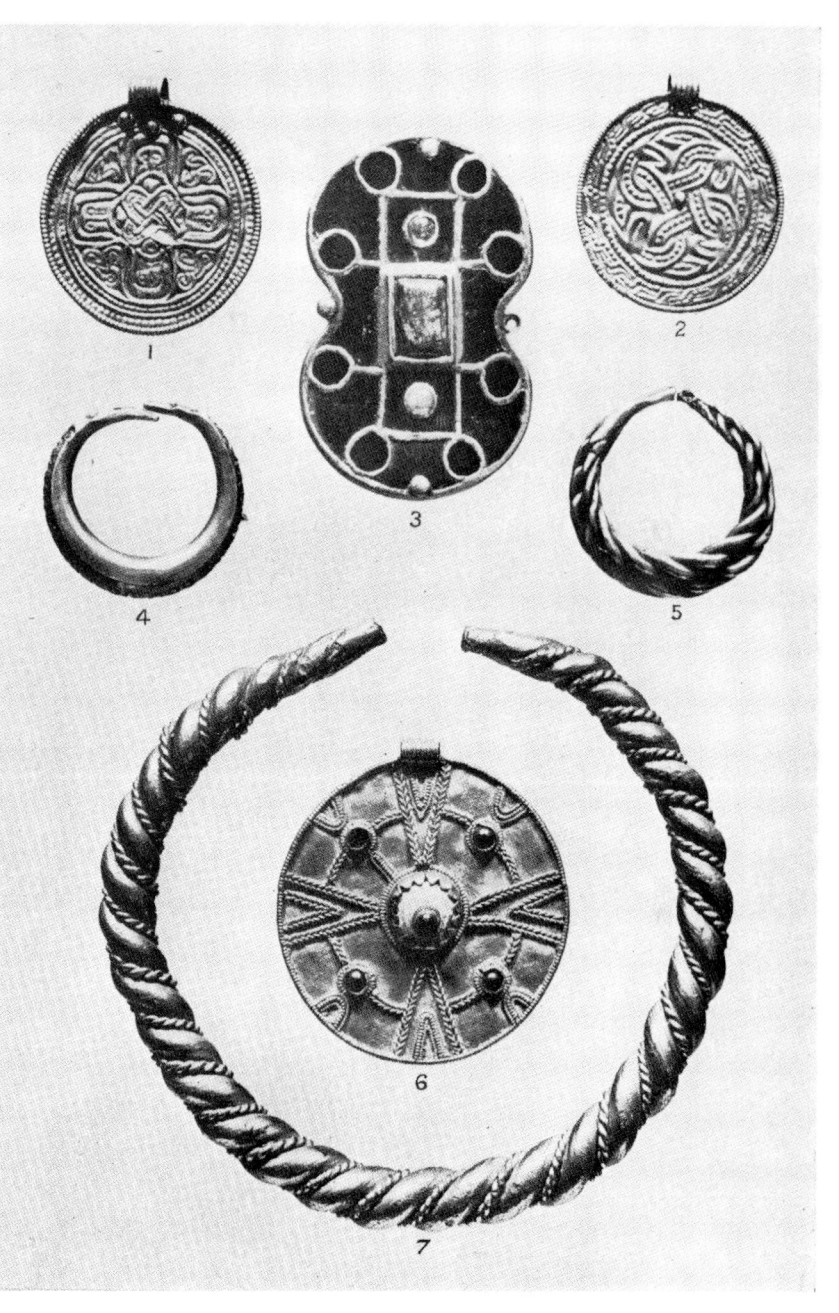

PLATE III. ANGLO-SAXON AND VIKING JEWELLERY FROM ENGLAND ($\frac{1}{1}$)
(Cases D and A 5, see pp. 42, 57, 62, 117)

The oblong plates (fig. 39) consisting of half-cylinders with rivets at either end for attachment to a belt are made of silver with zigzag borders in niello, and triangular panels with animals deeply cut and faceted. The oblong with its saltire and ring-and-dot pattern has a certain analogy to the bronze-plate just noticed (fig. 37); and this blend of classical and Teutonic motives may date from about 550 (Salin's Style I). More debased, and probably later, are pins of gilt bronze from this cemetery (figs. 40, 41), the heads being scarcely recognizable as quadrupeds; they may be assigned to the transition period (Style I–II), and date from the seventh century. The pointed jaw, which may be recognized in fig. 41, is better represented in a gold buckle from this cemetery which has two fairly complete animals in Style II flanking a fish (fig. 42); but the ring-and-dot above the point of the jaw should not be mistaken for the eye, which is within the right angle close to the outer margin.

FIG. 39. Silver buckle-plate, with side view, Faversham. ($\frac{1}{4}$)

The bird-headed pin, set with garnets, belongs to another

FIGS. 40, 41. Bronze-gilt pins, Faversham, Kent. ($\frac{1}{2}$)

category, and emphasizes the connexion between Kent and the middle Rhine at this period, as a bird of prey (perhaps the hawk) was a characteristic ornament of the Goths who moved west from the Crimea, and also of the Huns whose advance into Europe displaced many of the Teutonic tribes in the first half of the fifth century (p. 168). The garnet settings can also be traced to South Russia along the southern (central European) stream of influence (p. 156), which started about A. D. 400.

Another type represented at Faversham is the so-called union pin, probably worn in the hair, consisting of two short pins united at the end by a chain. Specimens are generally imperfect, as from Breach Downs, Canterbury, and Lymne, Kent (Case D 4); and an exceptional example of late type, with gold links and jewelled centre, is exhibited in Case D 2 from Little Hampton Worcestershire, the closest parallel to which was found on Roundway Down (Devizes Museum). Needles or bodkins of bronze are xhibited with the pins in Case 49 ; others from Kempston in Case 42.

Gold braid or flat wire has been found on Kentish and other sites in this country, and has evidently been worked into a fabric on the loom : to judge by its position in the graves, this was generally the head-dress. The silk, linen, or wool with which it was incorporated has decayed, but the gold remains unchanged ; and reference may be made to the ephod made for Aaron (Exodus xxxix. 3) : 'And they did beat the gold into thin plates, and cut it into wires, to work it in the blue, and in the purple, and in the scarlet, and in the fine linen, with cunning work.' It is evident that such rich

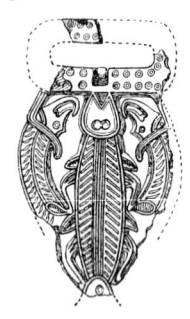

FIG. 42. Bronze-gilt buckle, Faversham. ($\frac{1}{1}$)

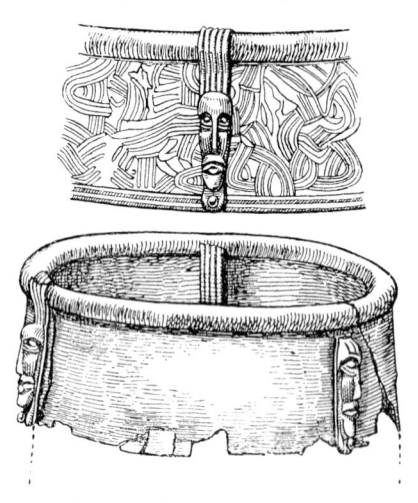

FIG. 43. Mount of drinking-cup, Faversham. ($\frac{3}{4}$)

FIG. 44. Bronze pyramid, with side and base. ($\frac{1}{1}$)

material was not used exclusively by women, as it was found in the warrior's grave at Taplow, and in the coffin of St. Cuthbert at Durham (died 687).

COLLECTION FROM FAVERSHAM 45

Attention may be drawn to the handsome series of horse-trappings in gilt bronze (Case 48), perhaps buried with the horse in its master's grave. All the disks had a garnet set in a boss of white material (p. 37) at the centre, and a star pattern of four points with corresponding projections from the edge. The front was heavily gilt, and engraved silver plates enrich the borders, while the ground is filled with pure (not animal) interlacing, as seen for example on some of the Caenby pieces in Case C (fig. 103). A debased example of this interlacing (fig. 43) is the silver mounting of a wooden cup or drinking horn (as Taplow, fig. 72), with human faces in relief at intervals, a tradition that evidently survived till the ninth century (fig. 127).

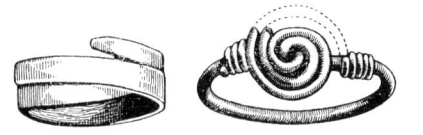

FIG. 45. Silver finger-rings, Faversham. ($\frac{1}{1}$)

Three hollow pyramids of bronze (fig. 44) have a bar across the back, over which a strap was no doubt passed in use. Such ornaments are sometimes found set with garnets, as in Devizes Museum from Salisbury race-course; and one from the warrior's grave at Broomfield, Essex (Case D 1). They are sometimes found abroad, and a plain example from the Marne is exhibited in Case 57; but against the theory that they were connected in some way with the sword is the fact that one was found at Uncleby, East Riding, Yorks., in what was obviously the grave of a woman.

FIG. 46. Silver armlet, Faversham. ($\frac{2}{3}$)

Finger-rings of the pagan period were often of silver, and two are here illustrated (fig. 45). That on the left is the common form, as from Chessel Down, Isle of Wight, and Long Wittenham, Berkshire; and the other (right) is of wire with a coil to form the bezel and the ends wound round the hoop, like one from Sarre, Kent. This method of providing elasticity is also adopted in bracelets (fig. 46), and the simpler kind of ear-ring consisting of a ring on which is strung a single glass bead.

Articles of the toilet are often found attached to a ring in sets, as at Kempston, Beds. (Case 42), and separately in Case B; but a nail-cleaner is here illustrated (fig. 47) as it occurs without its companions at Faversham and needs explanation. Other articles

FIG. 47. Bronze toilet implement, Faversham. ($\frac{1}{1}$)

of silver are illustrated from the Champagne district of France, and the set generally includes an ear-scoop, toothpick, and tweezers. For the last several explanations have been hazarded; and though the removal of stray hairs is a purpose fairly obvious, the recent discovery of similar sets in use on the Tibet border of India shows that the tweezers might well have been used for the removal of thorns from the flesh. Part of a 'girdle-hanger' is illustrated (fig. 48) as perhaps the only example found south of the Thames. Under that name are included several patterns, all no doubt worn by women and attached to the girdle by a ring. They are often found in pairs, occasionally joined by a bronze band at the top (as fig. 107), and their exact use is unknown; but a plausible theory is that they represent the bunch of keys worn by Roman matrons as a symbol of domestic authority; and as the locks of early Teutonic peoples were of the simplest construction, the keys would not be required to do more than lift a latch after passing through the keyhole. The keys soon became merely ornaments or symbols, and small rings attached to the lower part of some specimens suggest that tassels or spangles of bronze were added (like the pins, fig. 87), or that fabric was sewn to the end to serve as a reticule.

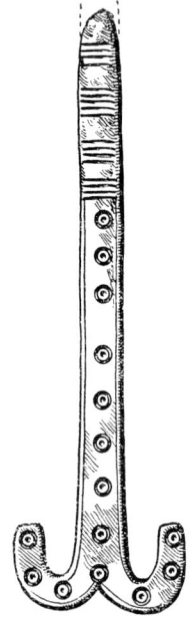

FIG. 48. Bronze 'girdle-hanger', Faversham. ($\frac{3}{4}$)

No precise use has yet been assigned to the crystal balls which are known in the Frankish area and are represented at Faversham; other examples in this collection come from the Isle of Wight (fig. 73), Bedfordshire (Case 42), and abroad (Case B). They are generally provided with a loop and bands of silver, and on more than one occasion have been found in the perforated bowl of a spoon, associated with a woman's skeleton. Crystal-gazing has been popular in many periods of history; but the spoon, which might give a clue to the use of such crystals in Anglo-Saxon times, is itself a still greater mystery. The stem is sometimes set with garnets; and as the bowl is pierced, it is safe to assume that the spoons were more for ornament than use. Portions of normal Roman spoons are exhibited from this site, and some Anglo-Saxon specimens were without the perforated bowl (fig. 88).

Crystal was one of the materials popular in the form of beads, and there is one spindle-whorl made of it in Case 48, others from the site being of amber and glass. The Kentish graves are specially rich in amethyst drop-shaped beads, which also occur on the lower Rhine, where they may have been derived from Roman centres. Amber beads are often roughly shaped, and the glass specimens are of great variety in several colours. Two other types are noteworthy—the 'melon' bead of turquoise-coloured glass dating from Roman times, and the multiple bead (several pearls moulded together in a row) which has a long history, being represented in the Bronze Age burials of Britain and in Egypt of the Eighteenth Dynasty (*Bronze Age Guide*, 2nd ed., fig. 89). It has been observed that, apart from the 'melon' pattern, small beads are closer to the Roman style in shape and colour, and therefore presumably earlier, than the large variegated examples of glass paste seen in the Faversham and Champagne series (Case B).

Apart from the jewelled specimens already mentioned (p. 39), the Faversham brooches are mostly small, and of several different types. The radiated specimens show both the straight and lozenge foot (p. 33), which belong to the first half of the sixth century, but are in a decided minority here, as elsewhere in England. Square or oblong heads are seen on several of silver and bronze, the latter in some cases gilt and set with garnets. The more ornate are similar to the Isle of Wight finds in Case 39.

Many of the smaller bronze brooches are difficult to classify, and some of them are almost equal-ended; but there can be no mistaking the long brooches of Scandinavian (probably Danish) origin occasionally found elsewhere in Kent. They are certainly smaller than the majority of Anglian brooches, but not of the earliest form, as the knobs are here cast in one piece with the head (p. 26). A similar brooch from Lyminge, Kent (Case D 2) is rather flatter; and two from Howletts, south of Canterbury, have lost the side knobs, which were cast separately.

Small penannular brooches belong to the type common throughout the Roman period, and may perhaps be attributed to the Romanized Britons of Kent, whose civilization would not have succumbed without a struggle. Others are included in the series from the Kempston cemetery, Bedfordshire, exhibited in Case 42.

Of rare occurrence are the annular or ring-brooches of silver (Case D 2) which have animal heads confronted at the terminals (fig. 49) sometimes with the pointed jaw of Style II. Besides

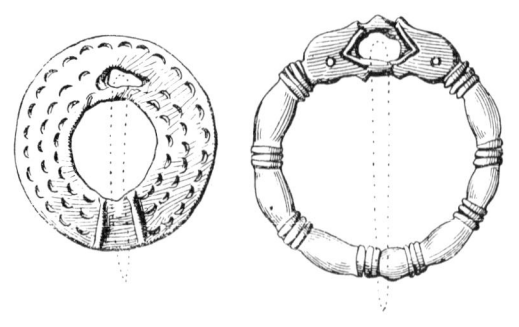

Fig. 49. Ring-brooches, East Shefford and Faversham. ($\frac{3}{4}$)

the few in Kent, there are some in York Museum from burials in what was originally a Bronze Age barrow (burial mound) at Uncleby, East Riding, Yorks., with other Kentish types.

The saucer-brooch is not generally regarded as a Kentish type, though several have been found in the county (p. 35). Those from Faversham are by no means early in the series, and one is remarkable for a setting of red enamel in the centre. Garnets are occasionally found in that position, and a small saucer (or button) brooch is exhibited with this added ornament: others in Case 47 from Longbridge, Warwickshire.

On the floor of Case 49 is a series of draughtsmen or gaming pieces made from horse-teeth (fig. 50), probably from Faversham, and to be compared with those from the Taplow barrow (Case 50) and the Island of Gotland (Case 55). Other links with Taplow are the bronze bowl with vandyke edge and open-work foot exhibited, with others of ordinary type from Faversham, in Case 41 ; the gold thread, and the jewellery (p. 64).

Fig. 50. Draughtsmen, Taplow and Faversham. ($\frac{3}{4}$)

Like most of the richer cemeteries, Faversham produced a certain number of swords, presumably from the graves of thegns or chieftains ; and these retain the cocked-hat pommel. The ornamented guards of two are in Case D 5. The ring-sword mentioned in *Beowulf* (p. 4) is taken to be the weapon with ring attached to the pommel, of the type represented specially in

Sweden, but also in Norway, Denmark, England, Germany, and Italy. Two at the top of Case 49 from Faversham, and specimens from Gilton, Kent (Liverpool Museum), and Bifrons (Maidstone Museum) are the only ones with the ring loose, and therefore available for use. Towards the end of the sixth century the ring and the loop in which it hangs increase in size and fill each other; both are then incorporated in the pommel, and are sometimes ornamented, the type disappearing before the end of the seventh century. A jewelled example in Case 61 (fig. 209) was found in Italy, and shows that in its later stages of develop-

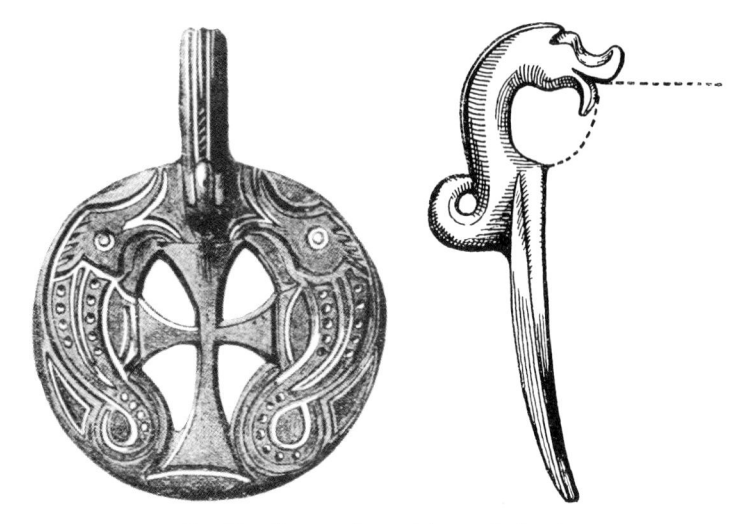

FIG. 51. Openwork escutcheon of a bowl, with side view, Faversham. (¼)

ment the ring was closed and would not even hold a sword-knot, or loop of leather to attach the sword to the wrist in action. In any case the knot could have been attached to the loop, as easily as to the loose ring, of the earlier examples.

More numerous than swords are the iron bosses of shields (p. 70) which formed part of the common soldier's equipment. Some of the Faversham examples show the grip in position underneath, the arrangement being seen in the diagram (fig. 111).

Of exceptional rarity is the Christian monogram (if such it be) on the end of a heavily gilt knife-handle, and there are a few other relics from the site that may date from the seventh century, after the conversion of Kent by Augustine. Of these the most convincing are three open-work escutcheons (fig. 51) from a bronze bowl, for attaching chains to the rim. In the centre is

50 DESCRIPTION OF CASES D 5, 48, 49

a Latin cross supported by two animals that may be meant for the hippocamp common in late Roman art. One of a set probably from Northumberland (fig. 52) with hook attached to

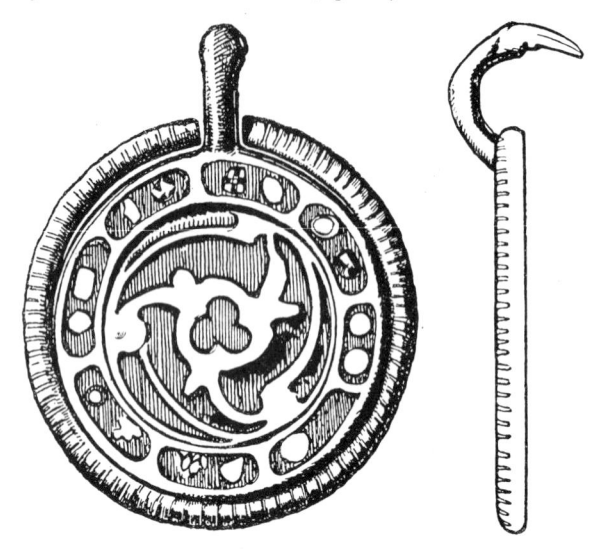

FIG. 52. Enamelled escutcheon of bowl, with side view. (¼)

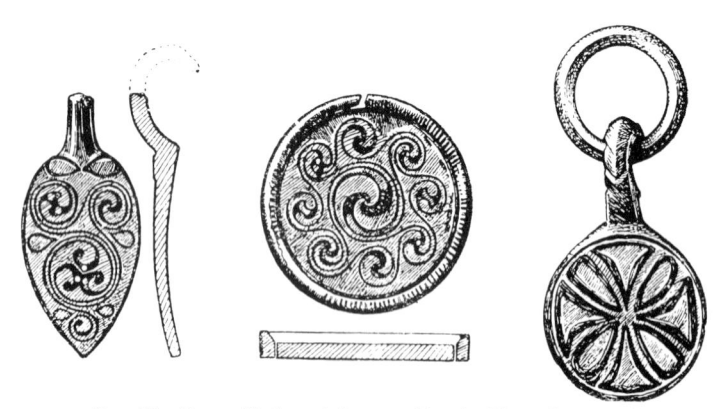

FIG. 53. Enamelled escutcheons of bowls, Faversham. (¼)

the frame is not in the best Irish style; it has, besides the enamel, slices of glass rods showing a chequer pattern. Some smaller disks (fig. 53) in Case 41, evidently for the same purpose, have a design that might also be taken for the Christian symbol.

Reference has already been made to the cruciform pattern in garnets on a brooch from this cemetery (p. 38), and the fish on a gold buckle (fig. 42) may also be a Christian symbol, as the Greek word for fish consists of the initial letters of a Christian confession of faith. Another buckle bearing a fish, from Crundale, Kent, is in the adjoining section 4 of Case D; and badges of this form are in Case 42 (fig. 85) and Case 51; also in Case A 1 (France).

At Faversham vessels of glass (fig. 54, c, f) formed one of the most important series, and differ in some particulars from those of northern France, though it is at present impossible to decide their place of origin. The colours are blue, bluish green, and

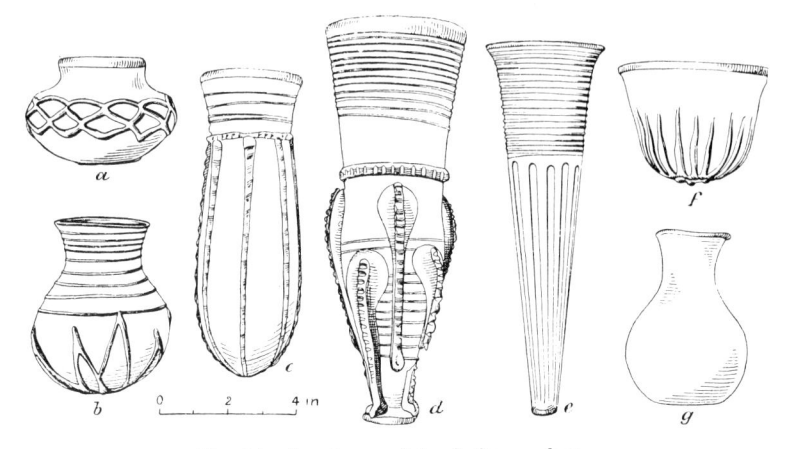

Fig. 54. Specimens of Anglo-Saxon glass.

amber; and the shapes are mostly without distinction, with globular bodies and short cylindrical mouths (as fig. 54, b, g), little more than jars in some cases. The drinking cups are generally mammiform (hemispherical with expanding lip, as fig. 54, f, whereas the Frankish pattern is funnel-shaped with rounded base (fig. 192, d); and in Case 47 there are a few Kentish specimens of the lobed beaker (as fig. 54, d), a tall vessel with one or more zones of hollow claw-like projections open towards the interior. These triumphs of the glass-blower's art are also found abroad (p. 157), and in England are common in Kent, but found sporadically as far afield as Winchester, Fairford, Northants, and Castle Eden, co. Durham. This method of decoration was perhaps suggested by a classical type with drop-shaped projections; two such specimens, from Thera and Cyzicus, are exhibited at the east end of King Edward VII gallery, in the standard-case of Roman glass. The more common drinking vessel is a tumbler in the original sense, having a pointed or rounded base that prevents it standing upright. The conical and ribbed patterns are here illustrated (fig. 54, c, e).

Finally the pottery from Faversham is remarkable and quite unlike the ordinary Anglo-Saxon ware in this country or abroad. Comparison is inevitable with the Frankish series in Cases 57-61; and much of it is clearly late classical, that is, Roman both in form and paste, probably produced locally by the Romanized inhabitants of Kent after the withdrawal of 410. Unfortunately there is no record of its association in this vast cemetery with any datable objects; but at Sarre the peculiar bottle-shaped vessel (as fig. 55)

FIG. 55. Pottery bottles of Jutish type. ($\frac{1}{5}$)

with zones of stamped or incised pattern was much in evidence; and Mr. Leeds has laid stress on its similarity to finds in the Eifel district and round Andernach on the Rhine. At home and abroad they seem to be found usually in the graves of men, and sometimes in association with pottery jugs with trefoil mouth. Most are of hard reddish ware and turned on the wheel, whereas the ordinary Teutonic ware is grey or black, and modelled by hand.

Other antiquities from Kent, presumably of Jutish origin, are exhibited in Case D, sections 2, 4, 5, and Cases 41, 47, 49; the Isle of Wight and Hampshire series being in Cases 39, 40, and D 6. Most of the groups contain circular brooches with garnet inlays of keystone type (fig. 33), also buckles with triangular plates bearing three bosses, and filigree or other decoration in the centre. A rarer type is the square-headed brooch with garnet inlay found in various sizes both in this county and in the Isle of Wight (Case 39). Three imperfect examples (fig. 56) are exhibited in Case D 2 from Milton-next-Sittingbourne; and are instructive as showing the gradual deterioration of the animal-ornament. Comparison with figs. 67 and 100 will help to elucidate the outer decoration both of the head and foot of this series.

Adjoining these is a group (including the whole contents of one

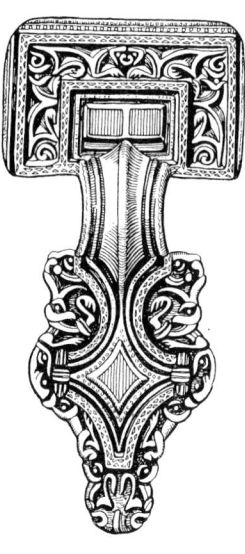

Fig. 56. Jewelled square-headed brooch, Milton-next-Sittingbourne. ($\frac{2}{3}$)

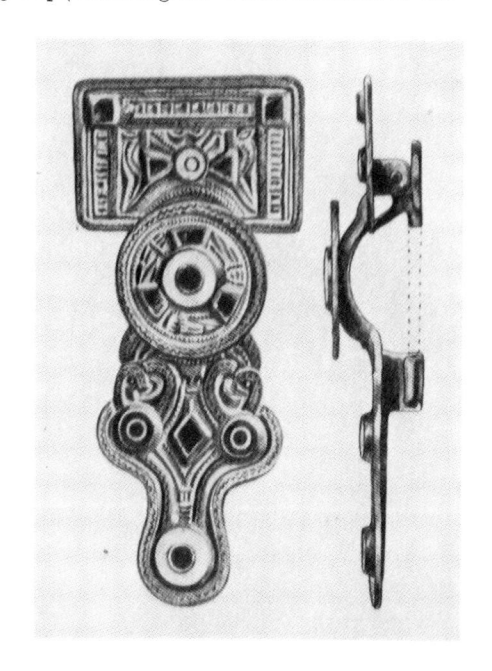

Fig. 57. Jewelled square-headed brooch with disk on bow, Howletts. ($\frac{3}{4}$)

grave) from a cemetery at Howletts, between Littlebourne and Bekesbourne station, in the Little Stour valley, where Anglo-Saxon sites abound. Besides the heavy buckle with violin-shaped tongue and shoe-shaped rivets (as fig. 35) may be mentioned the crystal hoop of a buckle, like that from the Marne district of France (Case 58). A bronze buckle has a half-cylinder on the plate, with a row of rivets like the silver specimens from Faversham (fig. 39) but less ornate. Besides the normal jewelled brooches there is a square-headed specimen of the same type as fig. 56, but half the length; a jewelled rosette-brooch of Frankish type (a cross with the arms filled with concentric rings, cf. Case A 6), a plain s-brooch with bird's-head terminals; and a square-headed brooch with a disk (resembling a keystone brooch) on the bow (fig. 57), in the Gotland style (Case 55). The radiated brooches are early and interesting: a pair with jewelled projections have a foot with parallel sides and square end (like fig. 26), but the other is of the central European type (pl. xiv, no. 8), with animal-head terminal to the foot, and lozenge or snake's-head knobs round the head, as no. 6 on the plate.

The small 'long' brooches have been already referred to (p. 47), and it remains to mention the quoit-shaped brooch of silver, with two zones of animal pattern (fig. 58), including the human face. This form of brooch is characteristic of Sussex and

FIG. 58. Details of silver quoit brooch, Howletts. ($\frac{3}{2}$)

therefore not essentially Jutish, but by far the best example comes from Sarre (fig. 59) and is exhibited with other objects in Case D 4. It is of silver, partly gilt, and measures just over 3 in. across, belonging strictly to the penannular type (as the internal ring is interrupted to admit the pin point), but generally classified as a quoit or annular brooch, as the outer border is a complete circle. This is engraved with animal pattern in two zones, each figure being independent and fairly complete, and on the base of the pin and near its point are three birds resembling doves, cast in the round and moving on pivots. It probably dates from about 550, but the animals are fairly naturalistic for Anglo-Saxon work, and an earlier date is possible, as similar animals serve as a border to an oblong plate from Bishopstone, Bucks. (Aylesbury Museum), very like fig. 37, and these seem to be not far from classical models. The border has a curious resemblance to that of a gold bracteate found near Lyngby, Ebeltoft, Jutland, of the early sixth century.

On the edge of the marshy ground drained by the Stour between Canterbury and Ramsgate (formerly the Wantsum, an arm of the sea separating Thanet from Kent), the village and neighbourhood of Sarre have produced some valuable jewellery, once deposited in graves. One of the richest groups was discovered in 1860, six feet below the surface of chalk-land, where a grave had been cut, the skeleton lying with the head NW. A fine jewelled brooch of circular form (fig. 60), 2¾ in. across, lay on the left breast, and

Fig. 59. Details of silver quoit brooch, Sarre. (¼)

closely resembles two found at Abingdon, Berks., one of which is in Case D. It has one large central boss of mother-of-pearl (or other white material) surrounded by four smaller bosses, all bordered with garnet cell-work on a gold filigree ground. A bronze bowl (like fig. 90) of the usual Kentish pattern with openwork foot, but of unusual dimensions (Case 41), contained bones of unnamed animals; and a necklace (fig. 60) consisted of coloured glass beads, with a central pendant of mosaic glass and four looped gold coins of the emperors Mauricius Tiberius (d. 602) and Heraclius (d. 641), with one of Lothair II, king of the Franks (d. 628). These were all barbarous imitations of the *solidus*, but serve to date the burial between 613 and about A.D. 650. Besides a few minor objects there was one of iron (as fig. 61) in the grave which was described as a sword, but was probably something more

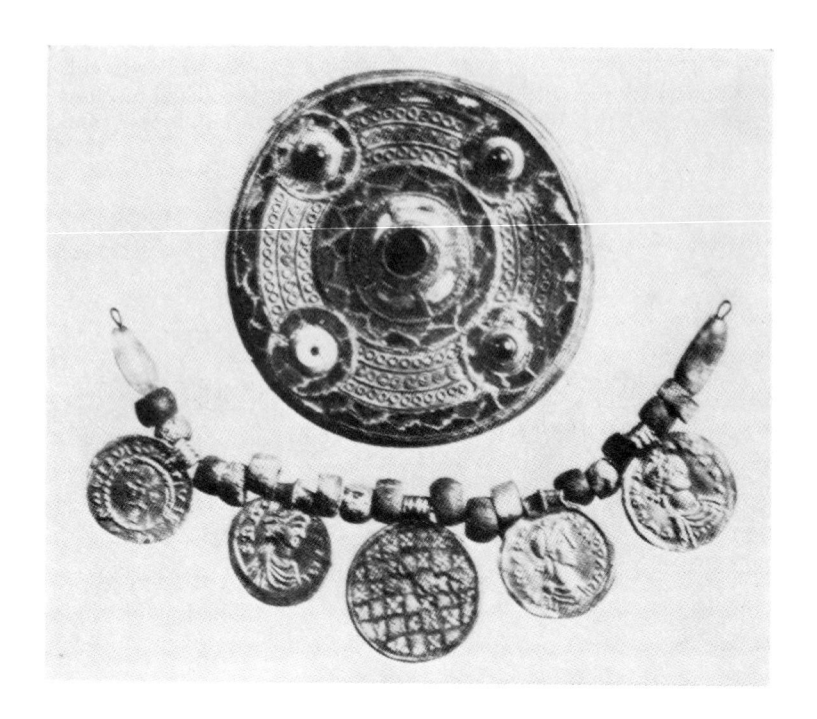

FIG. 60. Jewelled brooch and necklace of coins, Sarre. ($\frac{4}{5}$)

appropriate in a woman's grave. It has a blade like a short two-edged sword, but terminates at both ends in a tang, the longer no doubt being a handle. It is now commonly regarded as a reed,

FIG. 61. Iron weaving-implement, Chessel Down, I.W. ($\frac{1}{5}$)

lay, or batten for striking home the weft threads on a loom, and other examples have been found at Ozingell, Kent; Mitcham, Surrey; and Chessel Down, Isle of Wight, besides a Frankish example from Herpes, Charente, in Case 58.

From other Sarre finds a bronze strap-end or girdle-tab is selected for illustration (fig. 62) as a good example of animal-ornament in Style I (latter half of sixth century). Two of the Teutonic quadrupeds are here represented, one behind the other, the single fore-leg being extended in front of each: the eye and angular band behind it are easily recognized and may be compared with figs. 67 and 98. There are also ear-rings of silver with glass beads threaded on them, as well as larger beads forming a necklace; a gilt button-brooch with human face, two annular (ring) brooches which have lost their pins, and two small keystone brooches with garnets. A bronze bird, not of the raptorial kind as usual (Walthamstow, Case A 1), is moulded in low relief and has been used as a brooch, the pin now missing at the back.

Beside these are fragments of a bronze-mounted wooden bucket; iron disks probably from warrior's equipment, spear-heads, and knives of the type found in most Anglo-Saxon graves. The knife must have been carried on the person, for use at meals and elsewhere; and was so intimately associated with the individual as to be included in the grave even when other furniture was lacking.

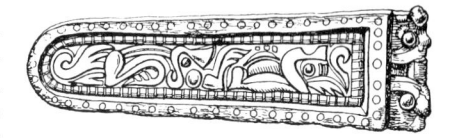

FIG. 62. Bronze strap-end, Sarre. ($\frac{1}{1}$)

Stodmarsh is half-way between Sarre and Canterbury, on the western edge of the low ground then covered by the river Wantsum. The Frankish buckles with violin tongue and the shoe-shaped rivets are normal, but there are two extraordinary brooches (one jewelled) from this site, also a triangular buckle-plate of silver with gold filigree, and a spoon with perforated bowl and a large triangular garnet at the base of the handle. It was in such spoons as this that several of the crystal spheres were found, and their significance is at present unknown.

The keystone brooch and triangular buckle-plate occur again at Ash (towards Sandwich), and with these are exhibited a gold pendant of the bracteate type (pl. III, no. 1) with human faces in the four arms of a cross; and an imperfect pair of brooches with garnets, a smaller version of fig. 56. This identical pattern occurs again at Ickham (Case D 4), with another square-headed brooch and a button brooch with human face.

Wingham, six miles east of Canterbury, is represented by a fine circular brooch (frontisp., no. 2) with four-pointed star of garnet and blue glass cell-work, and white bosses surmounted by garnets; also a pin (fig. 63) with splayed head set with garnets in the form of birds' heads, a later version of the motive seen in fig. 68. On plate III (no. 2) is one of the pair of gold bracteates with ser-

58   DESCRIPTION OF CASE D 4

pentine interlacing all over the front; and worthy of remark is the small bronze cross (fig. 64) evidently worn as a pendant by some early convert.

A number of grave-mounds (barrows, *tumuli*) were excavated on Breach Downs, four miles south of Canterbury, in 1841, and the objects found (Case D 4) were promptly published with

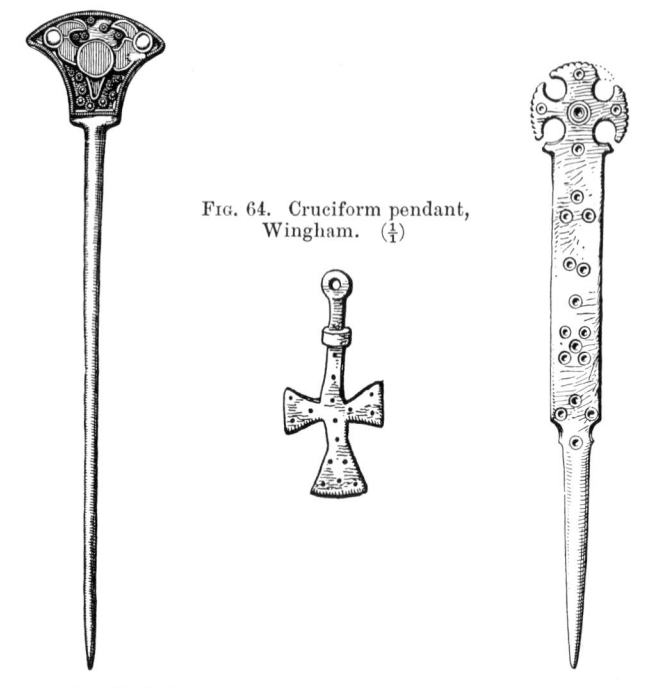

FIG. 64. Cruciform pendant, Wingham. (¼)

FIG. 63. Jewelled pin, Wingham. (¼)

FIG. 65. Bronze pin with cross, Breach Down. (¾)

illustrations. Of a group of thirteen the largest mound was 8 ft. high, the remainder being 4 ft. and less, to an elevation barely noticeable. Within each was found a grave cut in the solid chalk from east to west, and from 1 ft. to 2 ft. or even 4 ft. in depth. A gold disk, with loop for use as a pendant, has a cruciform pattern in filigree on the front and a cabochon garnet (carbuncle) in the centre; and the pattern may here be significant (p. 59). A buckle, with oblong plate now hollow, was probably set with a large slab of garnet, and can only be compared with one from Tostock, Suffolk, which still retains a garnet measuring 1·1 in. by 0·6 in. There are minute bronze buckles, also catches for a casket, and the union-pin already mentioned (p. 43). Beads are also conspicuous, consisting of amethyst, crystal, and coloured glass; and in a barrow on the same downs, and about the same time, was found the bronze pin (fig. 65) which is obviously of Christian origin. These interments probably belong to the early part of the seventh century, just after the coming of St. Augustine, but the east-and-west position was normal in Kent throughout the pagan period. A glass 'tumbler' from that site, in Case 47, has a conical body and rounded base, and belongs to a Merovingian type rarely found in England (Case 59).

Both Wye and Crundale lie west of Breach Downs, and the former site has produced, besides a cabochon garnet (carbuncle) in a gold setting, three gold disks mounted as pendants: one is divided into quadrants by applied wire, with an inner ring round a central boss; the second has empty cell-work resembling that of coin-pendants in the same Case; and the third has a distinct Greek cross, with interlacing in each arm, beaten up from the back as were the foreign bracteates. This last can hardly be anything but a Christian emblem, and has therefore a bearing on pl. III, no. 1.

The Crundale buckle with its fish in relief and silver counterplate has been already referred to (p. 51), and is a striking example of seventh-century work, with pure knot-work in filigree, and garnets arranged in a scale-pattern on the expanded base of the tongue. Another buckle is gilt, and is peculiar in having a crescent of garnet cell-work at the root of the tongue.

The large saucer-brooch with central stud from Dover has been already mentioned (p. 35), and there are the usual ear-rings and amethyst beads from that town; but special attention should be given to the jewelled brooch of the Sarre and Abingdon type, though finer than either, and an excellent example of Kentish goldsmith's work at the best period (about A.D. 600).

A kidney-shaped weight of bronze found at Grove Ferry, near Canterbury, has twenty-two impressions of the same stamp on both faces, but differently arranged, so that these are more probably ornamental than an indication of the standard. The weight is 576 grains or 37·3 grammes, exactly one-tenth of the Troy pound. As the history of Troy weight is obscure, this weight might be classed as mediaeval if it did not accord with the Anglo-Saxon standard deduced from the weights in a Jutish money-changer's grave at Ozingell, Thanet, eight miles from the site in question. Here among several weights of less significance were found three with the following values (G for grammes):

145 grains (9·39 G) marked with 3 dots,
    giving a unit of 48·3 grains (3·13 G);
243 grains (15·74 G) marked with 5 dots,
    giving a unit of 48·6 grains (3·15 G);
292 grains (18·92 G) marked with 6 cuts,
    giving a unit of 48·6 grains (3·15 G);

and the Grove Ferry weight is exactly twelve times 48 grains (3·11 G). In other words, the Grove Ferry weight is twelve times an Anglo-Saxon unit, and one-tenth of the Troy pound, which is now divided into 12 ounces. There is some independent evidence (collected by Mr. Wilfrid Airy) that in the time of the Saxons the Troy pound was subdivided decimally, and that Troy ounces (480 grains or 31·1 G) were also in use; as witness the Ozingell specimens given above, in which the ounce itself is subdivided decimally. The Grove Ferry weight therefore confirms the view that in Anglo-Saxon times both these systems were in use, at least for weighing small quantities:

1 Troy pound = 12 ounces   1 Troy pound = 10 G. F. weights
1 ounce = 10 units   G. F. weight = 12 units.

Lastly from Kent must be mentioned a group in Case 49 with strong continental affinities. The spear and shield-boss indicate

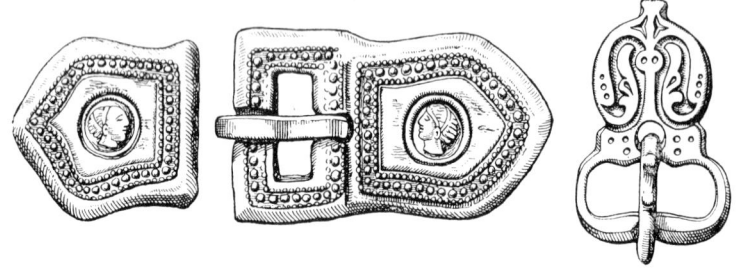

Fig. 66. Bronze buckles and counter-plate, Kent. ($\frac{2}{3}$)

the grave of a warrior, the knife is customary, but the four buckles (one with counter-plate) are unexpected finds in England. The largest (fig. 66) has a late classical appearance, with two heads in medallions apparently copied from antique cameos. A close parallel from Akmîm, Upper Egypt (Case 60), has interlacing instead of the medallion, and the style of decoration is in strong contrast to the Teutonic. The other three have openwork plates based on the classical acanthus, here split in two halves; and similar examples are exhibited from Sofia (Bulgaria) and Carthage (Case 60), and Kerch in the Crimea (Case 65). These were evidently manufactured in quantity somewhere in the Eastern Empire and traded far and wide.

Objects ornamented in the Kentish style have often been found outside the limits of the present county; and a few are exhibited in Case D. The most remarkable is the Abingdon brooch, one of a pair found at Milton North Field in 1832, evidently in an Anglo-Saxon cemetery. It is a disk about 3 in. across, with the usual white bosses surmounted by garnets, small garnet cellwork round the centre and edge, also in the arms of the cross;

and between the arms gold filigree in debased animal patterns (as on the Taplow clasps, pl. v, nos. 1, 3) that have become almost pure interlacing, and date the brooch about A.D. 620. Its fellow is in the Ashmolean Museum, Oxford, and one at least of them was found on the breast of a skeleton which lay due north and south at 2 ft. from the surface. Two iron spear-heads and a scramasax (sword-knife) from this cemetery are in Case 40.

The bronze oblong plate (fig. 67) from Barn Elms (on the Thames between Putney and Hammersmith), once attached to a leather girdle, has lost its central setting, but has a characteristic border of animal pattern in good Style I. There are two animals, and one eye of each can be distinguished, also the fore and hind legs, with the tail: and an outline of one animal is added to make clear the anatomy, which is more logical in this case and in fig. 62 than is usual in the sixth century.

FIG. 67. Bronze buckle-plate from Barn Elms. ($\frac{1}{1}$)

Much light is thrown on the garnet cell-work of the Anglo-Saxons by one of the gold coins mounted as pendants in Case D 2. It is a *solidus* of Heraclius I (610–41) with a double beaded border added by the goldsmith who enclosed it in a Greek cross with garnet inlay (pl. IV, no. 3). The obverse of the coin is on the under face of the pendant, and bears the effigies of the emperor and his son: the reverse, which forms the centre of the jewel, displays a cross upon a flight of four steps with the legend VICTORIA AVGVS-TORVM, an E which is probably the mint-mark, and the mysterious BOXX. The preference given to the cross on the reverse of the coin, as well as the form of the mount, show that the original owner was a Christian, but the jeweller has mounted it upside down, a blunder no doubt due to ignorance of the type. Another of the same emperor's coins was found at Sarre (fig. 60), and for reasons mentioned below (p. 80) the jewel may be dated about 630. Less attractive, but probably contemporary, are three other coin-pendants in this Case. That found on the beach between Bacton and Mundesley, Norfolk (pl. IV, no. 1), imbedded in seaweed, contains an imitation gold piece of the emperor Mauricius with his colleague Theodosius (between 590 and 602), struck at Arles, perhaps by a Merovingian king who copied the coinage of the Eastern Empire. This too must therefore be dated early seventh century;

FIG. 68. Jewelled S-brooch, Iffley. (⅟₁)

FIG. 69. Openwork jewel with garnets, Twickenham. (⅟₁)

and two similar pendants are probably contemporary, though one contains a coin of Valens (died 378). The other (pl. IV, no. 2) comes from Forsbrook, Staffs., and has the garnet inlay relieved by blue glass in the semicircular cells.

Another jewel (pl. III, no. 6) of somewhat rough execution was a chance discovery in a chalk-pit near some prehistoric barrows on Acklam Wold, East Riding, Yorks. It consists of a gold disk, 1·6 in. across, with a loop on the edge, and in front a cruciform design of plaited gold wire, with carbuncle settings between the arms and another in a boss of white material (p. 37) in the centre. At least three other gold pendants of this kind have been found in the county, and in Case C are exhibited three small jewels from Seamer in the North Riding, with three cabochon garnets placed as on Kentish buckle-plates.

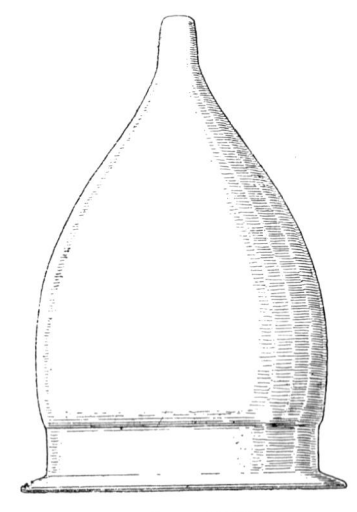

FIG. 70. Iron shield-boss, Twickenham. (⅓)

Another ornament that may have strayed from Kent is the S-shaped brooch with garnet inlay and terminals in the form of birds' heads (restored in fig. 68). There are plain S-brooches from Kent (Case D 2) and the Isle of Wight (Case 39), but the type is evidently continental, and is well represented in the series from Pontoise and Amiens (Case A 6), and the Marne (Case 57).

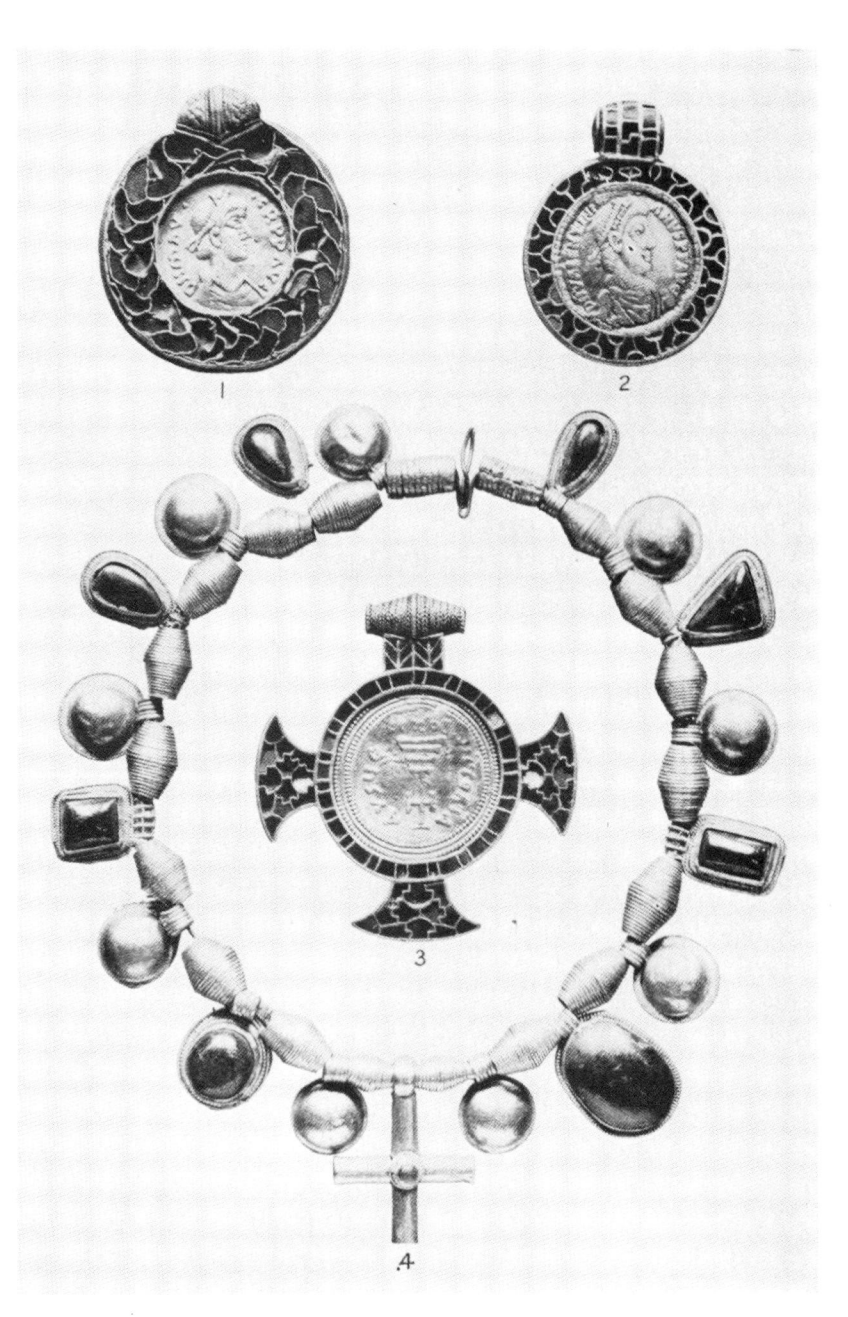

PLATE IV. PENDANTS WITH GARNETS, AND GOLD NECKLACE ($\frac{1}{1}$)
(Case D 2, see pp. 61, 75)

PLATE V. JEWELLERY AND BRONZE BOWL FROM GRAVE AT TAPLOW ($\frac{2}{3}$ AND $\frac{1}{4}$)
(Case 50, *see* p. 64)

The jewel (fig. 69) found at Twickenham, Middlesex, with a sword (Case 41), shield-boss (fig. 70), and a small spear-head, is possibly Kentish work of the seventh century. It is in openwork, with cabochon garnets set in rings of plaited gold wire; and the arrangement here, as often in Kentish jewellery, suggests the Christian cross. An approximate date is thus given to the shield-boss which has the unusual height of 7 in. and has parallels in Kent, Derbyshire (Tissington, in Case 46), and Kempston, Beds. (Case 43). It is in marked contrast to the ordinary varieties (fig. 111, and pl. x, no. 5).

Plaited gold wire is also seen on the pyramidal jewel (Case D 1) from the richly furnished burial at Broomfield, Essex, described by Sir Hercules Read in 1894. The purpose of such pyramids is at present unknown (p. 45), but its garnet inlay and the small piece of cell-work associated with it point to a Kentish origin, which is of interest in view of the paucity of relics from the East Saxon territory. The interment was found 6 or 7 ft. below the surface in a line ESE. and WNW., and it appeared as if a warrior had been placed in a wooden coffin and burnt on the spot, but the total disappearance of the skeleton has been often noticed in Kent. His sword was recovered, and near the centre of the grave was a bronze pan, 13 in. in diameter, with a pair of drop handles, resting on fabric of two qualities (Case 46). The vessel contained a cow's horn, two squat vases of blue glass (fig. 54, a), and two wooden cups, turned on the lathe and furnished with rims of gilt bronze (cf. figs. 43 and 72). As the pottery of the period outside Kent was hand-made, the use of the lathe may imply contact with the Jutish kingdom, which was then at its zenith (p. 4). The grave also contained two wooden buckets with iron mounts, 12 in. in diameter and 10 in. deep, which had been sunk into the floor; and a hemispherical iron cup on a tall stem terminating in four feet. This has a height of over 11 in. and may correspond to the bronze vessel of the Taplow burial (pl. v). There were in addition a deep cylindrical cauldron of iron holding about 2 gallons, a shield-boss with indications of a wooden shield, and a grey wheel-turned vase with impressed chevrons, singularly like one from the King's Field, Faversham (Case 48).

In Case 50 are exhibited remains from an artificial mound or barrow, roughly circular with a diameter of 80 ft. at the base and with a flat top 15 ft. above the level of the old churchyard adjoining Taplow Court. It occupied the centre of a prehistoric fort on high ground overlooking the Thames, and elaborate grave-furniture suggests that the name of the chieftain here buried is preserved in the place-name, the syllable *low* being equivalent to the Anglo-Saxon word for burial-mound. To construct such a barrow the adjacent soil must have been removed to a considerable depth and previous occupation-levels exposed: during its exploration in

1883 worked flints of the prehistoric period were found in the upper levels, and Roman relics below, but the date of the mound was settled by the discovery, 6 ft. below the original surface, of the primary and only burial, over which the mound had been raised early in the seventh century. At 20 ft. from the summit several strands of gold thread were noticed (like that from Faversham, Case D 5) ; and further digging revealed a rectangular grave 12 ft. long and 8 ft. wide, approximately in an east-and-west line, as at Broomfield (p. 63), but with the head at the east end contrary to the Christian rule. The spear had evidently been inverted, and at the side lay a sword in its wooden scabbard, with the grip under the arm. The gold buckle of Kentish type

FIG. 71. Bronze-gilt mount of drinking-horn, Taplow. ($\frac{2}{3}$)

(pl. v, no. 2) is in excellent condition, set with garnets and lapis lazuli, with filigree on the triangular plate ; and the pair of bronze-gilt clasps (nos. 1 and 3) have filigree in the same style, with little trace of animal-ornament surviving. Above the head, on the right, were two shield-bosses, the wooden framework of the shields having perished ; and close to these was an iron knife and ring $4\frac{1}{2}$ in. in diameter. Near the south-east corner was a bucket of about 12 in. in diameter, with an iron frame and ashen staves, having thin embossed plates of bronze outside ; next, a standing bowl of bronze 12 in. high with vandyke rim, pair of drop handles, and openwork foot (pl. v, no. 4), which lay on its side over a small drinking-horn with silver-gilt bands and terminals. Some feet farther west were the fragments of an olive-coloured glass cup with two rows of claw-like projections round the body (fig. 54, *d*) ;

and at the west end lay a large tub in a very crushed condition, which must have been placed over the thighs of the warrior. It had an iron frame, and contained two glass vessels like that illustrated, also two large drinking-horns with vandyke mounts at the mouth (fig. 71) and exceptionally fine terminals (fig. 5) marking the transition to Style II (p. 11). There was a smaller drinking-horn with silver-gilt mounts, and two silver rims (fig. 72) which probably belonged to barrel-shaped cups of thin wood as at Broomfield, Croydon, and Faversham (fig. 43). Northwest of the large bucket was an iron spear-head 21 in. long pointing west, originally barbed and of the angon type (cf. pl. x, no. 1), which is found more commonly in Belgium and N. France, and was used to pierce the enemy's shield and impede his movements: near this was another bucket, and at the west end a fourth glass and drinking-horn, a second spear-head of ordinary type, a silver-gilt ornament, and about 30 cylinders of bone (fig. 50) about 1 in. high,

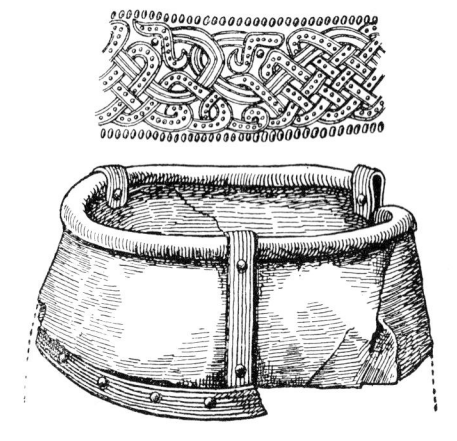

Fig. 72. Mount of drinking-cup, Taplow. ($\frac{3}{4}$)

with the ends closed by disks united by a silver pin. These last were doubtless draughtsmen, and may be compared with several from Faversham and Gotland (Case 55).

All the objects recovered were more or less crushed between stout planks which had been placed both above and below the body, and herein lies one of many resemblances to the interment at Broomfield (p. 63). Some connexion with Kent is not less evident; and the bronze bowl, with vandyke rim resembling one from Faversham (Case 41) was, like the Kentish bowls with open-work foot, probably of Coptic origin.

The Jutish cemetery on Chessel Down, Isle of Wight, has proved one of the richest in England, and is of importance ethnologically (p. 6). The finds collected and described by Mr. George Hillier are in Cases 39, 40; and one of the two large brooches has already been described (fig. 22), but is more characteristic of the Midlands and East Anglia than of the Jutish area. There are others of medium and small size, most of them set with garnets; and another still smaller series, one pair having garnet inlay and some with traces of gilding (as pl. xiv, nos. 1, 4, 5). The button-brooch occurs here, as in Sussex, with the human face, and a larger specimen has a garnet centre ; but several others find their counterparts in the Herpes cemetery, Charente (Case B, see p. 144); and in view of the Frankish character of most from that site, it is probable that this group was taken to France from the Isle of Wight either by emigrants or by raiders. The medium and small square-headed brooches, the equal-armed, rosette and radiated forms, and even the button-brooch with human face are common to the two sites, while another type from Herpes can be matched in Wilts. (p. 81). The buckles are mostly of Frankish types (as Case B) and the purse-guard is more common abroad (as fig. 194); but closer links with Kent are the keystone brooch, the crystal balls (fig. 73) and perforated spoon, shoe-shaped rivets and bird brooches. The beads of glass and amber are comparable with the Faversham series ; and besides the usual spears and shield-mountings, there is a throwing-axe (*francisca*), and seven swords, including one with elaborate decoration and runic inscription (fig. 74) that reads ÆKOSŒRI but has defied interpretation.

FIG. 73. Crystal sphere with mounting, Chessel Down. ($\frac{3}{4}$)

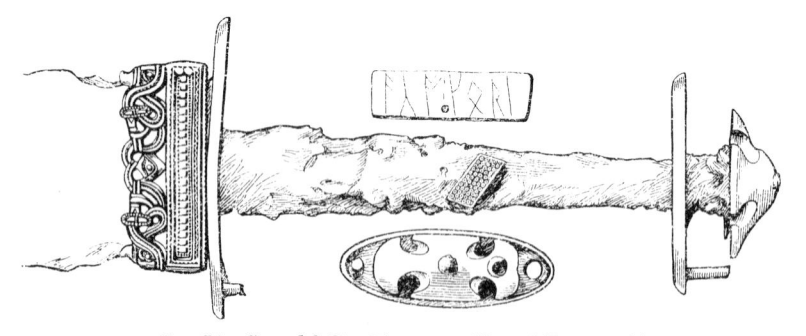

FIG. 74. Sword-hilt with runes, Chessel Down. ($\frac{1}{2}$)

Some arrow-heads are also preserved, and a bow 5 ft. long was traced in the grave, but the weapon was not in common use here in the pagan period. The pottery is obviously of Roman origin, like a boat-shaped pendant that may be derived from the horse's barnacles (*Guide to Roman Britain*, p. 48); and an early British terret is no doubt a survival, as it is at least five centuries earlier than the cemetery. One of the two bronze buckets has the figure of a panther executed in dotted lines, evidently not of local but late classical work; and finally there are certain objects that require explanation. One is of iron in the form of a short sword with a prolongation of oblong section at this point (fig. 61), now recognized as a weaving appliance, for compressing the weft threads on the loom (p. 56). Some gilt disks, each with a long hole near the edge, were evidently once hung on the side

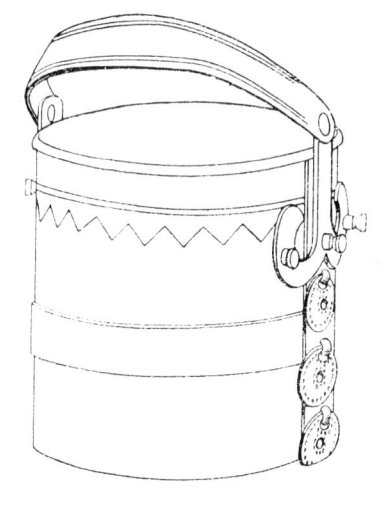

FIG. 75. Gilt pendant from bucket, Leagrave. ($\frac{1}{1}$)

*FIG. 76. Bucket with pendants (Maidstone Museum).

of a bucket below the attachment of the handle, as is shown by an extant specimen at Maidstone (fig. 76). Comparison may be made with some from Leagrave, Beds., in Case D 1 (fig. 75).

Droxford is in the Meon valley, 12 miles north of Portsmouth, and evidently in the Meonwara district, the relics showing a connexion with Jutish finds in Wight and Kent that Bede's statement (p. 1) would lead us to expect. A cemetery there was discovered in 1900 during the construction of the railway, and the shallow burials had no regular orientation. A crossbow brooch is a survival from late Roman times; and beside the usual button-brooches with a face was a small saucer-brooch with scrolls, of a type common in the Upper Thames valley; but the shoe-shaped rivets, the white-metal buckles, and small square-headed brooch are all represented in the Isle of Wight. Other small objects of note are the openwork wheel ornament with three spokes; the disk and ring (annular) brooches; the bronze mounts of a bucket, and a silver finger-ring with plaited wire bezel. Swords were plentiful in proportion to other weapons, and six are shown in Case 41, more than might be expected in what was by no means a rich cemetery. Among the iron objects in Case 51 should be noticed the handle of a shield (fig. 111) with extensions that indicate the size of the shield (about 18 in. across); also a number of shield-bosses, lances, and horse-shoes that may be contemporary, and finally some iron spear-heads, including the

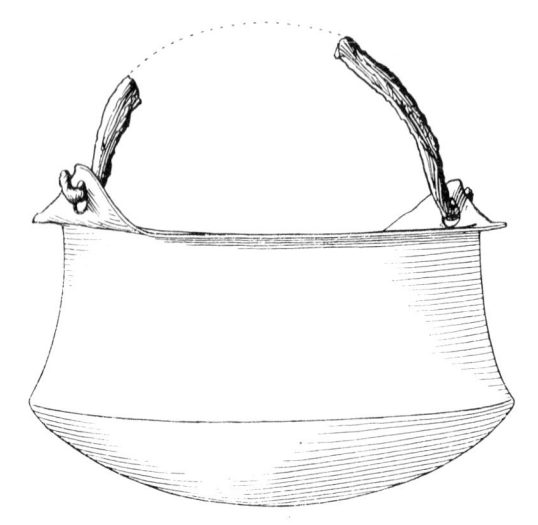

FIG. 77. Bronze bowl with iron handle, Long Wittenham. ($\frac{1}{4}$)

type with the blades in different planes, perhaps to give a spinning motion in flight. The series was collected and presented to the Museum by Mr. William Dale, F.S.A.

A typical West-Saxon cemetery was explored in 1860 at Long Wittenham, Berkshire, and described by J. Y. Akerman, the author of *Pagan Saxondom*. The site is south of the village, which lies on the right bank of the Thames midway between Abingdon and Wallingford. Abundant traces both of burnt and unburnt burials of men, women, and children were discovered; and of the 188 inhumations, 96 skeletons lay with the head at the west end of the grave, 54 pointed to the south-west and 27 in other directions, while 11 were insufficiently preserved. Children had in most cases been buried north and south; and towards the north end of the field the orientation became more exact, and an obviously Christian interment (no. 95) was found to be strictly east and west. The skeleton of a boy lay with the head at the west end, and at his feet was found a bronze cauldron (fig. 77) resting on a slab of wood, by the side of which was a spear-head about 6 in. long, with the point downwards. A small iron knife

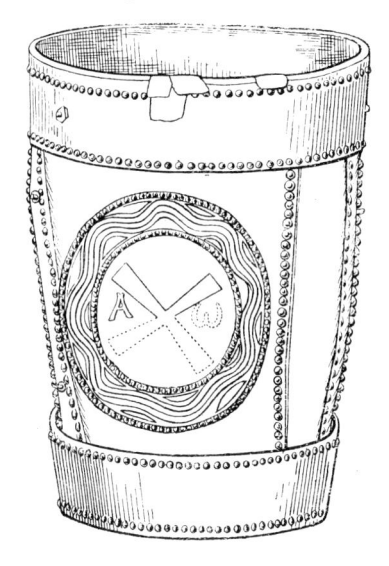

FIG. 78. Stoup and details, Long Wittenham. ($\frac{1}{2}$)

lay on the breast, and to the right of the head stood a beaker or stoup (fig. 78), 6 in. high, formed of hoops and staves, and covered with thin bronze plates which are embossed with scenes from the Gospel history. The four panels contain (i) the monogram or cross between the letters Alpha and Omega, the whole enclosed in a nimbus; (ii) the Annunciation; (iii) the Baptism of our Lord, above which appears an attempt to form the Greek word

ΙΩΑΝΝΗΣ (John); and (iv) the marriage at Cana in Galilee. A bucket remarkably similar was found in a Merovingian cemetery at Miannay, near Abbeville, Dept. Somme, and may well have come from the same Frankish workshop. Part of another embossed beaker, with Adam and Eve and the symbolic letters A and Ω, has been found in Rhenish Hesse.

Exactly one-fifth of the total number of interments were by way of cremation, and several of the cinerary urns are exhibited. As usual, these contained very little beyond calcined bones, but as elsewhere bronze tweezers and a bone (or ivory) comb were among the fragments; and a small knife with blunt blade (as at Kempston) should be mentioned. The urns were not confined to any one part of the cemetery, and had sometimes been disturbed and in one case replaced above an unburnt body. Inhumations were found on the drift gravel 2 or 3 ft. from the surface; and belonged to a tall and robust race, the thigh bones of the men measuring fron $20\frac{1}{2}$ to $17\frac{1}{2}$ in. (stature of 6 ft. 1 in. and 5 ft. 5 in.) and those of women from 18 to 14 in. (stature of 5 ft. 6 in. and 4 ft. 8 in.). The ovoid type of skull specially characteristic of the Anglo-Saxons was found to be fully represented.

At Long Wittenham brooches were as usual confined to the graves of women, and were worn in pairs, one on either shoulder. One of the commonest forms in the country—the flat bronze disk (fig. 32) engraved with circles or other geometrical patterns—were here in a minority, also the small square-headed variety (fig. 79). More characteristic are the saucer and applied brooches, as at Kempston, both these forms being sometimes found in one grave, sufficient proof that they were contemporary. An exceptional brooch, inherited from Roman Britain, is of oval form originally set with a carbuncle or glass paste (as fig. 76 in *Guide to Roman Britain*), and this or the circular form seems to have been popular among the Anglo-Saxons. Roman influence is also seen in a bronze buckle which has animal heads on the terminals of the hoop.

Of special note are the roughly faceted beads of amber, a pair of ear-rings with cubical pendants, a pair of bronze scales such as a goldsmith would use, and a scramasax or sword-knife of rare occurrence in Anglo-Saxon graves, but common abroad.

In the case of men, the spear and shield were the principal items of grave furniture; and the disposition of the studs found with some of the bosses showed that the shields were oval, not circular, as seems to have been the case among the Jutes of the Isle of Wight. The occurrence of only two swords in so extensive a cemetery led the explorer to combat the widely accepted view that this weapon betokened the high rank of its possessor, and that the thane wielded the sword on horseback while the ceorl went into battle on foot, armed with spear and shield. Iron weapons arranged, like the whole series from this site, according to graves (marked by numbers) are exhibited in the lower part of Cases 37, 38 ; and swords from other English sites are collected in Cases 39–42.

A series referable to the West Saxons is shown in Case D 1 from East Shefford, Berks., and includes both large and small square-headed brooches, the latter like some from Long Wittenham (fig. 79, *c*, *d* and *e*). There are ring (fig. 49) and disk-brooches, a small penannular specimen (as from Kempston), saucer and large 'applied' brooches, and a pair of hybrid type, cast in one

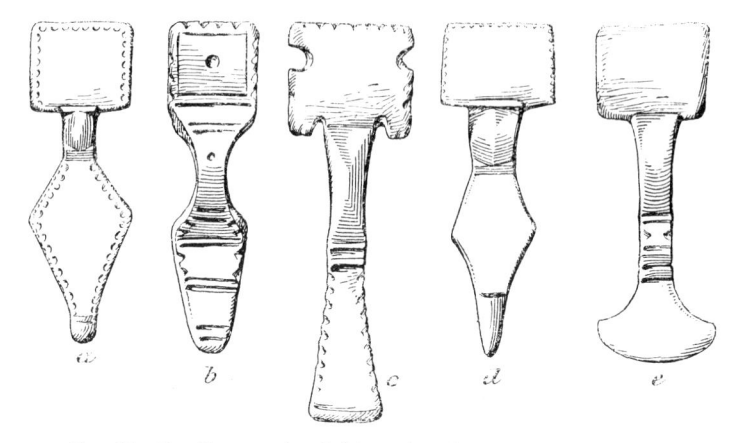

FIG. 79. Small square-headed brooches, Long Wittenham. ($\frac{3}{4}$).

piece but with a vertical collar like the 'applied' variety, and flat face with a yellow glass setting in the middle. One of three brooches of late Roman character (round and oval, as from Long Wittenham) has a glass intaglio representing a raven with its head turned back. There are several late Roman coins pierced for suspension, a set of toilet implements, glass spindle-whorl, and small pottery vessels in Case 43. The relics found in this cemetery were described by Mr. Walter Money, F.S.A., in 1890, and since then the remainder of the site, which is less than a quarter of an acre and now traversed by the railway, has been excavated. Most of the bodies had been laid east-and-west about 2 ft. 9 in. below the surface ; and while the male skulls point to a Saxon origin, the female are attributed to the native Romanized population.

In the same section of Case D are several disk-brooches (as fig. 32) from Gloucestershire, Sussex, and Somerset, the last county also producing a small gilt square-headed brooch like one from Chessel Down; saucer-brooches from Buckinghamshire, and a small group of brooches and beads from Hornton, Oxon.

Kempston, two miles south of Bedford, is one of the critical Anglo-Saxon sites and is well represented in the collection (Cases 42, 43). The cemetery contained a large number of burials varying in size, depth, and position, some being not more than 18 in. below the surface, others at a depth of nearly 5 ft. Skeletons of men, women, and children were directed to almost every point of the compass; some were laid at full length, others flexed, and there were many cinerary urns (pl. II, nos. 3, 5) containing the ashes of the dead, all lying near the surface and sometimes arranged in straight lines. Fragments of other urns could not

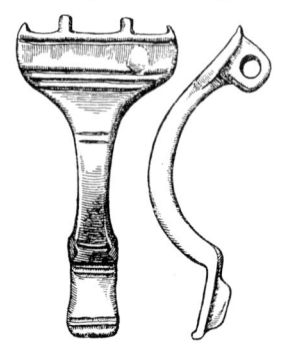

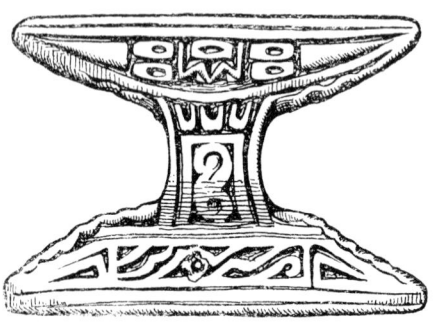

FIG. 80. Bronze brooch, with side view, Kempston. ($\frac{1}{1}$)

FIG. 81. Equal-armed bronze brooch, Kempston. ($\frac{1}{1}$)

be pieced together, and the conclusion was that many cremated burials had been disturbed when the ground was opened to deposit the dead of a later generation. Cremation was evidently the earlier rite and purely pagan; but there are no signs of Christian burial at Kempston, and the change to inhumation must therefore be placed in the sixth century. As already mentioned (p. 5), the locality is said to have come into Anglo-Saxon hands only in 571, but there are burials obviously earlier than that date, and two at least of the brooches (figs. 80, 81) are amongst the earliest Anglo-Saxon relics in the country. The first, with side view, has lost its pin and spiral spring, the latter having been held in position by the hooks projecting from the head; and the faceting of the foot is seen on the Roman crossbow brooch and on the earliest Teutonic varieties. The other brooch (fig. 82) is equal-armed and ornamented in a debased style, but belongs to a distinctly early class, represented also by two from Cambridgeshire but native to Hanover, where it exhibits the chip-carving technique (*Keilschnitt*) at its best, and dates from about 400. The origin of this type may be found in a Teutonic brooch of the late Roman period found near Marson, Marne (fig. 201).

The sepulchral pottery includes two urns already noticed (pp. 21, 22), and many forms with different ornamental motives. Some are quite plain, and one of yellowish ware is stamped with crescents and wafer-pattern.

Foremost of the ornaments are the saucer-brooches (in one piece) and the 'applied' variety (in three pieces), already described as common to ancient Wessex and to the eastern Midlands, but rare elsewhere (p. 35). Only one pair of button-brooches

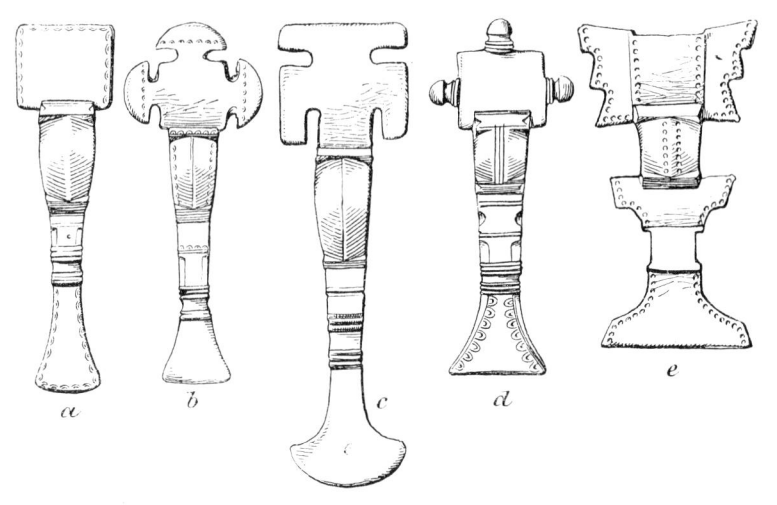

FIG. 82. Small bow-brooches, Kempston. ($\frac{2}{3}$)

appeared, and there is the middle portion of a large square-headed brooch characteristic of certain other parts of England (p. 65) but rather isolated at Kempston. On the other hand, the small bronze bow-brooch with square or cruciform head is plentiful (fig. 82), as at Long Wittenham, in undoubted West-Saxon territory. Small brooches of this kind have been specially studied by Dr. Haakon Shetelig, who refers to the Baltic area the crescent foot of the largest specimen (c), and the wedge-shaped foot of others (a, b, d) to Slesvig-Holstein. The brooch on the right (e) seems to be copied from the larger 'long' brooch dating after 550, when the wings appear below the bow and the foot undergoes expansion.

By far the richest grave was that of a woman, with whom had been buried no less than 120 beads of coloured glass, crystal, and amber, some lying near the left wrist. A ring of toilet articles and a carbuncle pendant set in gold were also found, as well as a remarkably well-preserved glass cup (fig. 54 e) of conical form and pale green colour, 10½ in. high, with fine threads of glass

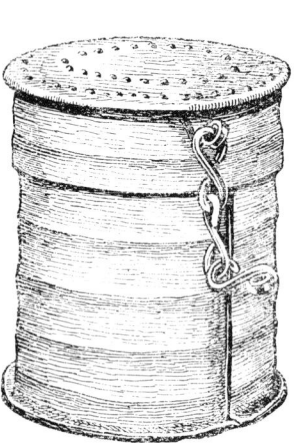

FIG. 83. Bronze work-box, Kirby Underdale. (¾)

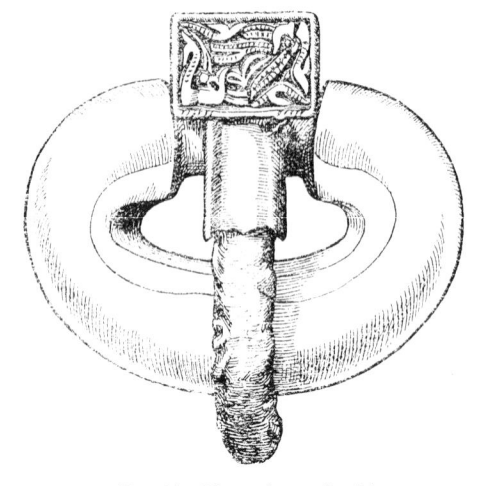

FIG. 84. Meerschaum buckle, Kempston. (¼)

attached to the surface. Others of this form have been found in Kent (Case 47) and Sussex.

In other graves were three small cylindrical boxes with lid attached by a chain (as fig. 83), and used as work-boxes. One

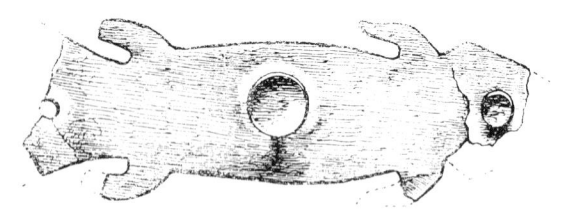

FIG. 85. Badge in form of fish, Kempston. (⅔)

that had been highly gilt lay by the right arm of a skeleton, and contained some spun thread and wool of two twisted strands: both parts were attached by separate chains to the girdle-chain. Another contained linen fabric of three qualities; and as thread, and even needles, were sometimes included, there can be little doubt as to their purpose. Other specimens are grouped in Case 46.

Among the varieties must be mentioned a buckle of meerschaum (fig. 84), with animal ornament on a gilt panel at the base of the tongue; a tin-plate badge (fig. 85), in the form of a fish (possibly a Christian symbol) formerly affixed by rivets, probably to a shield; and an openwork ring of bronze (fig. 86) that may represent the continental form with Daniel and the lions, the gryphon at a manger, &c. (Cases 57, A 6). The crystal sphere is fairly common in the Jutish area (p. 66), but rarely found elsewhere in England. The two burials of women found in 1908 on Leagrave Common, Bedfordshire, a few yards north of the Icknield Way, and close to the British camp called Waulud's Bank, are unusual as having the body contracted, not laid at full length. With one having the head at the west end were two disk-brooches with iron pins, a gilt disk (fig. 75) with heart-shaped openings (as from Chessel Down, and originally from a bucket, like fig. 76), and a pin (fig. 87) with three (now two) spangles that had stained the left clavicle. Pins with hanging attachments are seldom found in

FIG. 86. Openwork bronze ring, Kempston. ($\frac{2}{3}$)

FIG. 87. Bronze pin with spangles, Leagrave. ($\frac{1}{2}$)

this country, though the practice was common later in Livonia (Cases 65, 66), but there are examples exhibited from Searby, Lincs. (Case 51), and Kempston, Beds. (Case 42). The second burial had a pair of disk brooches on the shoulders; and possibly from a third came the bronze *stylus* (for writing on wax tablets, as fig. 138), and part of an ivory armlet, originally measuring $4\frac{3}{8}$ in. across outside, and 1 in. less within. This is by no means an isolated instance in England, and reference may be made to ivory fragments from Kempston (Case 42) and Harnham Hill (Case 47).

Two out of about sixty interments at Desborough, Northants, contained some unusual relics exhibited in Cases D 2 and 46. The gold necklace (pl. IV, no. 4) lay disconnected near the head of a skeleton, at the west end of a grave. It consists of thirty-seven pieces—barrel-shaped beads of coiled gold wire, two cylindrical beads connected with the clasp, nine circular pendants, eight others of various shapes and sizes set with garnets, and in the centre a gold cross formed of two cylinders with a small garnet in

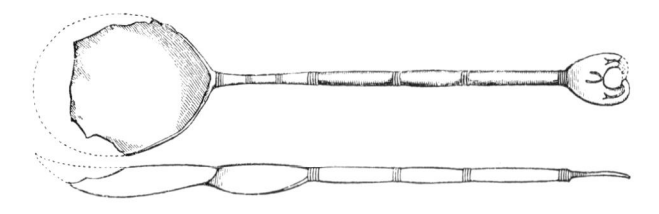

FIG. 88. Spoon, with side view, Desborough. ($\frac{1}{2}$)

bead-work at the intersection, originally on both sides. This evidently belonged to a Christian, and its date is indicated by the contents of a neighbouring grave. A saucepan-shaped vessel of very thin bronze, with rounded bottom and broad flat handle expanding towards the end into a disk is a native reproduction of a Roman type of skillet. With it was a delicate pair of scales in fragments, the pans $1\frac{3}{4}$ in. in diameter; a spoon of base silver or white metal, with both ends imperfect (fig. 88), remotely resembling a Roman type; a hinge or clasp of white metal

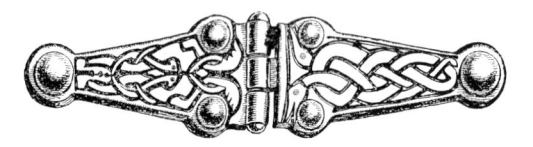

FIG. 89. Hinged clasp, Desborough. ($\frac{1}{1}$)

(fig. 89) with animal interlacing characteristic of the early seventh century; and lastly, two well preserved glass drinking-cups of an amber colour, the larger being no less than $7\frac{1}{2}$ in. in diameter. Both are of the mammiform type (as fig. 54, *f*), and like most Anglo-Saxon glasses are tumblers in the strict sense of the word, as the round base prevents them standing upright.

Bronze bowls of the Saxon period fall into two main divisions, one of foreign and the other probably of home manufacture. Those of fairly thick metal with a pair of drop-handles and an open-work foot (fig. 90) are now thought to be from Egypt, where this type of vessel was common among the indigenous Christian population known as the Copts; and it is interesting to find a specimen from the Rhine (Case 62) of the same class, possibly indicating the route taken. These bowls are common in Kent, and six are exhibited in Case 41 : three being from the Faversham cemetery already described (one containing filbert nuts), one from Wingham (found on the breast of a skeleton), and a large one

FIG. 90. Bronze bowl, Faversham. ($\frac{1}{3}$)

from Sarre, 15 in. across, associated with the jewelled brooch and necklace in Case D 2 (fig. 60). Sir Martin Conway has quoted several cases in support of an Egyptian origin, and illustrates one in Cividale museum (Prov. Udine), nor can his parallel between the

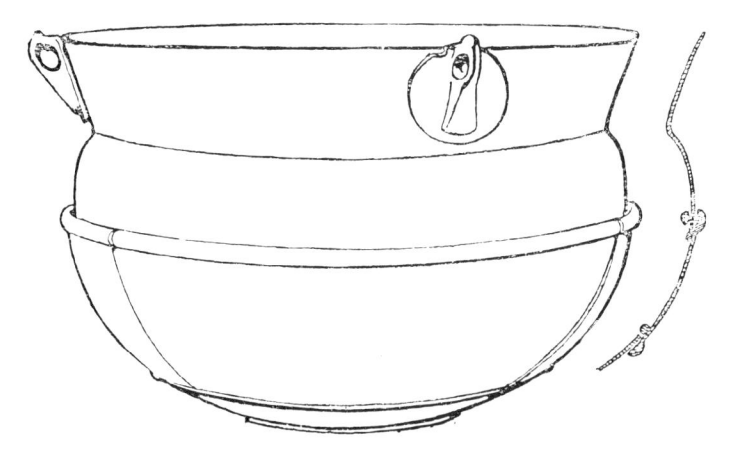

FIG. 91. Bronze bowl with escutcheons, Ewelme. ($\frac{2}{3}$)

Taplow bowl (pl. v) of the same style, and several in Cairo Museum be neglected in this connexion. The occurrence of such bowls in Kent is one more argument in favour of a Rhenish stage in the Jutish migration.

The other bowl-type is a home product, and both in form and decoration can be traced back to Early British (pre-Roman) times, this being one of the few cases in which indigenous art survived the four centuries of Roman domination. The date of several is put beyond reasonable doubt by the discovery of either bowls, or the enamelled escutcheons peculiar to them, in burials of the sixth or seventh century (as for example, the Barlaston group, Staffordshire), and later specimens or imitations of the type in Norwegian graves of the early Viking period; but an early stage in their evolution is marked by the Ewelme bowl (fig. 91) which is made in sections, and has three escutcheons for suspension. The chains have not survived, but these were clearly hanging-bowls intended to be seen inside and outside, as there are enamelled

FIG. 92. Bronze hanging-bowl, Hawnby. ($\frac{1}{3}$)

disks above and below the base, and often attached to the chain-hooks. These escutcheons are usually circular (as figs. 51, 52), but occasionally heater-shaped, pointed oval, or bird-shaped (as fig. 53); and the bowl from Hawnby, N. R. Yorks. (fig. 92) is so provided, though it was never decorated with enamel. There were usually three chains for suspension, but the large specimen from Sleaford, Lincs., needed four, two of the escutcheons surviving. The enamelling is anything but Anglo-Saxon in style, and is evidently related to the contemporary art of Ireland, in which country the Early British craftsman had taken refuge with the Kelts in the Roman period. In some cases the design is inferior (fig. 52), but the best examples (fig. 93) show the peculiar scrolls and trumpet-pattern, that can be traced back to classical times, and in the early Christian period dominated the art of

Ireland. In Scandinavia and Ireland itself hanging-bowls are of later date than the series in Case 41, and the enamelled fittings are almost confined to England (one at Brussels from Lede, Belgium). Their use is no more evident than their origin; and though hanging-bowls, apparently used as lamps, are depicted in some of the illuminated manuscripts, it may be that the bronzes were hung about the level of the eye, and used to contain holy water, as any opaque liquid would obscure the enamelled disk inside. The circumstances of their discovery throw little light on anything but their date. The Hawnby bowl came from a grave-mound (barrow) with a brooch and knives; and the Basingstoke fragments, which show a geometrical pattern inside the base,

FIG. 93. Enamelled escutcheon of bowl. ($\frac{3}{4}$)

FIG. 94. Bronze ewer, Wheathampstead. ($\frac{1}{4}$)

accompanied a skeleton, with an iron vessel, knife, spear, and lance-heads (Case 46), and several bone draughtsmen. The Sleaford specimen, which is without the usual hollow moulding below the lip, was found under a very large cairn with a bronze-mounted bucket lying about 1 ft. from the feet of a skeleton, and a pair of bronze tweezers at the hips. The Barlaston bowl is heavier than usual, and is cast, not wrought like the others: with the fragments are exhibited its enamelled mounts, which were found near the head of a skeleton in a north-and-south grave, with a typical Saxon sword, and the usual iron knife. These cases do not point to a Christian origin, but some Faversham escutcheons have a cruciform pattern, and a Latin cross between two fish-like creatures; and the Keltic scroll-work on others closely resembles that used to ornament religious manuscripts of the eighth century. Bowls of this kind in Norway may be regarded as Viking loot from monasteries in Britain and Ireland.

The bronze ewer (fig. 94) and glass cup from Wheathampstead (Case 45) were secured for the national collection by the joint efforts of Sir Hercules Read and Mr. A. F. Griffith, and were found about 1886 with several human skulls, bones, and rings of bronze (perhaps the hoops of a small wooden bucket), but the record is incomplete. Except for the lid, the bronze is cast in one piece, and was no doubt imported from the Rhine, as similar specimens have been found in Rhenish Hesse and in Baden, in both cases associated with bronze bowls having drop handles and openwork foot (as those from Walluf and Kent). The peculiar feet resemble those of a bronze bowl from Faversham (Case 41) which can no longer be claimed as Kentish work. As this is the only specimen in England, it is clear that the ewer and bowls were not home products, and the distant origin of the latter has already been indicated (p. 77). The glass tumbler is, on the other hand, frequent in England, and in this case is of green colour, 4·7 in. across the mouth. A date for this deposit is furnished by the discovery of a similar ewer in eastern Würtemberg with typical Alemannic relics including a stirrup and pair of spurs. Till the latter half of the seventh century one spur was preferred, and that on the left heel, so as to drive the horse to the right and thus present the shield-arm to the enemy. A similar argument as to date has been drawn from the presence of a stirrup, which seems to have been adopted in Europe about the same time as the pair of spurs, and is first mentioned as being of metal by the emperor Maurice (582-602). Further, with the ewer in a woman's grave in Hesse was found a gold coin of Heraclius mounted in a ring, and the popularity of that emperor as the champion of Christendom against the Persians was confined to the years 628-634.

The preservation of the relics from Croydon (Cases 44, 45) was due to Mr. Thomas Rigby, who presented them in 1895. When Edridge road was being laid out, a number of interments were found, both skeletons and burnt bones lying about $2\frac{1}{2}$ ft. from the surface. All the objects exhibited are of the pagan Saxon period; and besides the usual swords, shield-bosses, and spear-heads, they included specimens of rare occurrence. The 'angon' head is 38 in. long, of a type already referred to (p. 65) as intended to pierce and bring down an opponent's shield, the long iron socket preventing it being cut by a sword ; and one of the three axe-heads might rank as a throwing-axe or *francisca* (pl. VI, no. 6). A bronze bowl was of a type represented at Long Wittenham (fig. 77), with triangular ears for an iron handle ; and an open-work disk with triskele may have served the same purpose as fig. 86 or the Droxford wheel (p. 68). A flattened tube with loops and projections is probably an accoutrement, and is more ornamental than the example from Droxford (Case D 5), but their precise use has not been explained. The saucer-brooch (size of a florin) points to Wessex, and the broad ring-brooch of tinned bronze is of a Sussex type ; but it would be unwise to assign these burials to any particular tribe on that account alone. The largest cinerary urn has been already mentioned (p. 21), and there is another stamped with a reed to form the ring-and-dot pattern : others are plain and there is one small cup.

The Harnham Hill cemetery near Salisbury is in an isolated position and has long been a problem, three explanations having been offered : (i) that the site was occupied by West Saxons from the Upper Thames Valley about 550 ; (ii) that the West Saxons reached it by way of Southampton Water ; and (iii) that the settlement was Jutish, due to an advance inland from the Isle of Wight and the adjacent coast of Hampshire. An examination of the series exhibited in Case 47 shows West Saxon and Jutish affinities, as if the inhabitants had been influenced from the north and south-east, but a single raid in either direction might account for the ornaments included in the graves. The saucer-brooches, almost unknown in Hampshire, are not in the earliest style, but the applied brooches are embossed with the star pattern and have a cabochon setting in the centre, the absence of animal pattern suggesting a date before 550.

On the other hand, there is a pair of small gilt brooches (like pl. XIV, no. 2) as found at Bifrons, near Canterbury, where there is also a close parallel to the bone buckle with minute oval opening and tongue. Button-brooches with the human face and an equal-armed brooch resembling Frankish specimens in Cases A 1 and 6, and part of a small debased radiated brooch also point to Kent. Ring and disk brooches are not such good evidence, and small square-headed specimens are found in many districts (p. 73), as are gold and silver finger-rings, ear-rings, and ivory armlets (p. 75). There is a comb, and also a spindle-whorl of bone ; and an iron fork (originally two-pronged) in a handle of deer antler is a distinct rarity, whereas implements of the toilet on a ring, amber and glass beads, and iron weapons are normal. A strike-a-light is accompanied by flint flakes, and relics of the preceding civilization are two Roman brooches and a lion's-head boss of bronze, all of which were found in the graves, but had no doubt been collected as curiosities. Once more on this side brooches were found in pairs, one resting on each shoulder; and it was clear that beads had in some cases been worn as bracelets. Except beads there was no glass, no pottery, and stranger still no swords: here, as occasionally elsewhere (as Kempston, Lewes, Long Wittenham, and Droxford), the blades of spear-heads were in different planes, a peculiarity that has been supposed to make them rotate when thrown. A gilt ornament (fig. 95), apparently the head of a pin, has a pair of animal heads with open jaws, and transverse hatching on the neck anticipating the Jellinge style (p. 17). One skeleton was doubled up and lay north-and-south, but there were few exceptions to the east-and-west rule, with head at the west end, and the orderly arrangement of the graves was

FIG. 95. Bronze-gilt head of pin, Harnham Hill. (¼)

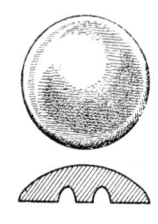

FIG. 96. Bone draughtsman and section, Pensthorpe. (¼)

particularly noticed; but there is little real evidence of Christianity on this site, and the settlement may have resulted from the capture of Old Sarum (near Salisbury) from the Britons in 552.

Remains from the eastern counties and Anglian district generally are exhibited in Case C and Cases 46, 47, 51 adjoining.

As already stated (p. 20) cremation was specially characteristic of the Anglian tribes, and seems to have been given up sooner in the south than in the north. Thus there are whole cemeteries containing no skeletons, and very few objects in association with the ashes in the urns. A good example from Eye, Suffolk (fig. 12) has been adduced as evidence of the early date of a certain type of urn, as the comb is a late Roman model; but generally there is little evidence of date beyond general considerations. A favourite addition both in England and Scandinavia was the gaming counter, sometimes several together with dice. The Romans preferred them of glass, but these are of bone, with two small holes in the flat (under) face to hold them on the lathe during manufacture (fig. 96). Specimens in Case C come from Pensthorpe, Norfolk, where a typical cremation cemetery has been discovered. A number of mounds could be traced over several fields, and had (before being levelled by the plough) been pierced a few feet deep for the insertion of cremated remains in urns placed upright: one of these is exhibited in Case 45.

The Anglian burial-place at Kenninghall, Norfolk, lies about half a mile west of the church, and produced nothing but inhumated remains with rather rich furniture (Case 51). A hook-and-eye clasp with spiral ends (fig. 97) served the same purpose as the wrist-clasps; and the bronze and silver badge in the form of a fish may be compared with others in the collection (p. 51). There are a few slight ring-brooches and one good example of the early 'long' brooch with the loose side-knobs missing; but the find is remarkable for its four square-headed brooches of different

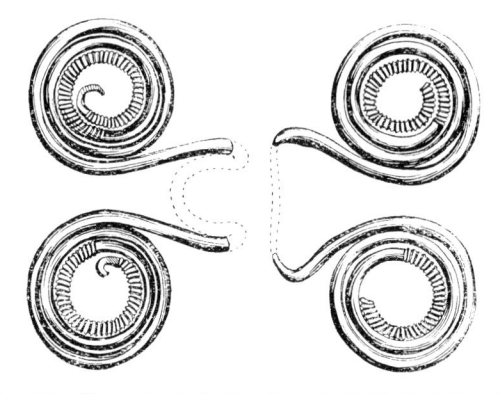

FIG. 97. Clasp of spiral wire, Kenninghall, Norfolk. ($\frac{1}{1}$)

patterns. One has been already noticed (fig. 21), another is similar; the third has garnet settings in the head (late sixth century), being really an ornate example of the 'long' brooch; and the fourth is smaller, with disks at the angles of the foot originally plated with silver, as were the two earlier specimens. Silver plates are also seen on bronze disks which have rivets at the back and are not disk (or applied) brooches, but ornaments from a shield. There is one still on the top of the shield-boss, and a more elaborate example from Barton Seagrave is in Case C.

A variety of the 'long' brooch is included in the series from Brooke, Norfolk (Cases 46-7), all dating between 500 and 550. Some of the knobs were originally loose and are now missing, others are cast in one piece with the head. An imperfect cruciform brooch is of debased style and presumably later, but may have been damaged in the funeral pyre, like the square-headed brooch with disk attached to the bow. Another imperfect brooch has flat spreading knobs on the head, like one found at Woodstone, Hunts. (Case C). A small brooch is of a common type, with trefoil head, and there are ring-brooches and the local wrist-clasps ; also shoe-shaped rivets, rather unexpected in East Anglia. The cemetery also produced the usual weapons, beads, and part of a girdle-hanger (p. 46), but was not properly described, and no further details are available.

A brooch-type with strictly local distribution is illustrated from the vicinity of Farndish, Beds. (fig. 98), where it was found with amber and glass beads in a woman's grave. The site is in the north-west angle of the county, near Irchester, and the occurrence of such brooches at Soham, Cambs., and Kenninghall, Norfolk, again serves to link Bedfordshire with the Fen district (p. 73). The clasp here represented is not found in Wessex or Mercia, rarely in Kent and Sussex, but abundantly in the eastern Midlands ; and the small triple 'pearl' beads are regarded by Professor Baldwin Brown as usually an early feature. A pair of bronze tweezers and small iron knife complete the equipment of this grave.

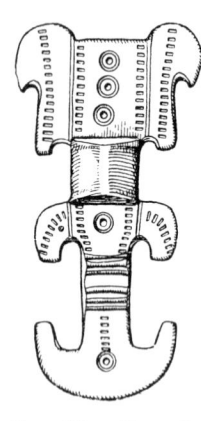

FIG. 98. Horned brooch, Farndish, Beds. ($\frac{3}{4}$)

A good example of the wrist-clasp (fig. 99) is exhibited in Case C from Cambridgeshire, and dates from the late sixth century. Other

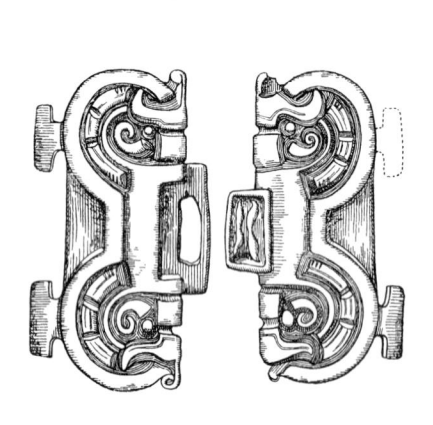

FIG. 99. Bronze-gilt clasp, Cambridgeshire. ($\frac{1}{1}$)

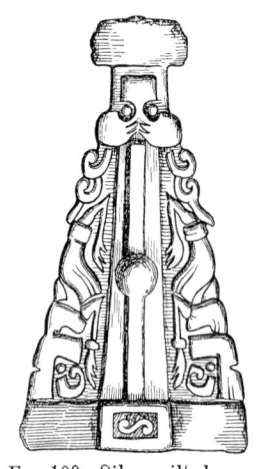

FIG. 100. Silver-gilt sleeve ornament. ($\frac{1}{1}$)

finds in that county make it clear that the gusset of the sleeve was covered in some cases with a triangular plate in the same style as the clasps and surmounting them in use. One of these plates is shown from a burial from Malton near Barrington; and one of silver-gilt, obtained in Winchester and possibly found in Hampshire, is illustrated (fig. 100). This is a good example of the Teutonic animal and may be compared with the oblong panel from Barn Elms (fig. 67). Clasps are rare south of the Thames, but two pairs are included in the local collection at Bifrons, near Canterbury. It may be observed that the S within the small panel of fig. 100 is on a ground of red enamel; and the apex may be intended to represent the human face.

The series from Longbridge (Case 47) has some features of special interest. In 1875 an Anglo-Saxon cemetery was discovered by accident at an angle of the Castle park on the north bank of the Avon, one mile west of Warwick; and the relics, presented by Mr. John Staunton, have an important bearing on the ethnology of the district. The skeletons lay about 2½ ft. below the turf, and not more than 1 ft. in the gravel: some had the head at the east end, others had evidently been interred in haste, possibly after a battle, as at Holdenby, Northants. Besides the usual shield-bosses and handles, spear-heads and knives, there was a sword, retaining traces of its wooden scabbard and ornamentation, indeed the remains were sufficient to show the original form of the handle and scabbard. The total length was 2 ft. 10 in., and the blade was 2½ in. broad from the guard almost to the point. The pommel seems to have consisted of two parts: a wooden bar, surmounted by a square piece of bronze brought to a point, recalling the jewelled pyramids sometimes found in this country (p. 45). Of the three buckets one had the staves replaced by bronze ornamented with beading, and held in position by three hoops. The other two had staves, which appeared to be of yew, fastened to the hoops with square-headed rivets; and inside one was a piece of fine linen, 1 in. square, adhering firmly to the wood.

The brooches link the Warwickshire Avon with the upper Thames, these being of the saucer type, and including not only the star and chip-carving patterns, but a large pair with a circular garnet setting at the centre. Part of a glass drinking-cup resembles that from Kempston, and a cinerary urn of more than usual size has impressed ornament in chevrons on the shoulder.

Most important of all was the last grave opened, that of a lady of distinction. She had worn a cruciform brooch which is probably the longest (7¼ in.) in the country, but not of the best workmanship; also a silver bracelet formed of a strip of metal originally 15 in. long, and bent to form a double loop, expanding on one side to a width of 1½ in. with six flutings, like specimens in Cases C and 38. The decoration was done with punches, as was the case with the gold bracteate 2 in. in diameter (fig. 101), which probably formed the centre of an amber necklace, and is only a debased copy of the horseman type described below (fig. 213). It is here figured to facilitate comparison, the loop being at the side, not at the top as when in use. The grave also contained a silver bracteate with punched design.

FIG. 101. Gold bracteate, Longbridge, Warwick. ($\frac{3}{4}$)

FIG. 102. Embossed silver disk, Caenby, Lincs. ($\frac{1}{1}$)

As the cruciform brooch must be one of the latest of its class (p. 28), it may represent some Anglian influence or invasion in the seventh century, when the valley had been in West Saxon hands since the Britons were expelled about 584 ; and the same may possibly apply to Cambridgeshire, as it was from Malton, near Barrington in that county, as well as at Long Wittenham, Berks., that the silver bracelets cited were discovered.

*FIG. 103. Frieze of animals, Book of Durrow.

The Caenby barrow (*tumulus*), situated $\frac{1}{4}$ mile east of the Ermin Street, and 10 miles north of Lincoln, was explored by Rev. Edwin Jarvis in 1849. The mound was 340 ft. in circumference, and about 8 ft. high in the centre, where the burial of an Anglian warrior was discovered. He had been placed in a sitting position on the original surface, with a shield on his knees and a sword probably on his right side. The mounts of the shield survive, and are of exceptional character. The only silver disk (fig. 102) formed the centre of a star-pattern, with rays like the fragment illustrated (fig. 104, right). The zone of animal pattern is embossed in a style recalling that of the Crundale pommel (fig. 6) and a frieze in the Book of Durrow (fig. 103) which dates from about A. D. 700, but the burial is probably fifty years earlier. Each animal had its jaws round the body of its neighbour ; and the lappet (p. 17) and interlacing hind-leg of the Durrow parallel show the decorative tendency of the period. The inner contour line of figs. 6 and 103 are due to the influence of Style II, which characterizes the seventh century abroad; and the pure interlacing of the other Caenby mounts (fig. 104) also points to central Europe, where it first appears towards the end of the sixth century, and to some extent combines with the Teutonic animal style, giving rise to Style II. A curious parallel to fig. 104 may be seen on the famous Lullingstone bowl.

As Prof. Baldwin Brown has pointed out, interlacing and animal-ornament have a totally different origin and early history; and instead of interlaced ribbons being merely extended and

FIG. 104. Bronze-gilt mounts, Caenby, Lincs. ($\frac{1}{1}$)

simplified animal-forms, it may be that animal interlacing in Christian miniatures and gravestones was in some cases due to the addition of heads and tails to the braiding of Italy and southern Germany.

The large series from Sleaford, Lincolnshire, represents all but the earliest phase of Anglian civilization before the conversion of England; and the excavations of 1881 have been adequately published. The cemetery is computed to have covered 3,600 square yards, now intersected by the railway; and about 600 graves were found, arranged in rows at intervals of about 10 ft., without any superficial indications. With about twelve exceptions, the skeletons were doubled up, with the knees bent and hands before the face, the head at the west end facing north, about 2 ft. 9 in. from the surface. It was noticed that the south-west angle was barren of grave-furniture; graves of women, as indicated by beads, brooches, and small pottery vessels, were mostly at the west end of the area, and those of warriors at the east, but not one of them contained a sword. Six cases of cremation with urns were found, and charcoal occurred with many of the skeletons, perhaps due to a symbolic use of fire at an interment when cremation had ceased. The exhibits are in Cases C and 51, the pottery being on upper shelves in Cases 45, 51, and 52. Clasps were found with remains of leather, and ivory rings (p. 75) apparently served to attach girdle-hangers to the girdle, though stout bronze rings with mouldings at intervals were generally used for this purpose. Six Roman coins were found in the hand of a child, and perforated coins were worn here as elsewhere on the necklace as pendants. From their position in the grave it was clear that glass and amber beads were worn, not round the neck, but in festoons attached in front of the shoulders (cf. Livonian chains in Case 64). There are several 'long' brooches, all with

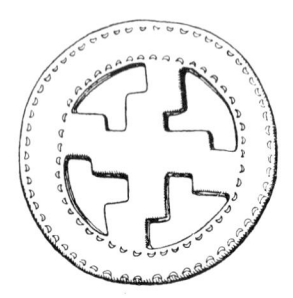

FIG. 105. Openwork brooch with swastika, Sleaford. (⅔)

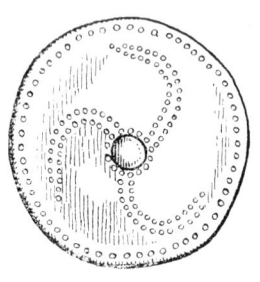

FIG. 106. Silver disk with triskele, Sleaford. (¼)

the knobs cast in one piece with the head; and large cruciform brooches of later date are heavily gilt. On the head of one of these (fig. 18) is engraved a swastika or fylfot, usually regarded as an emblem of the Sun, and sacred in many parts of the world from the earliest times. The same design occurs in openwork on a pair of circular brooches (fig. 105) in the same grave as two silver disks, one of which bears a triskele (fig. 106) or three-limbed device, which has survived in the arms of the Isle of Man. Two gilt disks with a single opening near the edge were probably attached to a bronze-mounted bucket as fig. 76, and the iron framework of a particularly large bucket is exhibited. The head of a large pin seems to be the broken foot of a gilt cruciform brooch remounted; and the girdle-hangers, in the grave of two women, have holes at the lower end as if for attaching a fabric of some kind. A pair in this Case from Searby, Lincolnshire, is unusually perfect, with arch above to unite the two arms (fig. 107). The moulded bronze ring probably held it at the girdle, and from the same grave came a pin (shaft missing) with three spangles of bronze attached to the head (as Kempston, p. 75). The gilt radiated brooch on the board came from another grave, and is a rarity in England on account of its animal-head terminal, a central European feature illustrated on pl. xiv, no. 8. It should date soon after A.D. 500. There is also a ring-brooch with ring-and-dot decoration, which likewise occurs on a silver disk larger than the Sleaford specimen (fig. 106).

Other Anglian specimens are exhibited in Case C, and it is difficult to account for their absence in the extreme north of England and the lowlands of Scotland, as Bernicia was founded (according to Bede) in 547, thirteen years before Deira. The latter is fairly well represented by brooches of the latter part of the sixth century, from Goodmanham, Bulmer, and Ganton Wold, Yorks., the last-named site and Moresby, Cumberland, producing two attractive spindle-whorls of glass. From Asgarby, Lincs., one of the two long brooches approaching the cruciform type is in its original condition—a golden bronze, but the other corroded. A delicate series from Wigberlow, Derbyshire, no doubt from a grave, includes a pair of pins with a cross at the head set with garnets; a pair of ear-rings, a gold disk with filigree, and a beaver's tooth mounted in gold. Horned brooches from Soham resemble fig. 98; and a penannular pin-head or small brooch comes from Woodstone, Hunts. An openwork swastika brooch from Malton, Cambs., resembles fig. 105, and the head of a radiated brooch and the oval foot of another of central European type (as pl. xiv, no. 11), should be noticed. A good series from a cemetery at Haslingfield, in the same county, comprises cruciform and 'long' brooches (with and without side-knobs), trefoil-headed and small square-headed brooches (as fig. 82, *a*, *b*), ring and disk brooches, a pin with polygonal head, toilet implements on a ring, and clasps as well as a gusset-plate like one from Malton (cf. fig. 100).

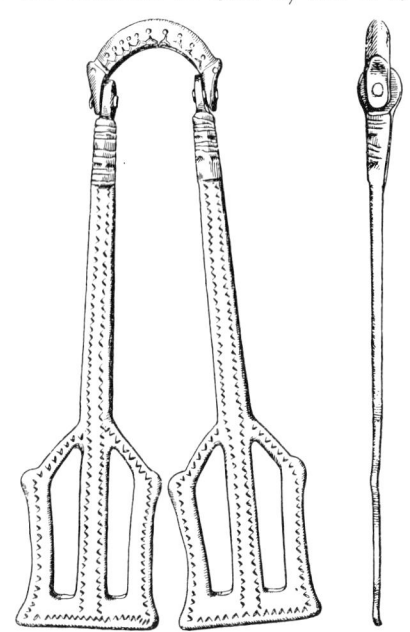

FIG. 107. Girdle-hangers, with side view, Searby. (½)

The small bronze buckle (fig. 108) with a pair of peacocks engraved on the oblong plate is of peculiar interest, but its history is uncertain, as its connexion with the Early British series from Stanwick is only a presumption, and the date is fifth century A. D. The

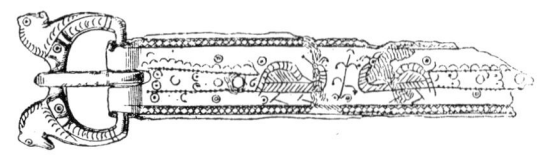

FIG. 108. Bronze buckle with peacocks. ($\frac{3}{4}$)

birds flanking a sacred tree are a common oriental motive, which occurs not only on an Early Christian lamp from Beyrût in the adjoining room (*Cat.*, no. 835), but also on the ring of Alfred's father (fig. 143); and the horses' heads projecting from the loop may have a similar origin. A close parallel in form, but without the peacocks, was found with another buckle, strap-ends, and bucket mounts, all of late classical style, at Dorchester-on-Thames, the find dating from the transition period between Roman Britain and Anglo-Saxon England, if not from the fourth century. Similar hoops without the ribbon-like plates have been found in Kent (Bifrons) and Rutland, and there is another in the museum at Périgueux, France.

Apart from history and the illuminated manuscripts, there is little known of the domestic life of the Anglo-Saxons, and the Christian period is not only devoid of objects buried with the dead, but is almost unrepresented by remains of dwellings, implements of any kind, or even by pottery, which is more durable than most metals.

*FIG. 109. Figure with axe. St. Gall MS.

Hoards of iron are of rare occurrence, and that found on the farm at Hurbuck near Lanchester, co. Durham, fortunately includes several types. There is a sword of the Anglo-Saxon form (p. 94) in fair preservation ; a long scramasax or sword-knife ; four scythes, a gouge and another tool, a buckle without its tongue, the ring of a bridle-bit, a spear-butt, and eight axe-heads, most of T-pattern, as illustrated in a St. Gall manuscript of the early ninth century (fig. 109).

Four iron stirrups of the Viking period are exhibited in Case 52, all of the same type, but two inlaid with brass in running scrolls (fig. 110) suggestive of fifth-century chip-carving (fig. 4), though probably five hundred years later, and derived from the vine-scrolls that characterize Anglian art between 670 and 870. There is ample evidence that the Danes copied these scrolls on their gravestones; but in course of time any connexion with the vine or other foliage was forgotten, and a purely geometrical pattern

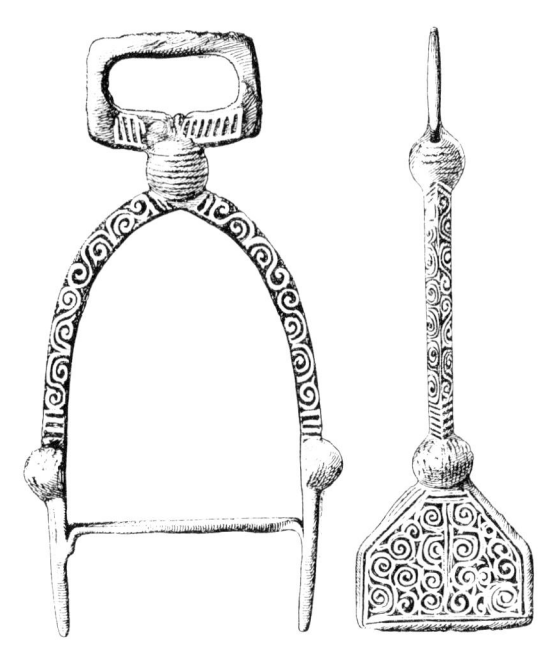

FIG. 110. Inlaid stirrup, with side view, Thames at Battersea. ($\frac{1}{3}$)

evolved. The transition may be traced on such Danish gravestones as those from Birstall and Gargrave in the West Riding of Yorkshire, also on the Deerhurst font; but account must also be taken of the Carolingian foliage or scroll-work, as on the trefoil brooch from Kirkoswald (fig. 122). It is significant that these stirrups were found in the Thames and the Witham, two of the principal approaches from Scandinavia. They are all of different sizes, the longest measuring $12\frac{1}{2}$ in., and the pattern is one of several found in Hungary, where it has been called Sarmatian, in contrast to the circular type of the Avars.

The spear was by far the commonest weapon of the Anglo-Saxons, and in the pagan period is easily recognized by the split socket, which was beaten out on a mandril, but not welded along the edges. Examples are illustrated on pl. vi, nos. 3, 8, the later type being much longer (no. 9), sometimes with the socket closed. Examples are exhibited in Cases D 6 and A 3, and a particularly slender specimen from the Thames has the socket inlaid with silver. In the manuscripts the spear has generally a thin crossbar below the head that may be nothing but an exaggeration of the pin that passed through a pair of holes to attach the head to the shaft; but the Corbie Psalter at Amiens (soon after 800: no. 18 in Catalogue) seems to represent a Carolingian type of wide distribution in the Viking period, with massive wings or bracket-like projections below the blade (pl. vi, no. 4). Examples are exhibited from Nottingham, and the City of London (Case A 3), one with silver rivets, and the other with longitudinal grooves, an

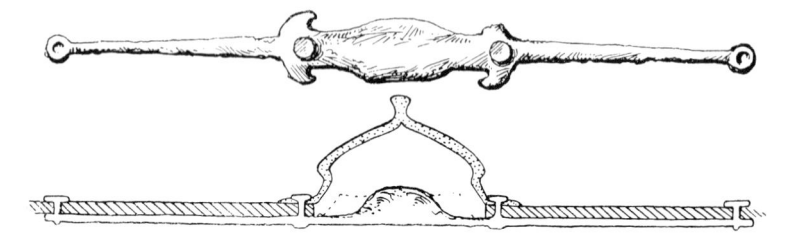

FIG. 111. Shield-boss, section and handle.

early feature assigned to the latter part of the ninth century. Most specimens, however, belong to the tenth, and foreign examples are shown from France (two in Case 57) and Norway (Case 56).

Reference has already been made to iron shield-bosses (pp. 49, 63), and many varieties are exhibited in the Wall-cases, but the most usual is here illustrated in section to show how it was affixed to the shield in order to protect and give room for the knuckles (fig. 111). The size and shape of the 'war-board' has been more than once observed in graves: a disk or oval, made up of sections joined by iron braces and perhaps covered with hide, had at least one dimension of over 18 in. (p. 68), and the thickness is given by the rivets often found in the edge of the boss. The handle crossed the opening of the boss, and had a wooden grip fitted between the upturned flanges, as illustrated.

The size and shape of swords found in the graves are fairly constant. The entire length is usually 36 in. (pl. vi, no. 10): in some cases the bronze pommel is preserved, and more often traces of the wooden scabbard, attached by rust to the blade; but for the grip recourse must be had to the jewelled specimen of horn from Cumberland (Case D 2, pl. vii), the shape of which

PLATE VI. TYPICAL IRON WEAPONS, ENGLISH AND FOREIGN ($\frac{1}{6}$)
(Cases A 3, D 6, 57, 45, see pp. 65, 81, 92, 148)

PLATE VII. HORN SWORD-HANDLE WITH GOLD FILIGREE AND GARNETS, CUMBERLAND ($\frac{1}{1}$)
(Case D 2, *see* p. 92)

SHIELDS & SWORDS

has been copied in wood for exhibition on an original blade. The garnet cellwork is probably of the early seventh century.

The unwieldy sword of the pagan period, with its long broad blade and slight cocked-hat pommel, eventually gave way to a more serviceable weapon with tapering blade (often grooved), and heavy pommel to serve as a counterpoise. There are two main types, with straight and curved guards respectively, and both are represented in Cases D 5, and 55, 56. A short straight guard and triangular pommel characterize the earliest Scandinavian double-edged sword (p. 160); but at a later stage, there and elsewhere, the pommel is more or less deeply cleft into three or five lobes, surmounting a straight or curved crosspiece corresponding to the guard. The change effected in two or three centuries can be appreciated by comparing pl. VII and fig. 112, the latter being a composite picture of the silver fragments found in Fetter Lane, London. It is complete down to the middle band of the grip; the lower part of the grip is the back view of the upper part, and the guard is copied from above, to give some idea of the original appearance of this work of art. The decoration, which is carried out in niello, is a curious blend of Irish animal-pattern and serpentine whorls with the ivy scroll-work of Merovingian manuscripts (p. 100); and the date is probably about A.D. 800.

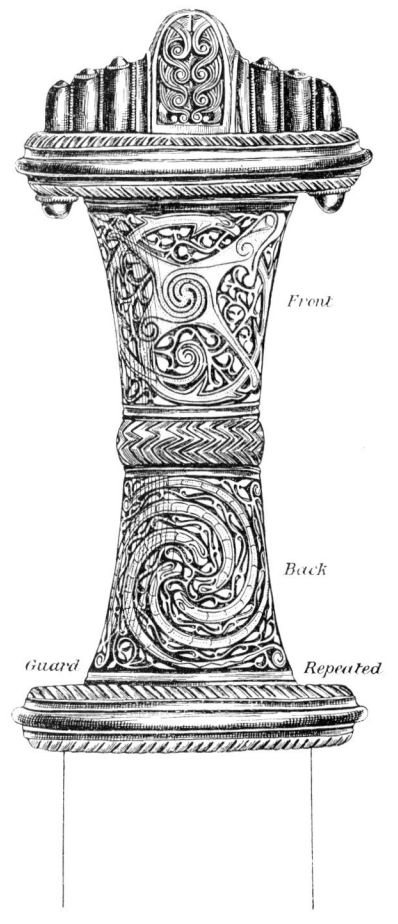

FIG. 112. Silver sword-handle (restored), Fetter Lane. ($\frac{2}{3}$)

The type best represented in England has a tapering blade, with the guard and pommel both curving outwards from the grip, the lobes of the pommel being more or less distinct. An indication of date is given by a representation of this type about 970 (fig. 8), and better by the discovery at Santon, Norfolk, of a specimen with a pair of tortoise brooches, a Scandinavian type dating 900–50: other examples of this sword come from Lanchester

FIG. 113. Sword from Thames, off the Temple. L. 33¼ in.

and Windsor (Case 52), and from the Thames (A 4); and in Norway the type is considered Anglo-Saxon, and assigned to the late ninth century. A development in this is seen in the flatter curve, greater projection, and broader face of the guard in a Thames specimen found near the Temple (Case A 4), the pommel also having a flatter base (fig. 113). That from Canwick Common, Lincoln, with silver lettering on the blade, is apparently a later variety of this type, and the guard projects further, and comes to a central point at the base of the blade. Except for this it resembles the sword of Goliath in the hand of David in an English manuscript of the eleventh century (fig. 7). The fine weapon from the Witham at Monks Abbey, Lincoln, has a lower pommel, lozenges of brass inlaid in the guard, and traces of a name damascened on the blade; and Ulfberht, who worked probably in France about 900–50, signed his productions in this way.

FIG. 114. King Canute (Stowe MS. 944).

Swords with straight guards are more definitely Scandinavian, as from Newark (Case 52) and Edmonton (Case A 4); and several from Norway are in Case 55. The best from England in Case A 4, comes from the Thames opposite the Temple, and has not only silver wire between and below the lobes of the pommel, but also round the grip, like some in Norway of the tenth century: the mouth and eyes of animals are still visible on the outer lobes of the pommel, as on one from France (fig. 205). The weapon held by Canute in the New Minster register of 1016–20 (fig. 114) may be meant for this type.

A bronze sword-guard from Exeter (fig. 115) is engraved on both faces with an angular fret-pattern, and bears on the top the Latin inscription **LEOFRIC ME FEC(IT)**. Leofric may have been the actual maker of the sword or had it made for himself, the names of both owner and maker appearing for instance on the Sitting-

SWORDS & SCRAMASAXES

bourne scramasax (fig. 116); and there is no doubt that Ulfberht was the maker, not the owner, of a number of swords bearing his name on the blade. That the inscription is in Latin, and not Anglo-Saxon as usual, suggests a connexion with some religious foundation; but whether it belonged to Leofric (appointed to the new see of Exeter in 1050) or to one of the local abbots (about 970), it should have had a cross at the beginning of the inscription (as on the seal of Godwin, fig. 137). The form of the guard suggests a date about A.D. 1000.

FIG. 115. Bronze sword-guard, Exeter. ($\frac{2}{3}$)

Two scramasaxes or sword-knives in the series exhibited (Case A 2) are worthy of remark, apart from the small specimen found with coins of Aethelred II (978-1016). Like most of the type,

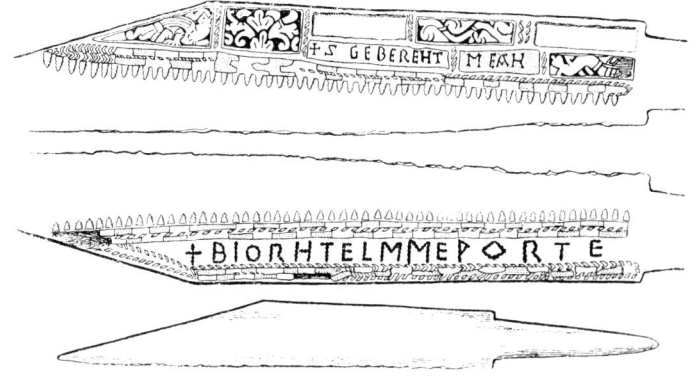

FIG. 116. Scramasax with inscription, Sittingbourne. ($\frac{1}{2}$ and $\frac{1}{4}$)

that from Sittingbourne (fig. 116) has a thick back and straight cutting-edge ending in a point; but the brass and silver inlay on both faces is unusual. On the front is inscribed +S GEBEREHT M EÂH (or ME ÂH) which is taken to mean *Gebereht* (possibly *Sigebereht*) *owns me*. It was no doubt made to order; but the maker Biorhtelm was careful to place his own name on the reverse like others in the tenth century. The decorative panel

96   DESCRIPTION OF CASE A 3

on the left of the front is in the style of Ethelwulf's ring
(fig. 143), and that above the inscription is analogous to the ivy-
scroll-work on one of the Trewhiddle mounts (fig. 120, no. 8); so
that a date between 850 and 900 is not improbable, especially as
the closest parallel for some of the letter-forms is afforded by
coins of Archbishop Plegmund (891–923).

The scramasax (fig. 117, pl. VI, no. 2) from the Thames, is a literary
document of great value, as it is inlaid with the Runic alphabet,
or rather *futhorc*, the series not beginning with A, B (Alpha, Beta
in Greek), but with F, U, TH, O, R, C. The lettering and
decoration are in brass and silver wire, the corresponding space
on the other side being purely decorative; and the date is thought
to be about A.D. 800. Earlier lists of the Runic characters are on
the gold bracteate found at Vadstena, Sweden, and on the back of
a brooch from Charnay in Burgundy, both dating about 600; but

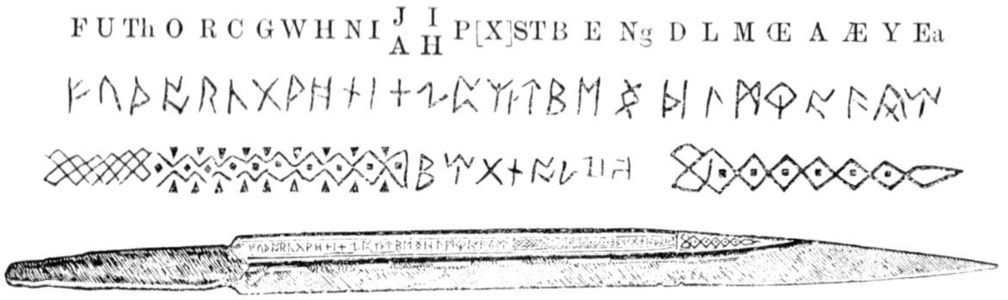

F U Th O R C G W H N I ^J_A ^I_H P[X]ST B E Ng D L M Œ A Æ Y Ea

FIG. 117. Scramasax from the Thames, with Runes. ($\frac{1}{7}$ and $\frac{1}{2}$)

this system of writing, specially adapted for carving on wood or
stone, goes back to the fourth century, and was probably based
on the Greek and Latin alphabets. It was known to all the
Teutonic peoples and originally consisted of twenty-four characters,
the last four on the upper line of fig. 117 being added to represent
new vowel sounds. During the eighth century runes went out
of general use in England with the exception of three which are
peculiar to the English hand in later manuscripts. These are
þ or ð, called *thorn* and retained till the eighteenth century in the
form of y, as in y^e, y^{at}; the *wyn* (p = w) and the *yok* (3 = y or
gh). The later runes (reduced to sixteen by the ninth century)
were known all over the Scandinavian world; and the Vikings
are responsible for their occurrence in the Orkneys and the Isle
of Man: examples in England are rare, as the gravestone from
St. Paul's Churchyard, and the Thorfast comb from Lincoln
(fig. 150).

On a pedestal between Cases B and C stands the Franks Casket
(pl. VIII), a Northumbrian carving in whale's bone of about A.D. 700,
full of interest from the literary as well as the archaeological point
of view. It was, early in the eighteenth century, in the possession
of a family in Auzon (Brioude, Haute-Loire, France), where it was

used as a work-box till the silver fittings gave way and it fell to pieces. All but the right side (replaced by a cast) were purchased by Sir Wollaston Franks in 1857 and presented to the Museum: the missing panel was subsequently found in a drawer at Auzon and bequeathed to the Museo Nazionale (Bargello) at Florence, where it now is. The following summary is based on descriptions by the late Prof. Napier, of Oxford (1900).

Some relief was given to all the carving by cutting away the ground, but there is little modelling of the figures. Of the top only the central panel remains (middle of plate VIII), representing Egil the archer, brother of Wayland (Weland), defending his wife and home against enemies in chain-mail, armed with sword, spear, and shield. Above the hero is his name in runes, ÆGILI. The front once had a lock at the top and consists of two panels surrounded by runes, which throw light on the origin of the casket, and have been translated : 'the fish-flood (sea) lifted the whale's bones on to the mainland ; the ocean became turbid where he swam aground on the shingle.' On the left is Wayland the smith holding in a pair of tongs the head of one of King Nithad's sons over an anvil. The skull was to be made into a drinking-cup, and the headless body lies below. The king's daughter Beaduhild is present with an attendant, and Egil is catching birds in order to wing his arrows. On the right is the Adoration of the Magi, as shown by runes above (MÆGI).

The left side is damaged but the central panel intact, with Romulus and Remus suckled by the wolf, with a second wolf and four huntsmen carrying spears and grasping boughs. The runes, inverted (as before) in the bottom row, are readily translated : 'far from their native land Romulus and Remus, two brothers ; a she-wolf nourished them in Rome city.'

The back has an inscription partly in runes and partly in Roman characters, the latter in the top right corner containing a mistake in the Latin : HIC FVGIANT (for FVGIVNT) HIERV-SALIM followed by AFITATORES (for HABITATORES) in runes. The remaining runes mean : 'here are fighting Titus and the Jews.' The allusion is to the capture of Jerusalem by Titus in A.D. 70 ; the runes for DOM in the left bottom corner may be descriptive of a court held to decide the fate of prisoners, and GISL in the opposite corner may mean Hostage ; but DOMGISL has been taken as the name of the craftsman. Mr. Bruce Dickins suggests that the central building is the Temple, containing the Ark of the Covenant with poles for carrying it : on either side the Cherubim, and underneath, the oxen below the sea of brass (1 Kings vii. 44).

The right side (cast from the Florence panel) has some arbitrary vowel-runes, and the inscription has been read thus : 'here (she) sits on the sorrow-hill, endures tribulation imposed upon her, rendered wretched by sorrow and anguish of heart'—but the meaning is uncertain. A figure sits on a burial mound or barrow, with a horse opposite and runs above (*risci bita*): the runes below (*wudu* = wood) may refer to the burial-place. Elis Wadstein connects the panel with the Sigurd (Siegfried) Saga. On the right Brynhild urges Gunnar and Hagen to murder the hero; in the middle is a tumulus with Siegfried's body within and the faithful horse Grane mourning above it; and on the left is Grane with a human body sitting on the mound, with the murderer Hagen standing in front. Why the horse is thus transformed is not clear, but a man with an ass's head had a long history before Shakespeare created Bottom the weaver.

In some cases there has been doubt as to the shape of the Anglo-Saxon shield (p. 92), but all represented on the casket are circular and used as bucklers to parry arrows. The swords have tapering blades, and the cross-pieces above and below the grip are quite straight (p. 94). The star of Bethlehem is a rosette, of rare occurrence before the later manuscripts, but seen on the mount of the Taplow horn (fig. 71); and on the angles of the front are animals with the head turned back to fill the space. Foliage is of rare occurrence in early Anglo-Saxon art, but is here treated naturalistically, not like the ivy scrolls seen elsewhere (figs. 112, 116); and in general the figures are in strong contrast to the dismembered animals of the pagan period. A new era has dawned, and contact with European civilization is proved by the subjects chosen from Roman history and the Bible.

The secular subjects were no doubt derived from some illustrated history of the world, based on that of the Patriarch Theophilus of Alexandria, who died in 412; and it is recorded that a cosmographical work of artistic merit was given to king Aldfrith of Northumbria by Ceolfrith, abbot of Wearmouth and Jarrow (690–716), in exchange for a piece of land—just when the Franks casket was carved.

The three linked silver-gilt pins represented in pl. ix were found at Fiskerton on the river Witham, east of Lincoln, in 1858, and presented by the Royal Archaeological Institute. The fine quality of the work gives them a prominent place among later Anglo-Saxon works of art, but at present there is little with which to compare the decoration. There is a similar disk-head in existence found at Ixworth, Suffolk; but the present design is peculiar in having a winged animal akin to the dragon, which was once considered a mark of the eleventh century; however, the pins have been more than once attributed to the early part of the ninth century. On the centre pin these animals are represented singly or in pairs on a background of interlacing formed by prolonging their tongues, wings, or tails, and reference may be made to the animals within the Temple on the back of the Franks

LEFT SIDE

PANEL OF TOP

RIGHT SIDE

PLATE VIII. THE FRANKS CASKET

(On ped

FRONT

BACK

[W]HALE'S BONE, NORTHUMBRIAN WORK (½)
see p. 96)

casket (pl. VIII). The best parallel is certainly the Croft stone (North Riding, Yorks.), which has not only birds but winged quadrupeds in this style, executed with the greatest precision and delicacy and evidently dating from the best period of Anglian sculpture (p. 13). The Croft stone has the ground occupied by foliage, which is probably earlier than the pure interlacing of the pins, which can be dated about 700, and compared with a solitary example in Trondhjem Museum.

The hoard of silver found at Trewhiddle, Cornwall, in 1774 gives an interesting glimpse of Anglo-Saxon art towards the end of the ninth century. Contemporary finds are scarce, and for that and other reasons of considerable importance: for instance, the Alfred jewel (copy in Case D 2), and the finger-rings of Alfred's father and sister (figs. 143, 144); but for artistic and ecclesiastical interest Mr. John Jope Rogers's gift of 1880 can hardly be surpassed. Tin-miners were searching for tin in a stream-work near St. Austell when they discovered 17 ft. below the surface a silver chalice (fig. 118) containing a variety of gold and silver objects covered by a slate in a heap of loose stones. Four articles of gold and silver were not presented with the rest, but in addition to the chalice and scourge (fig. 119), the bulk of the hoard is here represented, nos. 2, 6, and 7 (fig. 120) being borrowed from the original publication of 1788. A few of the 114 silver pennies are exhibited, and as only two occur of Alfred, the latest monarch represented, the deposit can be dated about 875, a coin of Ceolwulf of Mercia not being earlier than 874. The west of England was about that time much harried by the Danes, and the concealment by some priest of his little treasure can be easily accounted for. The chalice has been repaired, and was about 5 in. high, made in three pieces which were found apart. The scourge is probably the only Anglo-Saxon example surviving in a complete state, though what seems to be part of another has been found in the Scottish island of Islay.

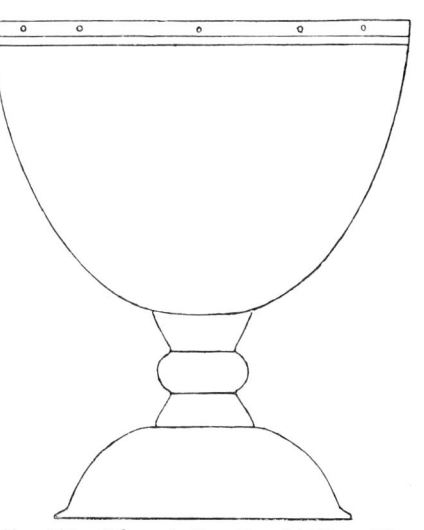

FIG. 118. Silver chalice, Trewhiddle. ($\frac{1}{2}$)

The Cornish specimen, without the four tails, measures 17½ in., and is made of plaited silver wire, with a glass bead at the end.

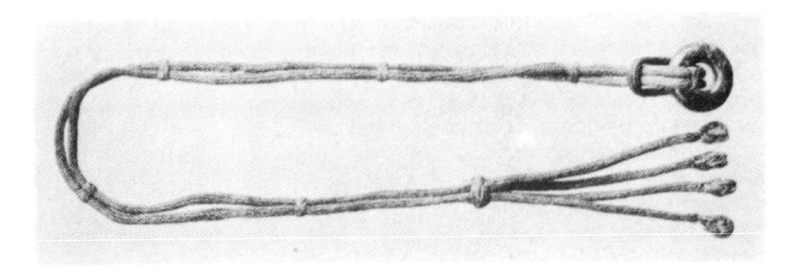

FIG. 119. Silver scourge, Trewhiddle. L 22 in.

Merovingian influence is evident in the animal motives of the silver mounts (nos. 3, 9, and 10) as well as the ivy-leaf scroll of no. 8; but the insertion of one animal, grotesque but complete,

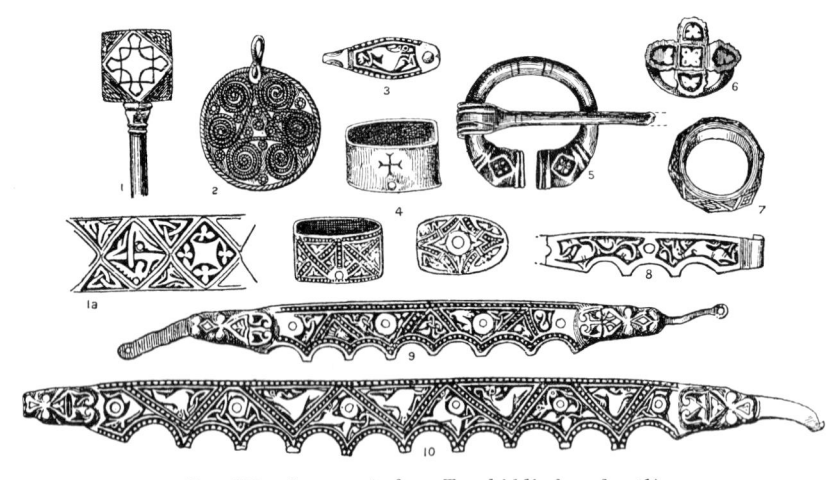

FIG. 120. Ornaments from Trewhiddle hoard. (½)

in each compartment of a series is now recognized as an Anglo-Saxon characteristic on sword-hilts found in Scandinavia. A fixed date is also welcome for the small capsule with cross engraved on one side (no. 4), the pin with polygonal head (nos. 1 and 1 a), and the small penannular brooch, the pin of which is imperfect. Traces of niello (a black composition inlaid in silver for contrast) can still be seen on the pin-head and the decorative

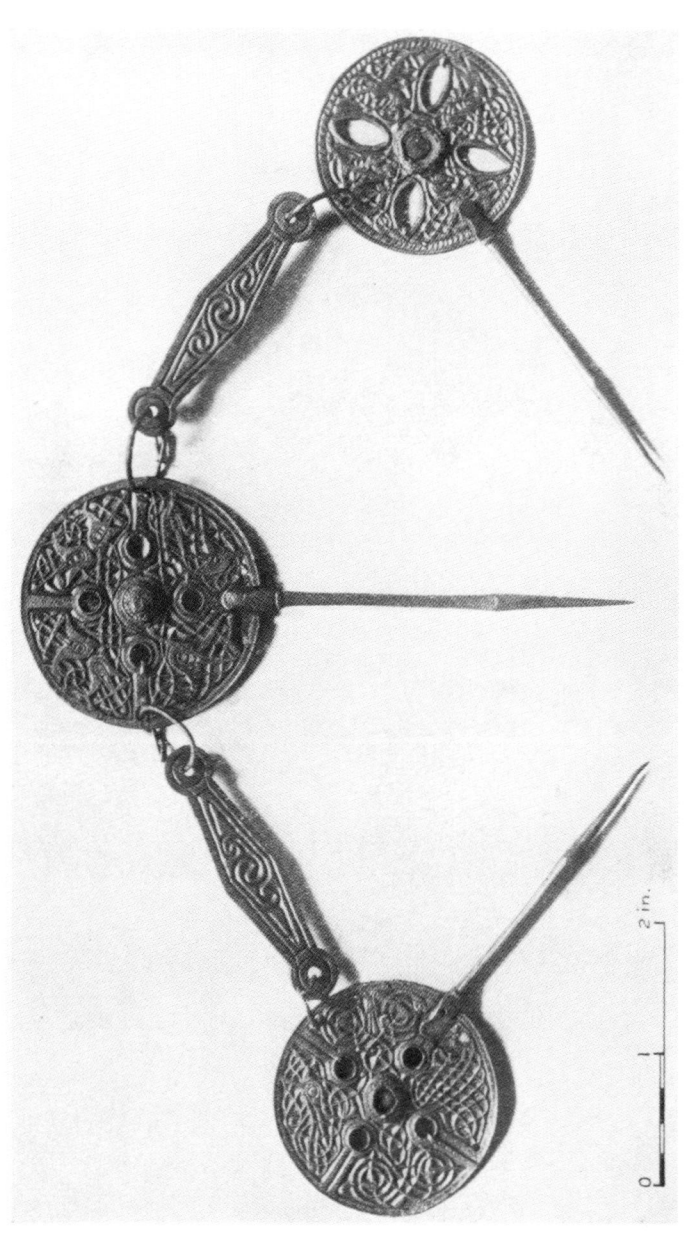

PLATE IX. SET OF SILVER PINS FROM THE WITHAM, LINCOLN
(Case D 3, see p. 98)

THE HAMILTON OR TOWNELEY BROOCH

THE CASTELLANI BROOCH

PLATE X. ENAMELLED BROOCHES, FROM SCOTLAND AND ITALY ($\frac{1}{1}$)
(Cases D 2, 61, see pp. 101, 155)

bands, the process having been known in Kent in the sixth century (p. 38). A silver parallel to the missing gold pendant with spiral filigree was found in the Baltic island of Öland with Cufic coins dating about 950; and the lozenge panels of the silver ring (no. 7) are not unlike those of the ring of Alhstan (Victoria and Albert Museum), who was bishop of Sherborne 823–67.

The two brooches on plate x are remarkable specimens of enamelling but of uncertain origin and date. The upper one is known as the Hamilton or Towneley brooch, and is said to have been found in Scotland, but is not so likely to be Anglo-Saxon as the Dowgate Hill brooch. It is flimsy in construction, but has in the middle a finely executed cell-work medallion bearing a floriated cross of dark blue, with red centre and yellow extremities on a translucent dark green ground. Round this is a zone of applied scrolls cut in strips of gold with seven pearls at intervals; and the border consists of gold hemispheres with similar applied scrolls and central pearls, alternating with flat disks of green enamel, each bearing a dark blue quatrefoil with a yellow centre. The style of the central design and its delicate workmanship are Byzantine of about the eleventh century; and the gold setting may have been produced in western Europe (probably Germany) at the same period.

FIG. 121. Enamelled brooch, Cambois, Bedlington, Northumberland. ($\frac{3}{4}$)

The gold brooch with enamel cell-work (*cloisonné*) from Dowgate Hill, City of London, collected and published by Charles Roach Smith, has a bust in the centre that has been variously interpreted, and though not of the highest quality is better executed than the Alfred jewel. The regal features are not in the Byzantine style, and the costume is that worn by Teutonic princes: hence it may be regarded as native work, perhaps of the tenth century. The openwork border with four pearls is very like a gold brooch found about a quarter of mile distant at St. Mary-at-Hill church, with coins of Edward the Confessor, Harold II, and William the Conqueror, deposited about 1075.

An interesting example of sunk enamel (*champlevé*) is a circular brooch (fig. 121) with bronze border in relief, the centre having the figure of a bird with a branch in its beak. Another, evidently from the same mould, was found near Hyde Abbey, and is now in Winchester Museum; and the date of both is approximately given by the bone comb of Scandinavian type, with whip-handle, found with the Cambois example in a barrow near Bedlington, Northumberland.

The trefoil brooch was a product of Charlemagne's time, and was eagerly copied by the Scandinavian peoples in the ninth century (fig. 212). A fine silver specimen from Kirkoswald, Cumberland (fig. 122), is exhibited in Case D 3, and was fortunately found with coins that date it about A.D. 850. Two bosses are now lost, but the whole face was once covered with a filigree pattern

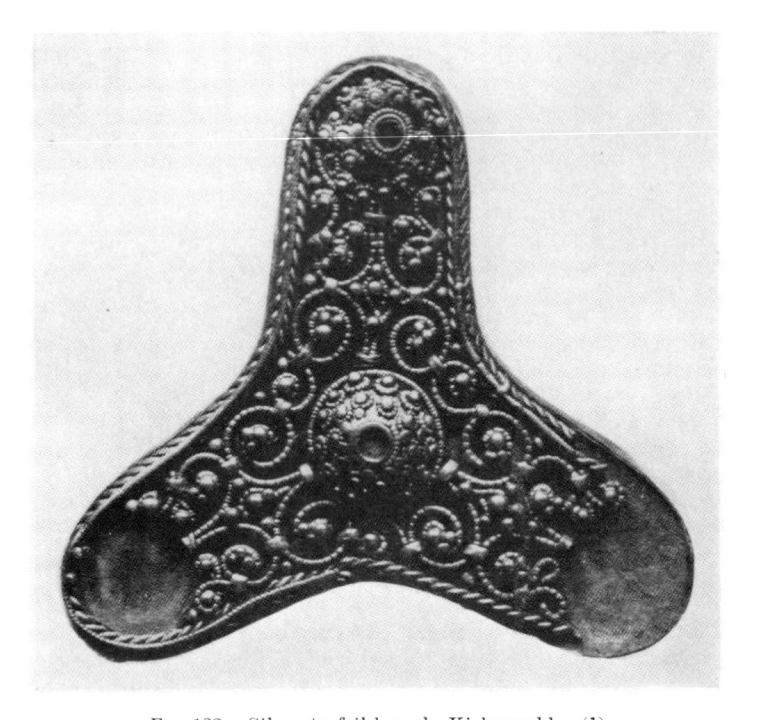

FIG. 122. Silver trefoil brooch, Kirkoswald. (¼)

of spirals springing from a cruciform centre, and bound together with collars like ornamental ironwork; and the four bosses were originally set with single garnets. The principal motive, better seen on the seal of Aelfric, is a translation into metal of the acanthus foliage seen in Carolingian manuscripts, and was adopted by the Winchester and Canterbury illuminators of the eleventh century (p. 15).

In 1838 a silver pendant (fig. 123) in the form of a Greek cross was dug up at Gravesend, Kent, with a quantity of coins that fix the date of the deposit about 874-5, closely corresponding to the Trewhiddle hoard. Of a total of 552 coins, 429 were of Burhred,

SILVER ORNAMENTS

king of Mercia (842–74), and only one of Ceolwulf II of Mercia (874). In the centre is a domed bead of blue and white glass, and on three of the arms chevrons have been lightly engraved, perhaps the beginning of a more elaborate pattern.

The openwork brooch of silver (fig. 124) found at Cuxton, Kent, belongs to a small class of inscribed ornaments of the later Anglo-Saxon period. In the centre is an eagle battling with a dragon, and round the border is engraved the legend ÆLFGIVV ME AH (Aelfgivu owns me), the formula occurring also in the Alfred jewel (reproduction in Case D 2 : original at Oxford), which, however, has the older form MEC of the pronoun.

FIG. 123. Pendant cross of silver, Gravesend. ($\frac{1}{1}$)

The name was a common one, but the owner of the brooch may have been the lady also called Emma, first the wife of Aethelred the Unready (m. 1002), then

FIG. 124. Silver brooch of Aelfgivu, Cuxton. ($\frac{1}{1}$)

FIG. 125. Bronze brooch, City of London. ($\frac{1}{1}$)

of Canute. Her death took place in 1052, and the style is not inconsistent with the early part of the eleventh century.

Pearled borders are common on ornaments of the later Anglo-Saxon period, and are often coarsely executed in bronze (fig. 125), lead, or pewter. The illustration shows a triangular device, like one from Cheapside in the Guildhall Museum ; but several are blundered copies of English and foreign coins. Smaller brooches of bronze often have a rude representation of a lion with head turned back, the attitude being perhaps dictated by the space available (as the small oblong panels on the front of the Franks casket). The same motive is found on a brooch from Borre, on Christiania Fiord, that is dated about 850, and is one of the earliest examples of the Jellinge style. It should be noticed that the series comes from London and East Anglia, but another has been found at Winchester. The Jellinge style is better represented on bronze book-clasps from Lincoln (fig. 126), Milton-next-Sittingbourne, and Peterborough, also on an openwork ornament from Ireland (fig. 188). The animal has contorted and interlaced limbs, and its head is normally seen from above, not in profile as abroad; and tombstones (as at Ramsbury, Wilts.) were sometimes carved this style during the tenth century.

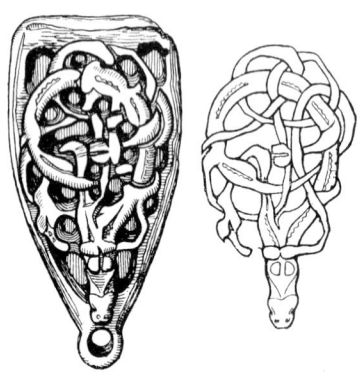

FIG. 126. Bronze book-clasp with design, Lincoln. ($\frac{3}{4}$)

The two silver 'thistle' brooches in Case 52 are probably the largest in existence, though a pin-head in the same style at Dublin no doubt belonged to a brooch with a pin about 2 ft. long. The brambled terminals are occasionally found in Scandinavia; and to judge from hoards (p. 109), this style of brooch, which may be called Cumbrian, belongs to the tenth century, when silver was coming in abundance from the East viâ the Black Sea and Baltic. The perfect specimen, found between Dacre and Greystoke, Cumberland, in 1785, had a pin 22 in. long, but this has been broken and soldered below the head and is now nearly 2 in. shorter. One of the terminals is missing from the specimen found near Penrith in the same county in 1830, though it was complete in 1859. The pin is 20·3 in. long, and the head is not brambled at the back (where it would be in contact with the clothing) but smooth and engraved in quadrants with interlacing bands. These large brooches seem to have been an indication of high rank, and legal enactments were found necessary to protect the public from pins that projected from the shoulder. Specimens from Cloneen, co. Longford, and Goldsborough, W. R. Yorks., are exhibited in Case A; and one was found with the Ardagh chalice (Dublin Museum), but may not be contemporary.

Stycas, the typical northern coinage before the penny (p. 12), were found to the number of 8,000 in a bronze bucket (fig. 127) at

Hexham, Northumberland, in 1832, three yards from the wall of the present church. More than 300 from the hoard are in the Department of Coins and Medals, and all were hidden in the earth about the year 867, the names of many kings and archbishops being recognized on the coins. The early English coinage of Northumbria was mostly silver; but after the sceatta had been superseded by the penny in the south, the styca was almost always

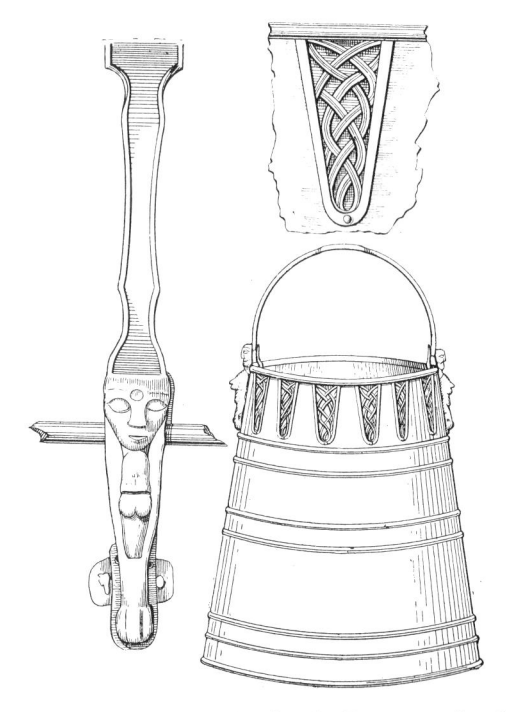

FIG. 127. Bronze bucket with details, Hexham. ($\frac{1}{2}$ and $\frac{1}{7}$)

struck in copper, and lasted till the Danish invasion of 867, the date of the deposit. The bucket is of bronze 10$\frac{3}{4}$ in. high exclusive of the handle, which is attached to the rim by plates bearing female busts: between the lip and upper cordon was a series of triangular panels enclosing plates embossed with plain interlacing.

From the same town comes an embossed silver plate (fig. 128) representing a saint set in a frame and wearing the pallium or band of fine white wool with crosses sewn on it, bestowed by the Pope on patriarchs and archbishops and buried with the owner.

Another interesting relic from Hexham is part of a leather scabbard, of which the ornamentation of both sides is illustrated (fig. 129). From the style it must date from the Viking period which has left very few relics of this material in England (similar at York).

A hoard of silver found in 1834 at Sevington, Wilts., contained seventy coins of kings and archbishops dating from Wulfred of Canterbury (806–32) to Ethelstan of East Anglia (878–90): a few strap-ends in various stages of manufacture; and a fork and spoon (fig. 130), somewhat surprising in a deposit of about 880. They are probably unfinished, the engraving being little more than a sketch; but apart from the Harnham Hill specimen (p. 81), the fork appears to be the only example fit for table use found in England till late in the Middle Ages.

Fig. 128 Embossed silver plate with bust, Hexham. ($\frac{2}{3}$)

The Sevington strap-ends are of the type illustrated from Stratton, near Cirencester (fig. 131, no. 3) with an animal head

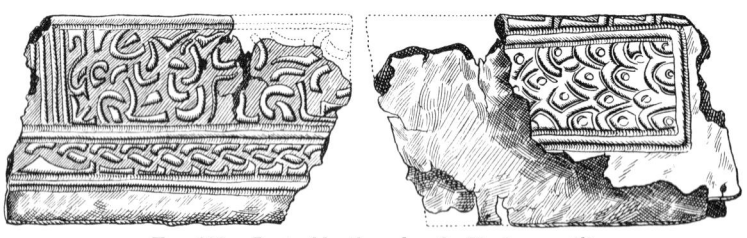

Fig. 129. Part of leather sheath, Hexham. ($\frac{1}{2}$)

(seen from above) in relief at the narrow end and two holes for rivets at the other. The panels form a cross at the centre, and this motive occurs on much work of the period, not only on these tags but on the hilts of swords of English origin both here and in Scandinavia. It is seen again on no. 2, which is of silver ornamented with niello, with a swastika in two panels and three rivets for attachment. The thin bronze example (no. 1) has an engraved pattern recalling that on the pin-heads of large penannular brooches (Case 52), dating from the tenth century; and no. 4 has an animal head of bold design like that on the end of

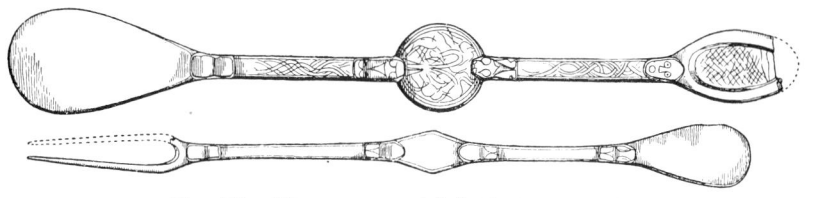

FIG. 130. Silver spoon and fork, Sevington. ($\frac{1}{2}$)

the Runic mount from the Thames (Case D 3), more Irish than English in origin.

The largest hoard of silver in the collection comes from Cuerdale, Lancashire, and was found in 1840 within a leaden chest near a ford across the Ribble, two miles above Preston.

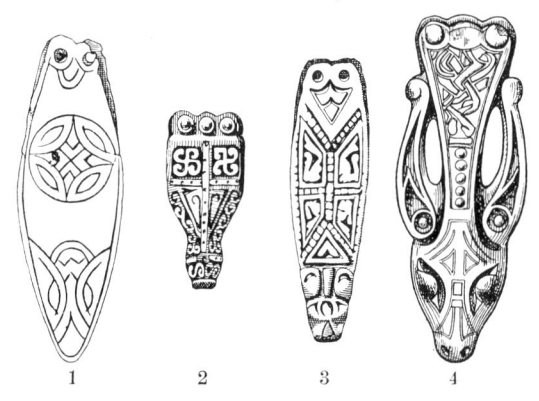

FIG. 131. Ornamented strap-ends.

It comprised about 10,000 silver coins of English, Northumbrian (Danish), continental, and oriental mints, and nearly 1,000 oz. of silver ingots and scrap-metal. Mr. W. J. Andrew, F.S.A., has suggested that this was the treasure-chest of the Danish host that was overtaken in its retreat to Northumbria in 911 and destroyed at the ford, the date agreeing with that deduced from the coins. A selection of the ornaments is illustrated (fig. 132) to show the stamped patterns of oriental origin that reached northern Europe overland by way of the Black Sea and Baltic (nos. 1, 3, 7, 8). Armlets and torcs (necklets) are of various patterns (nos. 1, 2, 9), one recalling the Faversham ring (fig. 45). No. 6 is of heavy squared metal with tapering and overlapping ends; no. 4 shows knobs surrounded by twisted wires—a coarse kind of filigree: and the strap-end (no. 5) is a good example of Anglo-Saxon design towards the end of the ninth century, with a cross in the middle forming four panels, as in fig. 131, no. 3.

An important silver treasure was found in 1858, 3 ft. deep, close to Goldsborough church, near Knaresborough, W. R. Yorks., and is dated by Cufic coins struck at Samarcand and Tashkent by the first four princes of the Samanid dynasty. The deposit was made about 925, and included half an 'offering-penny' of king Alfred and a coin of his son Edward. The scrap-silver (fig. 133) was intended to be melted down, but certain types are easily recognizable. There is a perfect example of the 'thistle' brooch, with the pin-head and hoop-terminals brambled; the hoop of

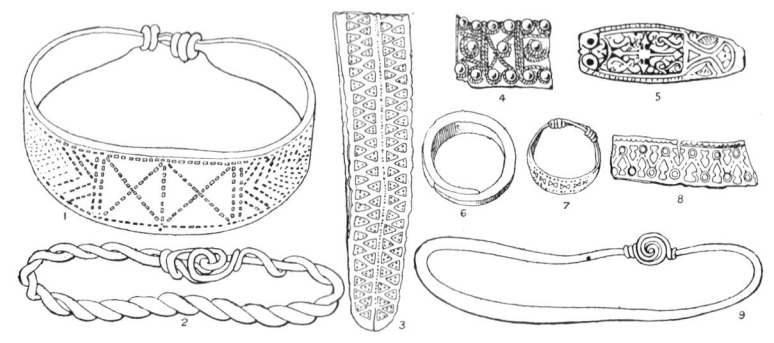

FIG. 132. Selection from silver hoard, Cuerdale. (nearly ½)

a second brooch with disk terminals and degenerate animal forms on the edge; and (right) the junction of hoop and terminal from a penannular brooch of Viking date like one from Ireland in Case A 2 (fig. 182). The fragments have stamped patterns like those of the Cuerdale hoard.

About fifty years later, as the coins indicate, was deposited the gold and silver hoard found at Douglas, Isle of Man. A long silver pin, with separate head engraved in quadrants, must have belonged to a large penannular brooch like those in Case 52; and the intertwining of thick and thin strands is exemplified in half a silver torc and a gold armlet which much resembles that from Wendover (pl. III, no. 7). Adjoining are two other silver ornaments from the Isle of Man—an armlet of the same technique but stouter with knob terminals, and a plaited torc like that from Halton Moor.

The silver-gilt cup (fig. 134) found in 1815 on Halton Moor, five miles from Lancaster, contained the adjoining torc of plaited silver wire, 860 silver pennies, and six pieces of stamped gold,

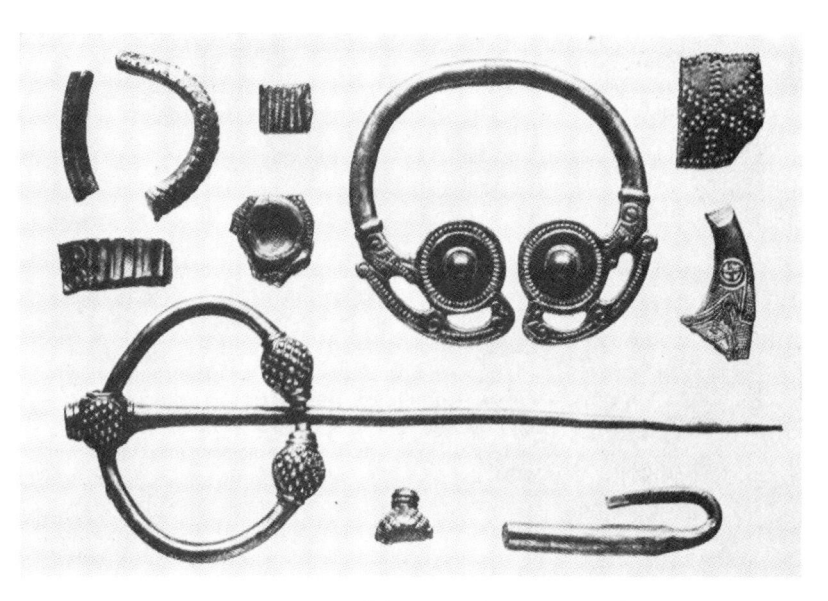

FIG. 133. Silver brooches and fragments from hoard, Goldsborough, W. R. Yorks. (½)

FIG. 134. Silver-gilt cup, Halton Moor, Lancs. (⅔)

one of which—a debased bracteate embossed with a human head—
is exhibited. The decipherable coins were of Canute who reigned
in England 1016-35, and a date is thus afforded for the remarkable
cup, which weighs over 10 oz., and is alloyed with copper. The
decoration consists of four medallions of grotesque animals with
foliage separating the medallions, and forming friezes above and
below. It is analogous to the Carolingian acanthus which was
often used as a border by English illuminators of the eleventh
century (p. 15), but has peculiar dog-like
terminals; and though the animal panels are
reminiscent of Sassanian work (A. D. 226-651),
it is difficult to decide whether the bowl is
of eastern or western origin.

The seals in Case D 3 belong to a small
and precious class that throws some light on
the public life and culture of the period.
It is unlikely that seal-impressions in wax
were attached to deeds before the time of
Edward the Confessor, though they may have
been used for sealing jars, boxes, or other
receptacles; and in any case they would have
belonged to persons of high rank in church
or state. A matrix of bronze, $2\frac{3}{4}$ in. high,
in the form of a cone (fig. 135) was dug up
about 200 yards from the site of the monastery
at Eye, Suffolk, and was afterwards thrown
into the fire by a child, but rescued in a
damaged condition. It has two tiers of pierced
arches, each containing an animal's head,
and at the apex there is a terminal like a
fleur-de-lis. The legend + SIG(ILLVM)

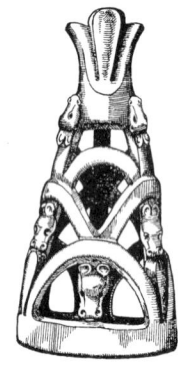

FIG. 135. Seal of
Ethilwald, Eye. ($\frac{2}{3}$)

EÐILWALDI EP(ISCOPI) shows that it belonged to Ethilwald, Bishop of Dunwich,
about 850. The see of Dunwich, created by St. Felix in the
seventh century, was ravaged by the Danes in 870, but the
monks of Eye possessed the site of the bishopric till it was
swallowed by the sea.

The bronze seal of Aelfric, found near Winchester, in the parish
of Weeke, belonged to a personage whose identity is practically
established. The dress resembles that on many coins of the
period (as of Aethelred II): the floral design was perhaps suggested by the cross fleury of the coinage; and the sword as a
symbol of authority limits the choice among many Aelfrics
known to history. The locality of the find, in the heart of his
aldermanry, serves to identify the owner as the commander of
Aethelred's fleet at London in 992, when he saved the Danish
host by treachery; and after similar conduct in 1003, was slain at
Ashington in 1016.

An original impression in lead (with cast to show reverse) shows that seals were sometimes used in England about 800,

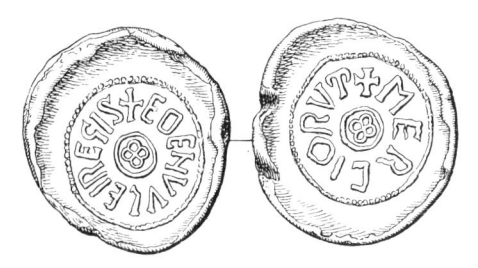

FIG. 136. Impression of King Coenwulf's seal. (¾)

FIG. 137. Ivory seal of Godwin with impression and reverse. (¼)

as this is clearly attributable to Coenwulf, king of Mercia, who reigned 796-819 (fig. 136). It was probably attached, like the papal bulls (*bullae* of lead), to some document requiring his signa-

ture or authority; and was brought to England in 1847 from Italy, where it had belonged successively to three famous collections. The legend is in Latin: +COENVVLFI REGIS MERCIORVM.
The ivory seal-matrix from Wallingford here illustrated full size (fig. 137) is cut on both faces, giving the accompanying impressions, and the handle is on one face carved in high relief with a representation of the Trinity, the dove having been broken off the top, and the figure below being probably Satan. The impression on the left shows a male bust with sword with Latin legend +SIGILLVM GODWINI MINISTRI, with B (perhaps for

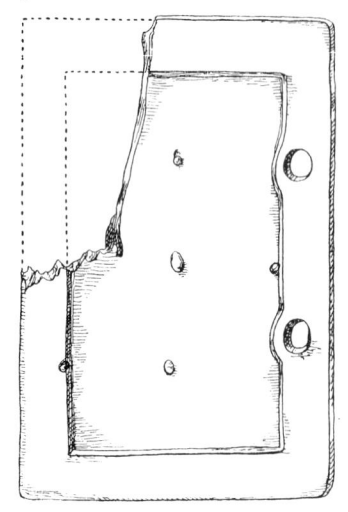

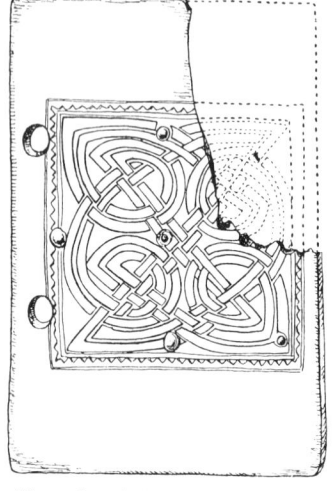

Fig. 138. Bone writing-tablet (inside and out), Blythburgh. ($\frac{2}{3}$)

BEATI) between the first two words. This Godwin was a minister of the king, but his identity is uncertain; and his seal was subsequently cut on the reverse for 'Godgytha the nun, given to God', the lettering being inferior to the obverse, and reading +SIGILLVM GODGYTHE MONACHE DŌDATE. She is represented seated on a cushion, and holding a book. Both seals are probably of the eleventh century, and Godgytha may have been abbess of a monastery founded by Godwin, who can, however, scarcely be identified with Earl Godwin, who married Gytha, the niece of Canute. With the seal, 4 ft. below the surface, were found a small bone comb and a perforated hone-stone.

The writing-tablet from Blythburgh, Suffolk (fig. 138), presented by Mr. Seymour Lucas, R.A., was evidently one of a pair fastened by two thongs at the side, as in Roman times. Wax was spread on the sunk panel inside to be written on with a stylus, and the

BONE ORNAMENTS

outside has a panel of angular interlacing in the style of the tenth century. This is the only Anglo-Saxon example known, and

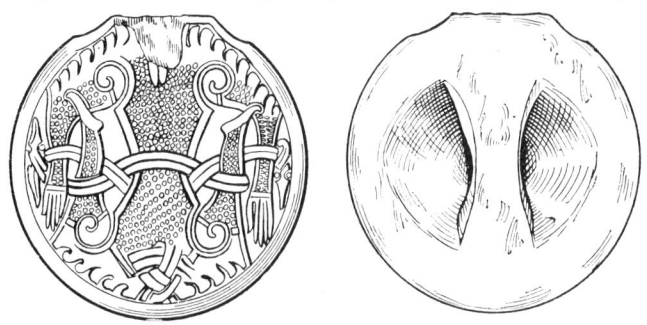

Fig. 139. Bone carving (front and back) from the Thames. ($\frac{2}{3}$)

bronze rivets in the decorative panel suggest that an equal-armed cross was subsequently attached to the outside.

London has produced some interesting specimens in bone, the chief of which is the disk (fig. 139) with bar at back as if for use as a toggle. On the convex front is the figure of a man, the head now missing: the legs are turned upwards and connected with the trunk and arms by two serpents, the heads of which are just within the margin. The granular pattern perhaps represents chain-mail, and the whole design recalls a wood carving from Queen Thyra's mound (p. 17) at Jellinge, representing a bearded man in armour; and in the same style is the crucified figure on the Jellinge stone, late in the tenth century.

The Ringerike style (p. 18) is represented by a bone pin from the Thames (fig. 140), and by the bronze model of a tombstone, from the Thames at Hammersmith (fig. 141), with its union knot at the top resembling a fleur-de-lis. The peculiar interlacing of the first half of the eleventh century, common in Scandinavia, and occasionally found in this country (as figs. 9, 159), is generally free of the animal forms inherited from Migration times; and tombstones of the period have been found upright at the head and foot of the grave in Sweden. Parts of an actual tombstone in this style (fig. 159) are exhibited in Case 34.

Fig. 140. Bone pin from the Thames. ($\frac{1}{2}$)

A trial-piece of bone (fig. 142), on which an engraver has been practising interlacing, is exhibited from the City ; and a lead dump, which has been stamped on both faces by a die for one of king Alfred's coins, and subsequently defaced, was found on the north side of St. Paul's Churchyard, London. It is a 'proof' of the moneyer Ealdulf, but no penny struck from this die is in existence, and the design was probably rejected.

Only a selection of the finger-rings (Case D 2) can be noticed here, and those bearing inscriptions have naturally a prior claim. Historic interest is not the only element of value in the ring of king Ethelwulf (836–58), father of Alfred the Great (fig. 143). It is of gold inlaid with niello, and bears a design that marks a definite stage in Anglo-Saxon art, while its chance discovery in a cart-rut at Laverstock, Wiltshire, in 1780 was a rare piece of good fortune. It was somewhat crushed in consequence, but its attribution is beyond all doubt. Attention has already been drawn (p. 90) to the Early Christian motive of two peacocks separated by a tree or vase, which is here executed in somewhat barbaric fashion. The inscription +ETHELVVLF REX is flanked by an ornamented knot with leaf-terminals, a rosette, and a cruciform design that occurs on several strap-ends of the period (fig. 132, no. 5).

A fitting companion is the gold ring (fig. 144) ploughed up between Aberford and Sherburn, in the West Riding, as it is attributed on sufficient grounds to Ethelswith, the sister of king Alfred, and wife of Burhred, king of Mercia. The Anglo-Saxon Chronicle states that the queen died on her way to Rome in 888–9, and her body lies at Pavia ; but it was suggested by Sir Wollaston Franks, who bequeathed it to the Museum, that she had offered it at some shrine in Yorkshire, and that a priest had engraved her name inside as a record of the gift. It reads +EATHELSWITH REGINA, and the bezel bears the Agnus Dei, accompanied by the letters A and D, the latter having a stroke through it, and representing the Saxon *Th* (Thorn). The initials are evidently those of the Greek words for ' Lamb of God '.

FIG. 141. Bronze model of gravestone, Thames at Hammersmith. (¼)

A plain gold hoop found in Lancashire has a mixed inscription in Saxon capitals and runes (fig. 145), which reads +ÆTHRED

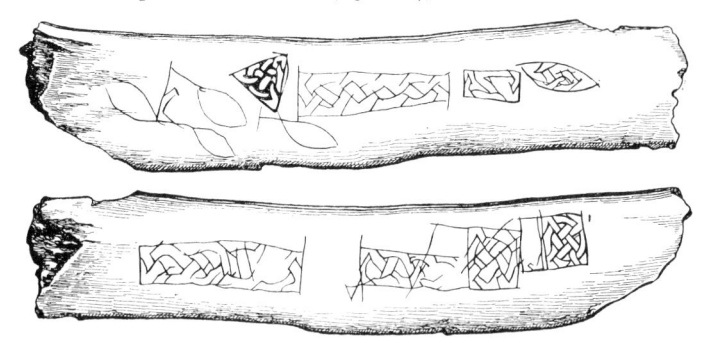

FIG. 142. Bone trial-piece from London. (½)

FIG. 143. Design on Ethelwulf's ring. (¼)

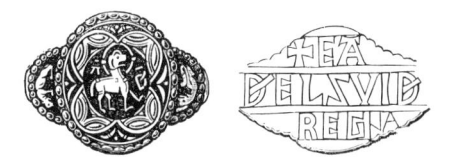

FIG. 144. Gold ring of Ethelswith, with interior inscription, W.R.Yorks. (¼)

FIG. 145. Inscription on gold ring of Aethred, Lancashire. (½)

MEC AH EANRED MEC AGROF (Aethred owns me, Eanred wrought me). The characters are reserved in the metal upon a background of niello; and the mention of both owner and maker recalls the Sittingbourne scramasax (fig. 116). The form

MEC of the personal pronoun is found also in the Alfred jewel, and is a sign of early date.

A broader gold ring (fig. 146) found near Swindon has the name BUREDRUTH between crosses, and the Greek letters Alpha and Omega (p. 69); and the character for *Th* used here is peculiarly English. The legend +EΛPEN MIEΛHS PETRVS STANCES on a gold hoop is a mixture of Roman and Greek characters, and has not been fully interpreted, but Stan may refer to the original meaning of Peter (a rock).

FIG. 146. Inscription on gold ring of Buredruth, near Swindon. ($\frac{1}{1}$)

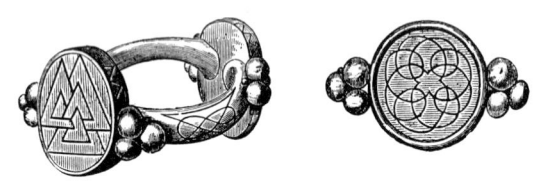

FIG. 147. Gold ring with engraved bezels, near Peterborough. ($\frac{1}{1}$)

(inside of ring)

FIG. 148. Gold ring with runes, Kingmoor, Cumberland. ($\frac{3}{4}$)

Of the ornamental series that from the River Nene, near Peterborough, is remarkable for its two bezels with engraved designs, filled with niello, and flanked by groups of three pellets (fig. 147). The Garrick Street ring closely resembles in form one from Bossington, Hants (Ashmolean Museum), which has a bust on the bezel within an inscription. One found near Faversham is set with a late Roman intaglio on sard—a trophy of arms.

The Runic finger-ring (fig.148) from Greymoor Hill, Kingmoor, near Carlisle, was found in 1817, and reads as follows: ÆRÜRIUFLTÜRIURIThONGLÆSTÆPON, and inside TOL; but no one has yet succeeded in making sense of the inscription. The bronze ring adjoining, with an identical inscription but sloping runes, has been traced back to 1745, but its earlier history is unknown. An agate ring (fig. 149), perhaps from the west of England, has similar lettering, but in small groups, and the division may apply to all these rings, which are probably magical. It has been read: ERÜRIUFDOL ÜRIURIThOL WLESTE-POTENOL.

Those in the Viking style are exhibited in Case A 5. The plaited gold specimen found in Hamsey churchyard, Sussex, is shaped like an ear-ring, but was probably worn on the finger,

FIG. 149. Agate ring with runic inscription. (1/1)

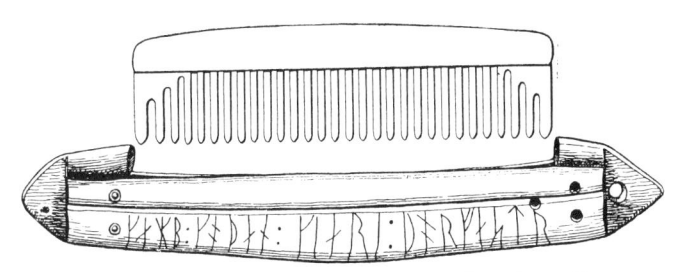

FIG. 150. Bone comb-case with runes, Lincoln. (2/3)

and resembles one from Soberton (pl. III, no. 5) found with coins of the eleventh century, and others from Oxford and Waterford. The second from Soberton (no. 4) is ornamented with stamped rings, and resembles in shape one from Thaxted, Essex. The twisting together of thick and thin strands of gold was a common process in the Viking period, and examples are shown from Wendover (pl. III, no. 7) and West Bergholt, Essex, as well as from Gotland.

Bone combs are of frequent occurrence and belong to two main types: (i) with a thickening at the back, and (ii) with a handle projecting from one end, like that of a whip. Sometimes combs of the first type fit into cases of symmetrical form, and one such case with inscription is illustrated from Lincoln (fig. 150), a specimen comb being supplied. The Runic characters are clear and record that 'Thorfast made a good comb'. The bone plate from Derbyshire of which both faces are illustrated (fig. 151) is without rivet-holes, and has a plaited border on the longer edges of the back. The runes have been interpreted by Mr. Bruce

FIG. 151. Runic inscription on bone, Derbyshire. ($\frac{2}{3}$)

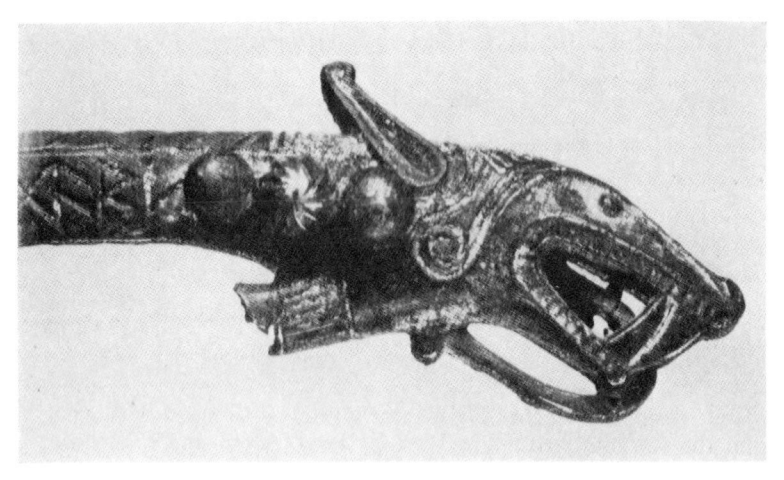

FIG. 152. Terminal of bronze fitting, Thames. ($\frac{3}{2}$)

Dickins: GOD GECATH ARÆ HADDA THI THIS WRAT, 'God saves by His mercy Hadda who wrote this'; and he suggests that the inscription is Northumbrian of the eighth century.

A bronze mount dredged from the Thames near Westminster Bridge in 1866 is incomplete at one end, and at the other has a gargoyle in the form of an animal's head in the Irish style (fig. 152), with eyes of blue glass. There are domed rivet-heads at intervals for attachment, perhaps to the gabled roof of a shrine, and part of a Runic inscription is plainly legible. Von Grienberger's reading of it is SBERÆDHTIBUAI ERHADÆBS, which he translates *Erhadus episcopus assequitur viam caniculae*, and supposes to have explained a scene on the shrine like that on the left side of the Franks casket (pl. VIII). It probably dates about the year 1000.

On two standing stones in this Gallery and on others in the Roman Gallery on the ground-floor are inscriptions in Ogham or Ogam characters, that are specially adapted for carving on wood or stone. This system of writing seems to have been invented in West Kerry, Ireland, by some one acquainted with Latin, or at least with the Roman alphabet. The principal characters are here given with their equivalents (fig. 153), the upright lines representing the front edge of a stone slab, for these inscriptions generally begin at the bottom of the left side of a gravestone and read upwards, then upwards or downwards on the right edge, some

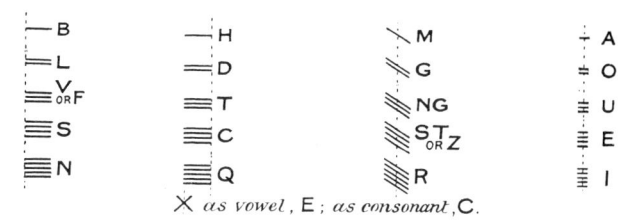

FIG. 153. Ogham characters.

of the letters encroaching on the thickness of the stone. The consonants are strokes and the vowels dots, the most frequent letters in Erse consisting of no less than five incisions; and what seems to be a waste of labour has been ingeniously explained by Bishop Forrest Browne as follows. The system arose from the use of the fingers and thumb of each hand to indicate letters (though the deaf-and-dumb alphabet was not invented till the eighteenth century); and it is easier to hold up the whole hand than to select one or more (especially three) fingers to hold up, and the later diphthongs had symbols derived from the use of both hands. These monuments go back to the sixth or even fifth century of our era, and are written in an early form of Irish, that language belonging with Gaelic and Manx to the Goidelic branch of the Keltic family, as opposed to the Brythonic Welsh, Breton, and Cornish. They are most numerous in South Ireland (especially near Corcaguiny), but many have also been found in Wales, and some in Scotland and England. One marking the south-east limit of the Ogham area was found in 1893 at Silchester in Hampshire. In some cases the name of the deceased was also written in Roman characters on the face of the stone, and the following is a case in point.

A standing stone of peculiar interest adjoining Case D comes from Pentre Poeth farm adjoining the parish of Llywel near Trecastle, Breconshire, and is known as the Llywel stone. It has been specially studied by Bishop Forrest Browne, who reads the Latin inscription on the north face as MACCUTRENI+ SALICIDUNI, the cross between the two names being the Christian symbol, usually placed at the beginning of an inscription, as in figs. 143-6. The corresponding Ogham characters, that here run up the right edge of the stone, seem to read MAQITRENI SALECEDUNI. The stone therefore is useful in giving the Latin equivalents of the Oghams, and the two inscriptions may be contemporary. The name Macutrenus incorporates *Mac*, the Gaelic for 'son' (Welsh *Mab*); and occurs on another Welsh monument, from Cilgerran, near Pembroke, which also has the name both in Roman and Ogham characters.

On the back are incised designs which (like the inscriptions) have been traced in water-colour for exhibition purposes. The stone has at some period been inverted, as the south face has figure subjects now upside-down, but their interpretation is a problem not yet satisfactorily solved. They are seen in perspective on the photograph (fig. 154), which is intended to show the Ogham characters on the edge.

FIG. 154. Llywel stone showing Ogham inscription. H. 6 ft.

At the west end of this Gallery is another grave-slab with

Ogham inscription, found in the crypt of a rath (earthen fort) at Roovesmore, Aglish parish, co. Cork. This and some others have been read differently by various authorities, and there is usually some doubt as to the translation, even if the characters are clear. The legend begins about one foot from the base on the left edge, and reads TOBIRA MOCOI SOGINI, VEDACU (downwards) being in the middle of the right edge.

On the ground floor, in the Roman Gallery opposite the busts of the Caesars, are five Ogham stones, of which the most interesting is from Fardel, Cornwood parish, Devon, as it bears, in addition to the characters for SAVAQQUCI MAQI QICI, a Roman inscription on the front — FANONI MAQVTRINI, and on the back, SAGRANVI. The second name has been variously read, but is undoubtedly the genitive of Macutrinus, a name spelt almost in the same way on the Llywel stone just described, there being now three instances of it recorded. Sagranus, who is here commemorated, bears a name that occurs also on a slab found at St. Dogmael's Abbey, Pembrokeshire. There are two more stones from Roovesmore, co. Cork, the larger of which has been read (left) MAQI ERCIAS, (stone of) the son of Erca; and (right) MAQI FALAMNI, (stone of) the son of Falaman. The other, which is seven feet high, has on the left Oghams for ANAFLAM-MATIAS MUCOI; but the right edge is damaged and the characters cannot be deciphered with certainty. Two others came from the parish of Aghabulloge, co. Cork : the larger, from a rath near St. Olan's church, Coolineagh, is also called the Glounagloch Stone, and has Oghams beginning as usual with MAQ (son of); the other, from a killeen (burial-ground) at Leades in the townland of Deelish, reads OT MAQI MAQI RITE (Ot, the son of MacRit).

From the literary point of view, the Ogham monuments are disappointing as they only record the name and kindred of the deceased, the formula being (name of) A, son of B ; or of the kindred (Mucoi) of B ; or descendant (Avi) of B. It is clear that Mac had already been incorporated into some of the names. With the possible exception of the Llywel stone, there is no trace of Christianity in these inscriptions, and the characters were apparently ousted by the Roman alphabet introduced from Britain by missionaries of the new faith.

Hartlepool has produced a number of small sepulchral slabs, of which six are exhibited (four originals and two casts). They are known as 'pillow-stones' because some are said to have been found under the skull in a number of Christian graves dug north and south in what was once the cemetery of a monastery for both sexes, founded by Heiu about 640. St. Hilda succeeded her as abbess in 649, but went to Whitby in 657, and the house had become a nunnery only by 686. It was probably destroyed by

122   DESCRIPTION OF CASES 34, 35

the Danes about 800, and the burials, which began to be discovered in 1833, date from the seventh or early eighth century, when the Christian orientation would have been expected. The slabs bear crosses and Christian inscriptions, four being illustrated as specimens. The names are Anglian, recorded in runes and Hiberno-Saxon lettering. Four different kinds of cross are repre-

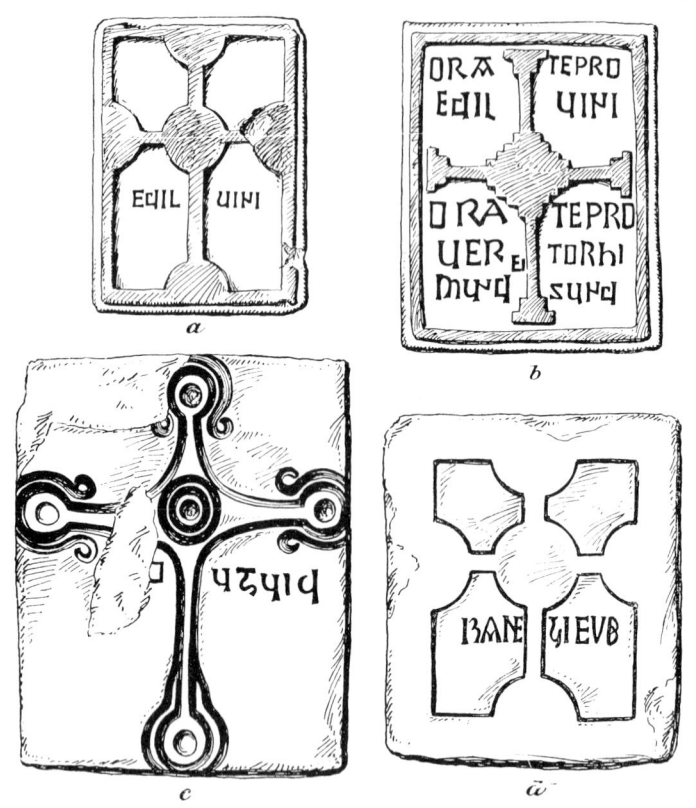

FIG. 155. Small gravestones, Hartlepool. (⅕)

sented, and suggest an Irish influence (pl. XIII). In fig. 155, a, the name is EDILUINI, which occurs again in b: ORATE PRO EDILUINI, ORATE PRO UERMUND ET TORHTSUID (Pray for Aethelwine, Waermund, and Torhtswith). Fig. 155, c, has the last letters of a name ——UGUID in minuscules; but Hübner's illustration shows lettering above the arms including Bregusu, which he identified as Bregusuid, the mother of St. Hilda; and d apparently reads HANEGNEVB. Similar stones but with rounded heads have been found at Lindisfarne, off the Northumberland coast; and to the same class may be referred the fragment (fig. 156) from Billingham, co. Durham, which belonged to a slab engraved with a cross, having Alpha and Omega above the arms, and round the edge an inscription in Hiberno-Saxon characters: **ORATE PRO F(RATRIBVS NOSTRIS ET PRO CVNCTIS CHRIS- TIANIS H)OMINIBVS**, according to Hübner (Pray for our brethren and all Christians).

The Monkwearmouth fragment may be part of a cross-shaft and probably comes from the cemetery of Biscop's monastery (p. 14).

FIG. 156. Gravestone, Billingham, co. Durham. (½)

On the front are two standing figures in low relief, holding an oblong object above a cross; and at the back is another human figure walking. A small panel is engraved with the name **TIDFIRTH** in Anglian runes; and the person to whose memory the monument was raised may have been the last bishop of Hexham, who was deposed about 821 and perhaps died at the monastery on his way to Rome.

The stone cross (fig. 157) found in 1807 at St. Mary's church-yard, Lancaster, is now 3 ft. high, the original breadth across the arms being 1 ft. 9 in. The raised knotwork of the head ends below in a bird's head, and encloses four bosses that were probably once set with glass or amber centres: the back is plain except for a

124 DESCRIPTION OF CASES 34, 35

double ring-cross (one within the other) incised at the centre. In a panel on the front of the shaft is a Runic inscription, asking for prayers on behalf of Cynibalth Cuthbertson; and the style of the monument points to the end of the ninth century.

The inscribed fragment (fig. 158) found about 1830 near Dewsbury church, West Riding, Yorks., formed part of the upper limb of a cross dating from the end of the Anglian period of sculpture, and therefore about the time of the capture of York by the Danes in 867. It has been described by Mr. W. G. Collingwood, F.S.A., as follows: One face has a late Anglian scroll (p. 13), with fernlike leaves set at right angles to the

FIG. 157. Stone cross with runes, Lancaster. H. 37 in.

FIG. 158. Inscribed fragment of cross, Dewsbury. H. 4 in.

CROSSES & TOMBSTONES 125

stalk, as usual in later forms of this design; the edge has a straight-line twist, and is unusually narrow, between cabled borders; and the inscription in half-uncial characters records its erection by some one to his lord (whose name ends in —*berht*): Pray for his soul. It reads: —— RHTAE BECUN AEFTER BEORNAE. GIBIDDAD DAER SAULE.

Fig. 159. Gravestone from City of London. ($\frac{1}{10}$)

Two pieces of a gravestone, now mounted together in Case 34 (fig. 159), are known to have been found in the City of London, and probably came from a Viking cemetery on the site of St. Paul's Churchyard, where the Guildhall stone was found. The slab is 8 in. thick, and carved on one face only, with a quatrefoil design evidently intended for the Christian cross. Two opposite angles are filled with something resembling a fleur-de-lis, and at the broad end is a good example of the union-knot (p. 113). The design is free of the animal motive, and can be therefore placed in the Ringerike period (1000–1050).

Four sepulchral monuments from the churchyard at Bibury, Gloucestershire, present various features of interest; and two are illustrated here of the same school or period. The first (fig. 160) shows the peculiar interlacing and scroll-work of the Ringerike style, but the presence of two human masks at the top, and confronted dragons below, points rather to the tenth century, about the date of the great Jellinge stone; and this slab may therefore be a little earlier than the other (fig. 161), which is ornamented on both faces with pure interlacing and scrolls, with rows of dots to fill the spaces. Domed studs (perhaps representing coffin nails) are seen along both edges of a recumbent stone, with arcading but without columns on one side, the other three being plain. The raised interlacing on the top is imperfect, but takes the form of two knots known as the carrick-bend; and the date is probably just pre-Norman. The fourth stone is again imperfect, and has a plaited serpentine pattern in the Danish style, the tail being visible at the lower corner on the right.

FIG. 160. Design on gravestone, Bibury, Gloucs. ($\frac{1}{8}$)

The cross-head from the churchyard of St. John's upon Walbrook, City of London, once surmounted a slender shaft, and is some evidence of a Saxon church on this site. It is 14 in. in diameter, and 6 in. thick, the shaft evidently $3\frac{1}{2}$ in. across. The design is virtually the same on both faces, and is rather unsymmetrical, the wavy border being unusual. Crosses in Wales and the Isle of Man often have large wheel-heads and slender shafts; and the date is probably just before the Norman Conquest.

The rough stone slab engraved with a bull (fig. 162) is one of a series found only at Burghead, Elginshire, and near Inverness;

the series being of uncertain date and meaning. The slabs, of which at least five are preserved, though about thirty small specimens were found in digging the harbour, are not trimmed as gravestones, and were never fastened in a wall. The figure is well cut in outline and made to fit the space; the tail being

FIG. 161. Design on faces of gravestone, Bibury. ($\frac{1}{8}$)

FIG. 162. Stone slab with bull, Burghead. ($\frac{1}{6}$)

thrown over the back, as in this example, or hanging down. The bull may for the present be regarded as a local and peculiar Pictish symbol, dating (according to the late Dr. Joseph Anderson) from the seventh or eighth century.

Scotland is not well represented in this collection, but a cylindrical stone in Case 53 reproduces on a small scale some of the Pictish symbols constantly found on gravestones of the later Iron Age. The specimen (fig. 163) is 5½ in. long, and was found probably at Portsoy, Banffshire : haphazard engravings on it suggest that it was a trial-piece, used for practice or for recording the traditional symbols, and the cross below one of the two human faces is more likely to be meant for Thor's hammer than the Christian emblem. The fish may imply a confession of faith (p. 51), and here appears with cross-hatching on one half, like a mackerel ; but usually there is only a line down the middle, suggestive of a haddock. Crescents, both plain and ornamented, are frequent on the Scottish monuments, but the meaning of

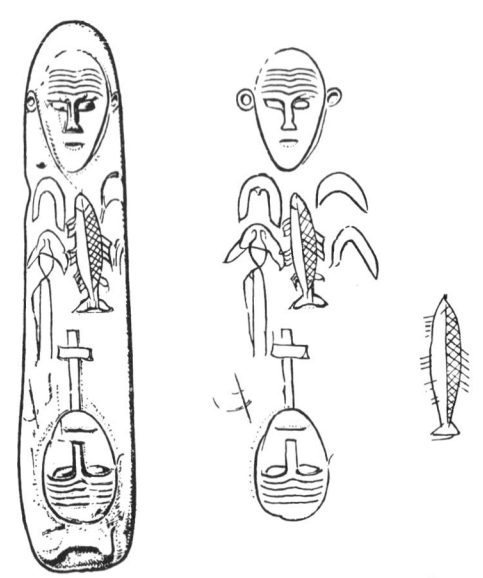

FIG. 163. Engraved stone with details, Portsoy, Banffshire. (½)

these and other symbols is at present unexplained ; and only an approximate date can be given—ninth or tenth century.

The Hamilton brooch (pl. x) has been already described (p. 101), and there are in Case A 5 two silver armlets with stamped patterns of the Viking period from Scotland.

An interesting discovery of Viking remains was made at Ardvonrig, in the Isle of Barra, Hebrides, in 1862 (Case 53). A standing stone surmounted a mound of sand, in which an aged man was found buried with a sword and possibly a shield. There were also two tortoise-shaped brooches of bronze (fig. 164), typical examples of about A.D. 800, when the grasping animal appeared in Scandinavian art in imitation of the Carolingian lion. With these were a bronze pin with loose ring-head, an iron comb (perhaps a 'ripple' for preparing flax), and a bone comb engraved with angular interlacing.

Reference has already been made to specimens of the Irish style in England, either in enamel (p. 78) or illumination (p. 14); and the enamelled disk (from a bronze bowl) formerly at Keswick (Case 41) may be contrasted with the animal subjects of the Anglo-Saxon repertory. Early Christian art in Ireland was a phenomenal growth, but was not truly indigenous; its roots were certainly in Keltic soil, but on the continent, whence Britain

FIG. 164. Tortoise brooch, with side view, Barra, Hebrides. ($\frac{2}{3}$)

no less than Ireland drew its inspiration in the period of La Tène. The development of early British art was interrupted by four centuries of Roman rule, but even without that hindrance Ireland did not produce her masterpieces till the Anglo-Saxons had done their worst to Britain, and civilization was once again restored in a Christian England. The angular fret and the spiral or trumpet pattern (both seen on a cast of the Turoe stone from co. Galway in this Gallery) were taken over from the linear art of the Early Iron Age, and brought to perfection by the Irish, who combined with these motives an animal scheme derived from elsewhere—possibly from the Anglo-Saxon world; but Ireland was seized at an early stage with missionary zeal, and had every opportunity of obtaining models from abroad. St. Gall, for instance, must have come into contact with other phases of art in the course of his journey to Switzerland (where he died about 645); and his master, St. Columban, who founded the monastery at Luxeuil, Haute Saône, in 590, and died at his Apennine monastery of Bobbio in 615, must have passed through the area of Lombardic interlacing (p. 153). There was much travelling in this period, and a close connexion maintained with the continent, as Bede's History proves, so that all the elements were available in the workshops and monasteries of Ireland before a new era of production began with the Books of Kells and Durrow about 700. There are few landmarks in the previous history of Irish art, but the origins of certain national types have been traced, and the various stages of development help to fill the opening centuries of our era.

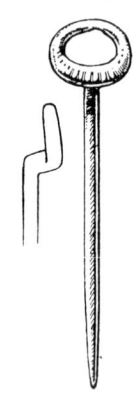

FIG. 165. Pin, Keady Mountain, co. Derry, Ireland. ($\frac{2}{3}$)

A series, mostly from Ireland but occasionally found in Britain, has received the name of hand-pins, from the resemblance of some specimens to the closed hand; and is capable of typological treatment. Fixed points are few, but the stages in its evolution are well marked, and the hand-pin can be traced from its beginnings in the Early Iron Age to the tenth century. From certain ring-headed pins in Case 26, with a shoulder below the head, seems to be descended the specimen (fig. 165) which resembles a tie-pin, and is of cast bronze, not made of wire like the earlier forms. About two centuries may be allowed for its evolution into fig. 166, which is probably about A.D. 200. Here the fingers are represented by bead-pattern, and the part corresponding to the palm is decorated. By the seventh century the opening has contracted as (fig. 167), and disappears probably in the next century, the pin-head becoming semicircular (fig. 168). The final change is to a circular head, with Irish scroll-work (fig. 169), and for some distance below the head the front of the pin is engraved in the late Irish style. It should be observed that the size of the hand-pin increases at each stage, and the final form here represented is nearly 13 in. long. It was

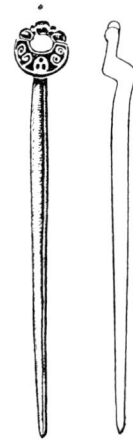

FIG. 166. Ornamented pin, Ireland. ($\frac{2}{3}$)

EVOLUTION OF HAND-PINS 131

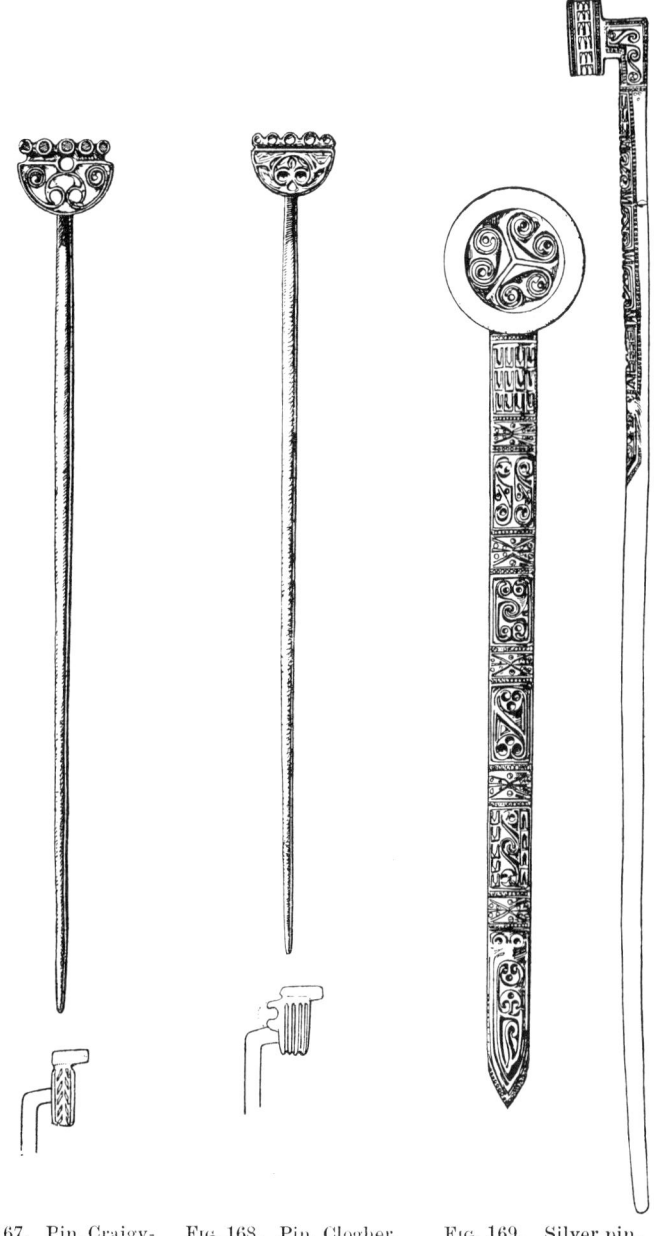

FIG. 167. Pin, Craigy-warren Bog, co. Antrim, Ireland. ($\frac{1}{2}$)

FIG. 168. Pin, Clogher, co. Tyrone, Ireland. ($\frac{1}{2}$)

FIG. 169. Silver pin, with detail, Ireland. ($\frac{1}{2}$ and $\frac{1}{1}$)

the age of enormous pins and brooches, as witness the two thistle-brooches in Case 52 and the Viking silver penannular from Galway (Case A 2).

Peculiar to Ireland are the bronze ornaments known for many years as latchets, but probably used to fasten the dress, not the shoe. The type began as a pin with a disk head and bent shaft (fig. 170) to secure it in cloth; but increased in size, and instead of piercing the dress was attached by two coils of wire (as on a large specimen in Case 54) which were passed through the fabric like a corkscrew, and left the whole latchet visible. The coils have in most cases perished, but the widening of one part of the stem was no doubt intended to prevent the pin from working free through the coils. The disk and expanded stem were soon decorated with incised geometrical patterns (fig. 171), sometimes filled with enamel; and the climax is reached before the ninth century, when the ornament is spread all over the additional

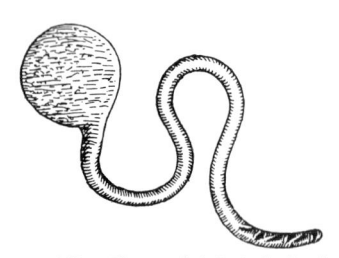

FIG. 170. Bronze latchet, Ireland. ($\frac{2}{3}$)

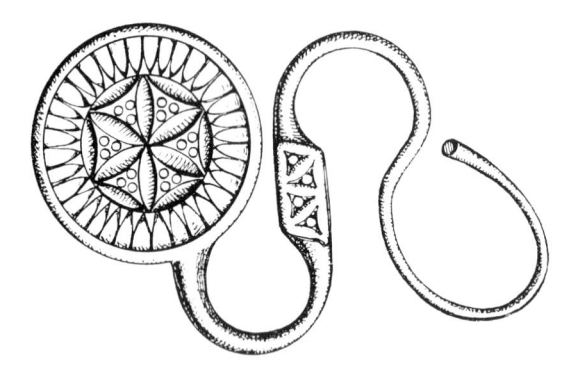

FIG. 171. Bronze latchet, Newry. ($\frac{1}{1}$)

flat surface provided by flattening the stem, and the two loops for the coils are replaced by two long holes in a solid plate (fig. 172).

The particular ring-headed pin from which the latchet was descended dates from the Early Iron Age (Case 26), and the evolution therefore occupied several centuries, like the penannular brooch, which is also in the main an Irish product. A pin with looped head moves freely on an interrupted hoop, which allows

EVOLUTION OF LATCHETS 133

the point to pass through, and locks the pin when turned round under the point. This ingenious method of fastening the dress was known before the Roman period on the continent, but first appears in Britain after the Claudian conquest (*Guide to Roman Britain*, fig. 64), and seems to have remained of small size till

FIG. 172. Enamelled bronze latchet, Dowris, King's Co. (½)

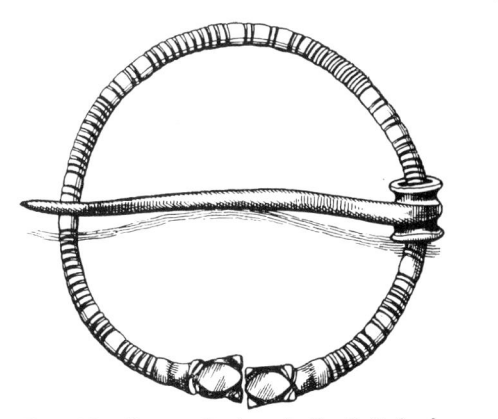

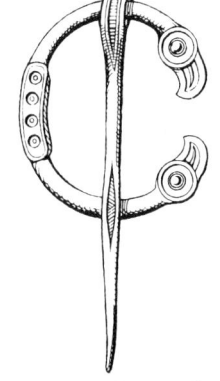

FIG. 173. Penannular brooch, Porth Dafarch, Holyhead. (¾)

FIG. 174. Penannular brooch, with birds' heads, Antrim. (½)

the fifth century, when a larger form appears (fig. 173), of British manufacture, contrasting with the imported brooches of the Anglo-Saxons. They are rarely found in Britain (only eleven are published), but the type was largely developed in Ireland, and enamel or glass inlay is sometimes found on the expanded terminals (as in the Abingdon specimen), more frequently in the ensuing stage.

A slender example (fig. 174) from co. Antrim has terminals in the

134   DESCRIPTION OF CASE A 2

form of birds' heads with amber eyes, in the Teutonic style; and an ornamented section of the hoop opposite the opening here makes its appearance. Many of the brooches have lost their pins, but the proper proportion is indicated in an Irish specimen of silver, dating from about 800 (fig. 175). The type becomes more solid and ornamental, and the head of the pin is widened and flattened to provide extra space for decoration. In Case A 2 specimens are arranged in chronological order, and a surprising development in form and splendour evidently took place in the eighth century, when Irish art in general reached its zenith. The finest example in existence is the Tara brooch at Dublin, now dated about 730–40; the silver-gilt specimen (pl. XI, no. 1), formerly in the possession of Lord Londesborough but with no other history, certainly belongs to the best period (about 740–50). The hoop had to be kept narrow to allow the pin-head to move round easily, and the growth of the terminals put such a

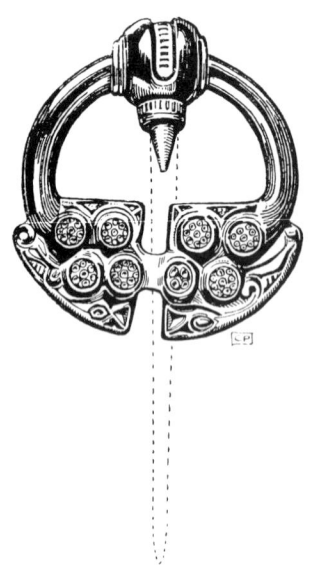

FIG. 175. Penannular brooch of silver. (1/1)

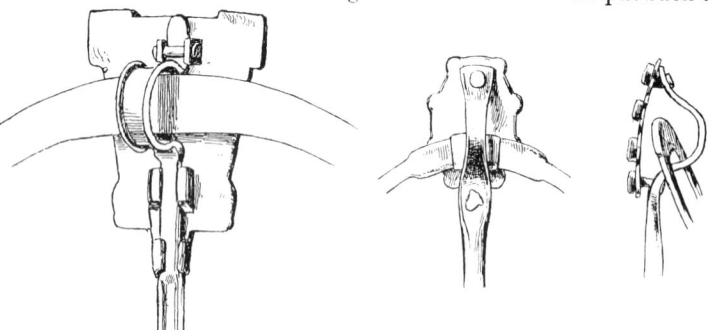

FIG. 176. Back of pin-head of brooches. (2/3)

strain on the hoop that they had to be joined, and the brooch was no longer penannular in the strict sense, but annular. As the way was barred for the point of the pin, the loop of the pin-head was made to open, and was closed in use by a rivet or bolt (fig. 176),

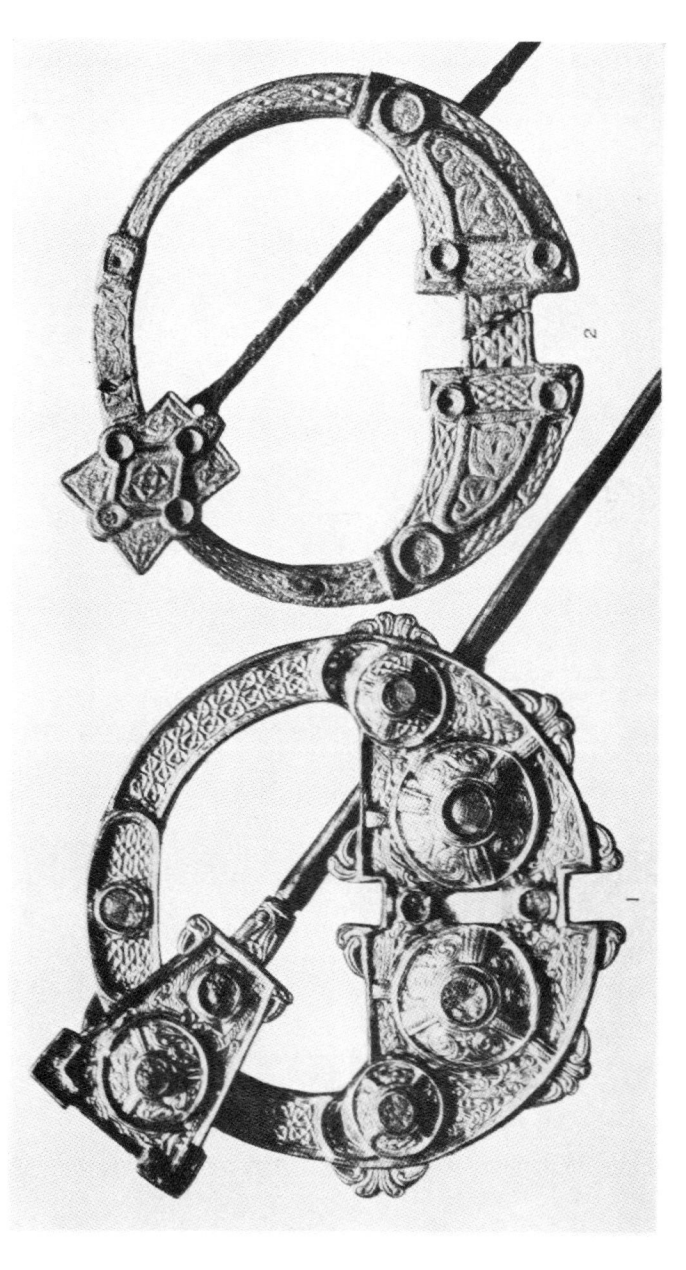

PLATE XI. GILT PENANNULAR BROOCHES, 8TH CENTURY (¾)
(CASE A 2, see pp. 134, 136)

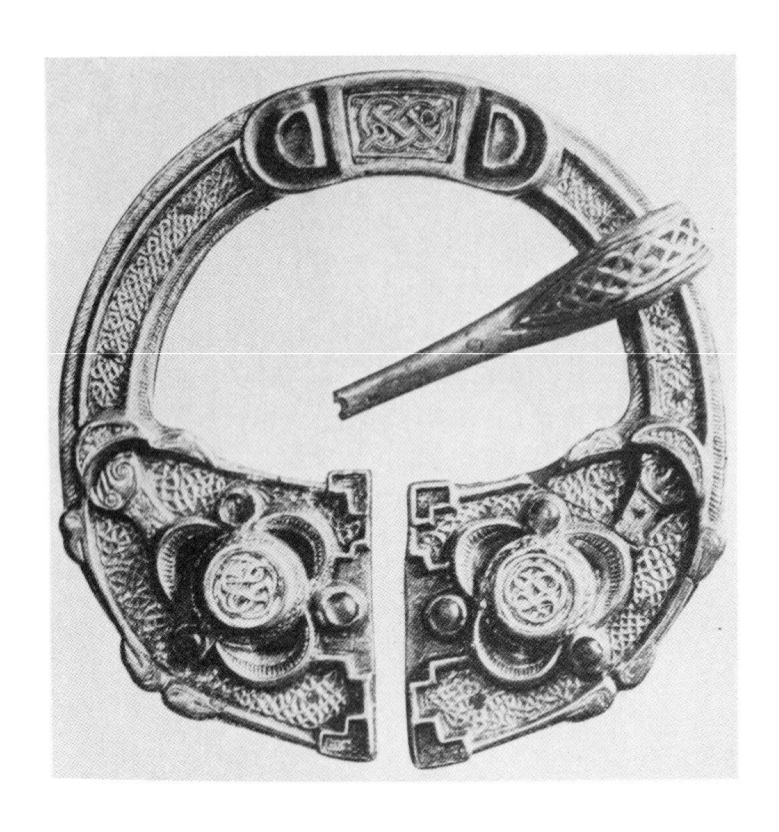

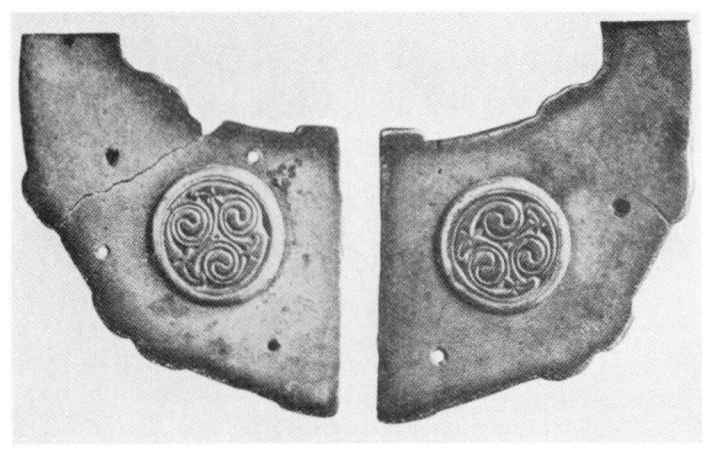

PLATE XII. THE BREADALBANE BROOCH, WITH DISKS ON BACK (NEARLY ½)
(Case A 2, *see* p. 135)

the brooch being now a mere ornament and seldom removed from the garment. Both the Londesborough brooch and another of silver-gilt formerly in the collection of the Marquess of Breadalbane (pl. XII) are even ornamented with disks of scroll-work on the

Fig. 177. Detail from Londesborough brooch. ($\frac{2}{1}$)

Fig. 178. Silver penannular brooch (back). ($\frac{2}{3}$)

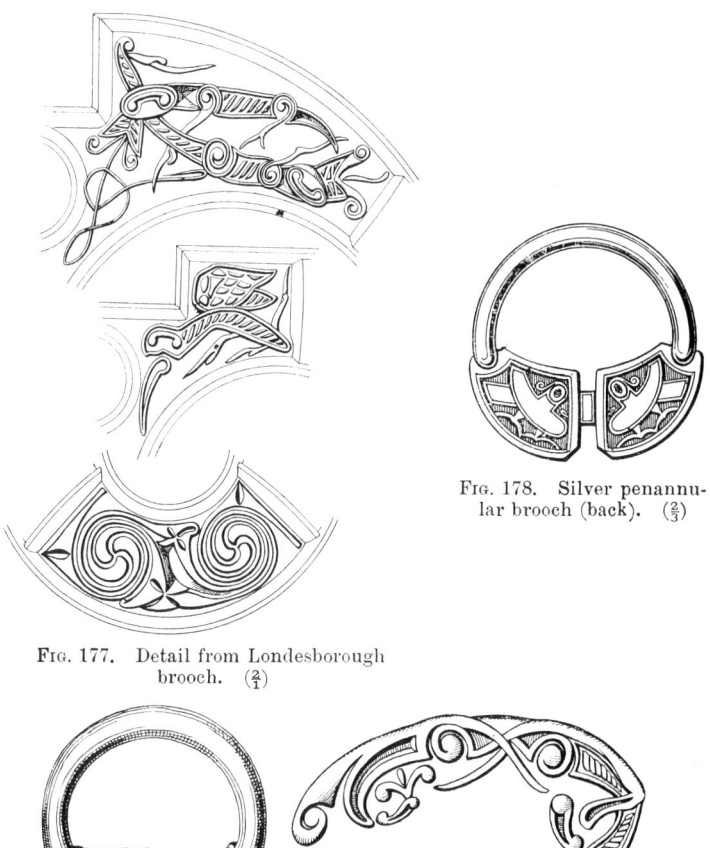

Fig. 179. Silver penannular brooch (back), with design on edge, Donegal. ($\frac{2}{3}$ and $\frac{2}{1}$)

back of the terminals, and both were heavily gilt all over the front, with settings of amber and glass. Details of the ornament are given on a larger scale, showing a pair of animals, a bird, and whorls with trumpet-pattern on the Londesborough brooch (fig. 177), also the backs of silver specimens (figs. 178, 179) and the animal fringe of that from Donegal, which may be compared with the Killucan brooch (fig. 180). The lozenge terminals of this and others can be dated approximately by the small brooch in the Trewhiddle hoard (fig. 120, no. 5); and the same motive is retained on the front of a fragmentary brooch from Westmeath (fig. 181), which has the back represented on the right to show the original form of the hoop. The decline of the style can also be seen in the Bonsall brooch (pl. XI, no. 2), which has the gilding much rubbed and nearly all the front occupied by simple interlacing. The purely Viking brooch of this pattern is of silver and generally of large dimensions; the debased animal design is engraved on the terminals, but gradually disappears, and the raised settings of the

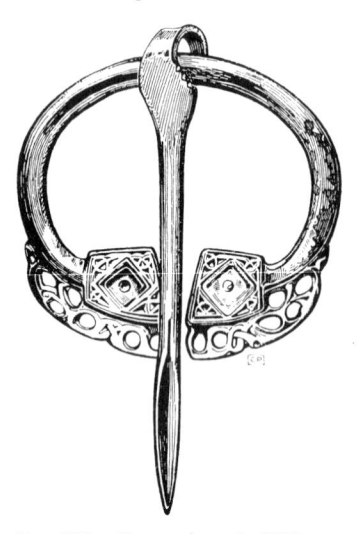

FIG. 180. Bronze brooch, Killucan, co. Westmeath. ($\frac{3}{4}$)

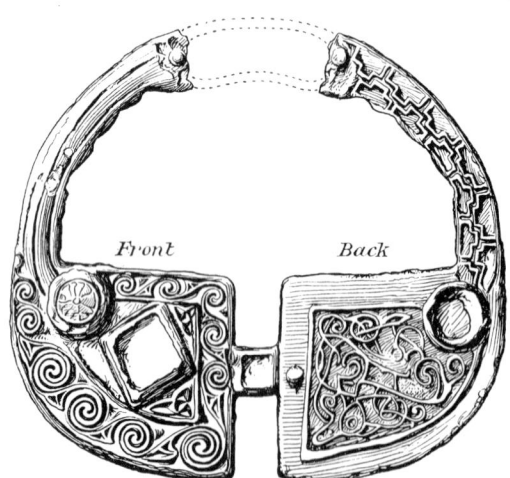

FIG. 181. Part of penannular brooch, co. Westmeath. ($\frac{1}{1}$)

best period give way to plain silver bosses (fig. 182). The pin is on the average twice as long as the diameter of the hoop.

Bronze pins from Ireland are in extraordinary variety and with few indications of date ; but a tentative sequence has been published by Mr. E. C. R. Armstrong, F.S.A., and the illustrated specimens will suggest a few parallels. To some extent the ring-headed pin develops on the same lines as the penannular brooch, and a case in point is fig. 183, *b*, which has the rare addition of garnet cell-work. A loose ring-head without ornament is quite common, and is found with Viking relics (one from Norway in Case 55) ; but there are penannular variants (as fig. 183, *a* and *c*). The polygonal head is a special form, the loose ring-head fitting closely

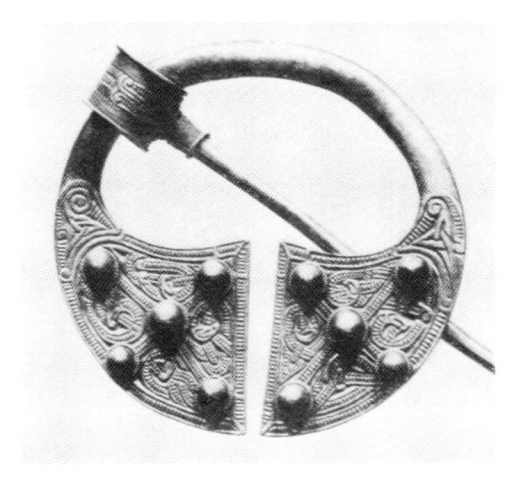

FIG. 182. Silver penannular brooch, Ireland. Diam. 3½ in.

and often ornamented (as *e* and *f*). Pins all in one piece also take several forms, and the twin-spiral head is found on Irish specimens (*d*) larger than those from East Anglia (Case C). Another pattern with polygonal moulding both on the stem and head (*g*) may be compared with Merovingian toilet-implements in Case 57, and are possibly contemporary. Large amber and glass beads are frequently found in Ireland, though the date is uncertain : one specimen of amber has an Ogham inscription, and is said to have been worn as a charm in maternity cases.

Though found below Steeple Bumpstead church in Essex, the large gilt boss in Case 53 is obviously of Irish origin and was perhaps looted by Vikings from a shrine like that of St. Manchan (copy in Victoria and Albert Museum), which has five bosses on an equal-armed cross. A diagram is here given (fig. 184) showing the form

138   DESCRIPTION OF CASE 53

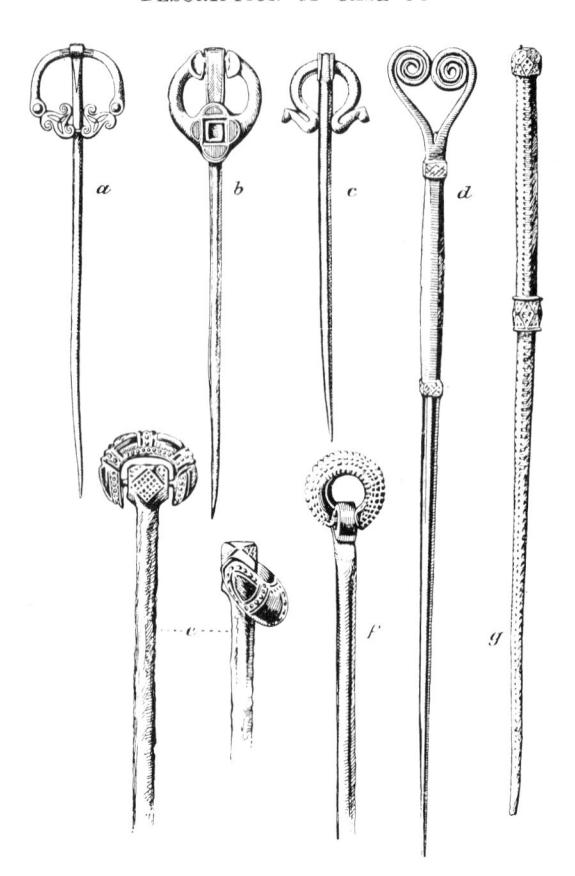

FIG. 183. Various pins from Ireland. ($\frac{1}{2}$)

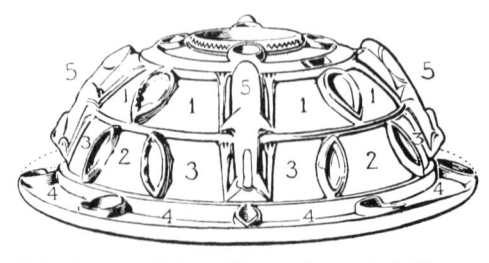

FIG. 184. Bronze-gilt boss, Steeple Bumpstead, Essex. ($\frac{1}{2}$)

and the arrangement of the various engraved patterns (fig. 185) numbered to correspond; also enlarged whorls selected from the border (fig. 186). The hole at the top was probably filled with a

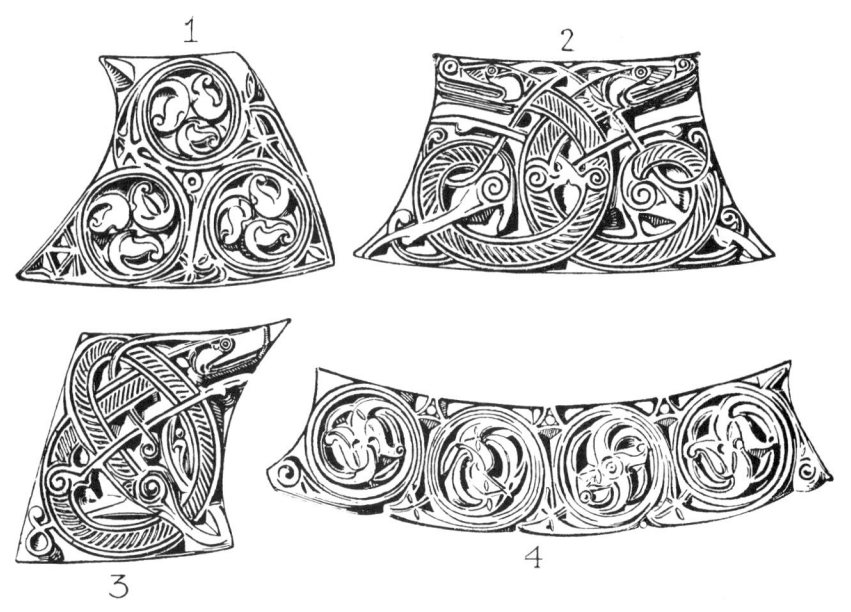

FIG. 185. Detail of Steeple Bumpstead boss. ($\frac{2}{1}$)

FIG. 186. Whorls on Steeple Bumpstead boss. ($\frac{4}{1}$)

crystal like that within the foot of the Ardagh chalice, with which it was probably contemporary. The serpentine forms have lappets behind the head, and spirals where the limbs are attached to the trunk; and the heads are here seen in profile, as usual in the

Jellinge style. To contrast with the gilding, niello was used in places, and the smaller settings were probably of blue glass and amber. The execution is remarkably good, and the animal and scroll patterns show the variety and precision generally found in Irish illumination. Works of art like this seem to have impressed the Scandinavian craftsman, for many were carried over to Norway, and the Jellinge style (pp. 16, 104) is attributed to Irish influence.

A good example of the Irish animal-style, in contrast to the mutilated and disjointed creatures of early Anglo-Saxon art, is a gilt

FIG. 187. Bronze-gilt mount, Phoenix Park, Dublin. (1/1)

FIG. 188. Stone trial-piece, Killaloe, co. Clare. (2/3)

mount, probably from a book cover, found in Phoenix Park, Dublin (fig. 187). The lappets springing from behind the heads of the two confronted animals interlace in the upper angle, and the rest of the field is ingeniously filled with the two bodies which have gaping jaws, and two legs each, with a whorl at the junction of each with the body (joint-spirals).

The chief design on both faces of the stone trial-piece from Killaloe, co. Clare (fig. 188), is in the Jellinge style, and the sketches of knot-work in the margin are consistent with a tenth-century date. An openwork ornament in the same style, with the head seen from above and the limbs coiled and interlaced, is here illustrated (fig. 189).

It is evident that the Irish saints and monks of the early Church in Ireland used ordinary cow-bells to summon their congregations to prayer; and that in course of time many of these bells came to be regarded as holy relics, and were encased in shrines of more costly materials but essentially of the same shape. The custom spread to Britain, France, and Switzerland, no doubt owing to the activity of Irish missionaries; and specimens of cast bronze were obviously copied from those of iron, but of reduced dimensions.

The iron bell of St. Cuilleann, coated with bronze, and enclosed in a shrine of the eleventh century (pl. XIII), was found in a hollow tree at Kilcuilawn in the parish of Glenkeen, co. Tipperary, and was used in the eighteenth century as a sacred object on which oaths were taken. The original handle is missing, but the maker of the shrine has added the traditional curve in openwork at the top. Two of the four bronze plates belonging to the sides now remain, one bearing an incised cross like some of the Hartlepool pillow-stones (fig.

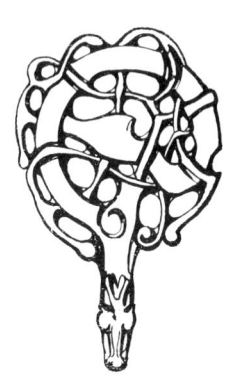

FIG. 189. Openwork bronze ornament, Ireland. ($\frac{1}{1}$)

155); and the upper mount is of stout bronze, inlaid with gold, silver, copper, and niello. At the spring of the arch on either side is a conventional head of an animal, with a small human head on the forehead; and between these heads is a fine example of the union-knot (p. 113), seen in a simplified form on many a Scandinavian tombstone. The upper mount was originally joined to the lower by angle-plates which depended from conventionalized animal-heads at the four angles. These suggest the Ringerike style, and the panels of interlacing show that the native art was nearing its final stage. On the upper face of the bow are three geometrical devices with yellow enamel, like those on the cross of Cong (twelfth century). St. Cuilleann was brother of Cormac, king-bishop of Cashel, who died in 908.

The bell of St. Conall, till about 1833 in the hands of its hereditary keepers the O'Breslens of Inishkeel (an island off the coast of Donegal), was enclosed in a bronze shrine decorated in the style of the fifteenth century, with the Crucifixion, various saints, and black-letter inscription. The bell itself, exhibited separately, is 7 in. high, consisting of an iron plate hammered into shape, riveted down the side and coated with bronze. A bronze cap was added, probably in the twelfth century, bearing an ornate cross on an interlaced background, each panel with a different pattern. One of these, forming a diaper of triangles, may be related to the Scandinavian chain or vertebral pattern of the tenth century seen on stone crosses in Cumberland and the Isle of Man ; but the saint, who was abbot and patron of the church, lived in the seventh century. Three other fragmentary bells of iron are connected respectively with St. Caimin (died 653), St. Molua (died 605), and St. Cummin (died 662). Examples in bronze are smaller, and one with a zoomorphic handle belonged to St. Ruadhan of Lorrha, who died in 584.

Iron bells were not the only cherished relics of the Irish saints and ecclesiastics : their walking-sticks were sometimes retained by the church, and encased in metal for their better protection. Ornament was lavished on the crozier thus formed, and the shape is still preserved in the pastoral staff of a bishop. A striking example of this practice is exhibited in Cases 53, 54, with an inscription soliciting a prayer for Maelfinnian and Condulig. The former was bishop of Kells, and died in 967 : Condulig was an ecclesiastic of the same monastery, and died in 1047. The knops have many facets, with well-executed animal and other ornament ; and the cresting is an open-work sequence of animal heads, one biting the other. Irish art was certainly in decline, but a century later was still capable of producing the cross of Cong.

Among other objects of interest from Ireland is a bronze-gilt cross with an oval setting at the centre engraved with a Cufic inscription that has been read *Bismi'llah* (In the name of God): the Mahometan formula is unexpected on a Christian emblem, probably of the ninth century. It was found in Ballycottin bog, Youghal, co. Cork, and another is of the Latin form in gold with filigree and blue glass centre, from Mellifont Abbey, co. Armagh. The gold bracelet from Virginia, co. Cavan, with wire lapped over a stout bar, dates from the Viking period and explains a fragment in the Dublin Museum. A gold necklet from co. Waterford is of unusual form, but is ornamented in the same way as a finger-ring from Harwich, Essex. Three rudely made bracelets of silver, two with stamped patterns, date from the Viking period in Ireland.

To a much greater degree than Britain, the Roman province of Gaul retained its independence and civilization in face of the Teutonic tribes that threatened its frontiers during the last two centuries of the Western Empire. The Franks from Germany, under pressure from the Saxons in their rear, occupied Roman territory on the lower Rhine early in the fourth century, and advanced

PLATE XIII. BELL OF ST. CUILLEANN IN ITS SHRINE (H. 12 IN.)
(Case 53, see p. 141)

PLATE XIV. JEWELLERY FROM HERPES, CHARENTE, FRANCE
(Case B, see p. 144)

through Gallia Belgica to the conquest of the Roman province. By about 430 they had reached the Somme, and in fifty years subdued the country as far as the Seine. The Loire was reached in 489, and within twenty years they made themselves masters of Aquitaine, in place of the Visigoths, whose history must be briefly noticed.

Nine years after their invasion of Italy in 401, Rome fell to the barbarians under Alaric. The Visigoths continued their march westwards, and in 412 broke into Gaul, soon capturing Narbonne, Toulouse, and Bordeaux, and then passing on into Spain, where they had been preceded by Vandals and Alans. The Visigoths were eventually given the country between the Loire and Garonne, with the district of Toulouse; but at the height of their power they were in possession of Gaul between the Loire, the Rhone, and the Pyrenees. A defeat at the hands of Franks and Burgundians in 507 left them very little in Gaul, and their headquarters were removed to Spain, where they maintained their independence till the Arab invasion in the eighth century.

The tomb of Childeric, who died in 481, was found in the seventeenth century at Tournay in Belgium, and is a fixed point of some importance in the development of Teutonic art in the West. His son Clovis (Ludwig, Louis) was recognized as the Frankish leader and advanced to occupy Roman Gaul, which was then bounded by the Somme, the Loire, and the upper Moselle. He defeated the Roman army of Syagrius at Soissons in 486, and after consolidating his conquests proceeded to drive the Visigoths out of the old Roman province. In this he was aided by the provincials, whom he led as an orthodox Christian against the Arian Goths. His baptism in 496 was thus a century earlier than the mission of St. Augustine to England.

The Frankish invasion of Gaul was not the forcible settlement of a migrating people, but an expedition led by Teutonic chieftains, and the distinction between Frank and Romanized Gaul survived in the names of Austrasia and Neustria for their respective areas within the Merovingian kingdom. As the antiquities recovered clearly show, there was a strong Teutonic element in the first half of the sixth century, but about 550 began what Nils Åberg has called the de-germanization of France, the conquerors gradually yielding to the superior culture of the native population. Frankish influence was on the wane in Central Europe, which gradually ceased to send its products to the West. During the seventh century the Merovingian power declined, and the Austrasian Pepin founded the Carolingian dynasty in 751 by deposing Childeric III and himself ascending the throne. Under his son Charles the Great (Charlemagne) the Frankish kingdom comprised the whole of Western continental Europe, except Spain: and to him we owe the revival of classical art in the West, known as the Carolingian renaissance. Though the Ostrogoths may account for examples both in South Russia and Italy, the Belgic area in Gaul seems to have been a centre for the 'chip-carving' (*Keilschnitt*) technique that was widely adopted in the fifth century, but after the Lombards had entered Italy, only survived in Scandinavia. Mention has already been made (p. 9) of the gilt specimens found at Vermand, near St. Quentin, and a distinction drawn between the angular patterns (pl. xiv, nos. 7, 8, 9, 11) engraved or cast in metal and the running scrolls (pl. xiv, nos. 6, 10) which, though less adapted to wood-carving, would present no difficulty to any one familiar with the *cire-perdue* process. Both patterns are often found in association with the animal ornament, to which they eventually succumbed (about 550 in the West). Garnet cell-work too was characteristic of the Franks (both the Salians of Belgium and the Ripuarians of the middle Rhine and the Moselle), and first appears among them in a developed form about 481, the date of Childeric's interment. In this treasure some of the cells are angular, forming a step pattern seen also on Anglo-Saxon jewellery ; and the industry flourished till about 550, though the standard reached was below that of the Lombards and Anglo-Saxons.

It is now agreed that the important cemetery at Herpes in the Charente (Jarnac, about 18 miles west of Angoulême) belonged to a Frankish rather than a Visigothic population, and the best relics recovered from it are clearly subsequent to the decisive battle of 507. No less certain is it that the collection from this site in Cases B and 59 contains some specimens that stand apart and have a different origin. Some of these are illustrated in the top row of pl. xiv (nos. 1–5), and attention has already been drawn (p. 66) to their identity with Isle of Wight specimens. There is some warrant for calling them Jutish, though the rosette brooch (no. 3) is common in the Frankish area.

The radiated brooch (no. 6) with blunt foot is certainly Frankish, but the angular knobs recalling a serpent's head are rare compared with those of nos. 7 and 8 ; and have been noted above in England (p. 89). The specimen with lozenge (diamond) foot terminating in an animal's head was probably imported from beyond the Rhine (p. 156), and the shape of the foot, with its lateral projections enclosing cabochon garnets, suggests an Ostrogothic origin, which is confirmed by the birds' heads round the head of no. 10. These two brooches date between 500 and 550, and nos. 9 and 12 are certainly earlier but point in the same direction. A close connexion with Hungary and the remote Crimea (fig. 24) is obvious, and the Szilágy-Somlyó find (just before 400) includes what are held to be the earlier and later varieties of this type (with the foot broadest near the terminal and near the bow respectively). As these silver brooches and gold buckles of a particular pattern also occur in Spain, the Visigoths may be credited with their circulation between the Black Sea and the Atlantic.

Many details of interest were noticed during the excavation of the cemetery. There were no coffins, but in nearly every case there was a pillow-stone, and sometimes the grave was surrounded by stones set upright: the Christian orientation was rigidly observed, the feet being at the east end. Nearly always a vase of earthenware or glass lay on the right or left side, occasionally at the feet. The men as a rule had large buckles of iron, bronze, or silver, and from the belt hung one or two single-edged knives in sheaths of wood or leather, with blades 10–16 in. long and wooden grips. At the right side was sometimes a spear or an axe of *francisca* or some other type: but no shields were found. Roman coins, some of them pierced, were found in the mouth or at the waist, and two crystal spindle-whorls

FIG. 190. Bowl, with pearled border, Herpes. Diam. 10 in.

were lying near the neck of males, no doubt worn as beads. Nearly every female grave contained a pair of tweezers, and many had girdle-hangers (*châtelaines*). Many finger-rings, mostly worn on the right hand, were recovered, but only four were of gold. Bracelets were rare, most of them silver, but beads worn on the wrist were common (p. 73). The brooches were never worn opposite one another (p. 70), but in pairs vertically, and the smaller were nearer the neck than the larger specimens. There were earrings of several types, and three or four cases of gold thread at the head (p. 44). Nearly all the coins were of the Roman Empire, the latest being of Justinian (565); and one grave contained a number of barbarous imitations. Many of the graves were therefore later than the battle of 507, and to the first half of the sixth century may be referred the four bronze bowls (Case 59): one resembles in form a small pottery vase, the others have a beaded horizontal border (fig. 190), with a rounded profile. The pottery consists mainly of angular bowls from 4–7 in. in diameter at the mouth, which expands slightly: the shoulder is generally ornamented with repetitions of a single stamp. A small urn and one of several jugs are illustrated (fig. 191, *b* and *d*), the latter being of black, red, or yellow ware. The glass is well preserved and of many forms, three being chosen for illustration (fig. 192, *a–c*), but the Frankish tumbler (as *d*) was perhaps the commonest, with rounded or angular profile. Two elaborate chains are exhibited, one with

FIG. 191. Frankish pottery. H. of jug, $6\frac{1}{2}$ in.

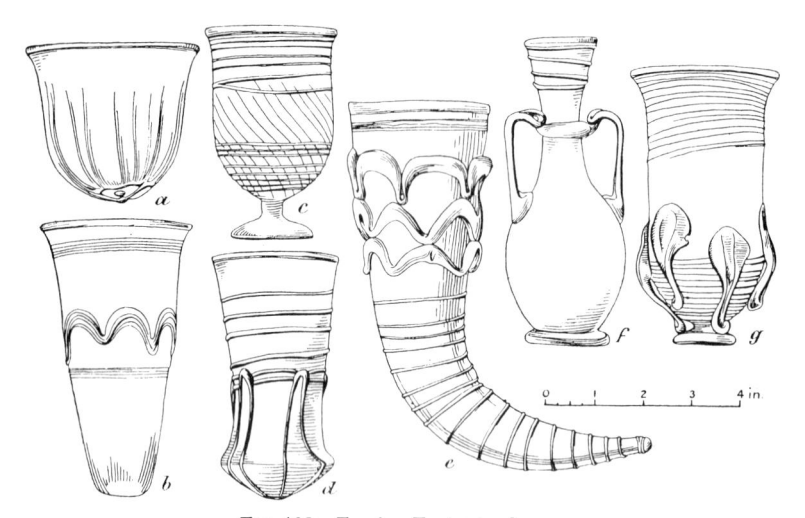

FIG. 192. Foreign Teutonic glass.

a cross at one end: both have long hooked terminals for attachment. The buckles are mostly large, of bronze with engraved ornament, one in imitation of garnet cell-work (fig. 193, left); and either of round or triangular form, with domed bosses at the angles. The smaller objects are in Case B, and typical of the Franks are the purse-mount (fig. 194), toilet implements (fig. 195), and hooked clasp for fastening the dress (fig. 196). An armlet

FIG. 193. Frankish buckles from Charente and Marne. ($\frac{2}{3}$)

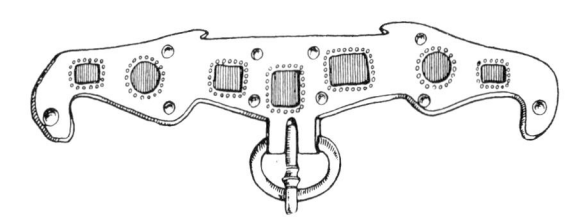

FIG. 194. Purse-guard set with garnets, Herpes. ($\frac{2}{3}$)

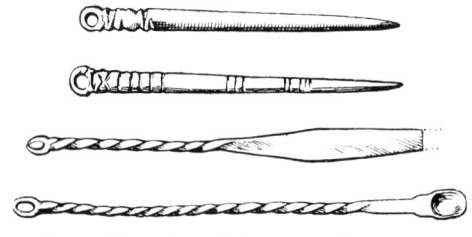

FIG. 195. Toilet implements from cemetery, Herpes. ($\frac{2}{3}$)

with swelling ends is of silver, but many of the buckles are of white metal (p. 41), and the variety is extraordinary. There are

L 2

148 DESCRIPTION OF CASES 57, 58, A 1

spindle-whorls of shale and amber, two dice (fig. 197), a crystal sphere unmounted (as in the tomb of Childeric, 481), jewelled ear-rings with polygonal ends, beads, combs, and what may be a Gothic buckle with garnets in a pattern like one from Ringwould, Kent. Iron specimens exhibited in Case 58 comprise a sword and angon (both otherwise unrecorded from the site), axe-heads, and weaving-implement like those from England (p. 56).

The important collection acquired in 1901 from M. Léon Morel of Rheims includes many Frankish specimens, mostly no doubt from the Champagne (Dépt. Marne), but only three grave-groups are recorded, two being from Bréban. With a warrior had been buried the head of an angon 38 in. long (pl. vi, no. 1), the long head of a spear, and two lance-heads, as well as a shield of which the boss (pl. vi, no. 5) and handle survive, the latter being the same length (17½ in.) as the Droxford specimens. The furniture of a woman's grave consisted of a pair of gold ear-rings with jewelled polygons, an amber necklace, a bracelet of coloured glass beads, a pair of radiated brooches with birds' heads, another pair of rosette brooches and one circular specimen with garnet cell-work, a bronze pin behind the head (worn in the

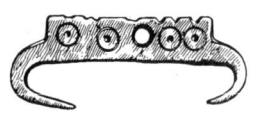

FIG. 196. Bronze clasp with hooks, Herpes. (¼)

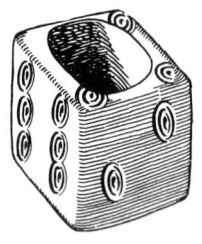

FIG. 197. Bone die, Herpes. (¼)

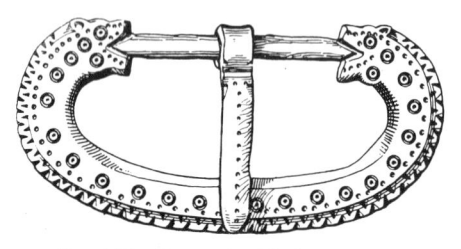

FIG. 198. Bronze buckle from grave, Gourgançon. (⅔)

hair), and a silver blade in the hand. Both burials probably date between 500 and 550, and Ostrogothic influences may be traced in the head and lateral settings of the larger brooches (p. 144).

The third grave was at Gourgançon (Dépt. Aube), and contained another warrior, armed with an axe (pl. vi, no. 7) and scramasax; two knives, a large iron buckle and a smaller one (fig. 198) of bronze (late Roman pattern, cf. fig. 4) were included, also a brown pottery bottle, and a black vase of the ordinary ware, with bands of stamped pattern between cordons.

In Cases 57, 58, and A (section 1) are exhibited series of objects collected by M. Morel. Scramasaxes are numerous, and were evidently the favourite weapon of the sixth and seventh centuries in this area. 'Damascened' buckles of iron had silver foil beaten into the roughened surface, and then ornamented with geometrical or animal designs ; they may be attributed to the seventh century, which is marked by the violin-shaped tongue (p. 41). One plate is encrusted with a cruciform pattern. Axes are of various shapes besides the throwing-weapon (*francisca*) with its flowing curves (as pl. vi, no. 6), and the type of fig. 109 is represented. The winged spear-head from the Morel collection is not in such good preservation as one from Amiens, like pl. vi, no. 4. Several ear-rings with polygons of garnet cell-work are characteristic, also long pins with scoop at the head and polygonal moulding on the stem, sometimes engraved with a cross. The open-work bronze plates are of various patterns— triskele, cruciform, horse (or gryphon) at a manger, Daniel between two lions (like representations of St. Menas and his camels) barely recognizable in fig. 199. One of these objects has a double buckle at the top, and all were no doubt worn on the girdle, forming with the various objects on chains the châtelaine of the housewife (cf. Case 63). A buckle of rock-crystal is remarkable, and the beads are particularly large and brilliant.

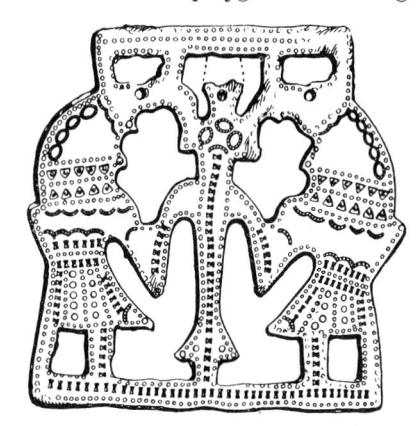

FIG. 199. Open-work bronze, with Daniel and the lions, Amiens. ($\frac{2}{3}$)

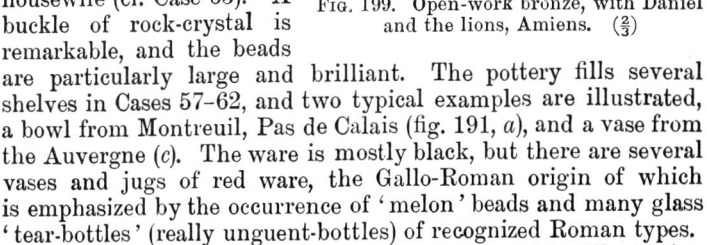

The pottery fills several shelves in Cases 57–62, and two typical examples are illustrated, a bowl from Montreuil, Pas de Calais (fig. 191, *a*), and a vase from the Auvergne (*c*). The ware is mostly black, but there are several vases and jugs of red ware, the Gallo-Roman origin of which is emphasized by the occurrence of 'melon' beads and many glass 'tear-bottles' (really unguent-bottles) of recognized Roman types.

Buckles are of the usual types, and one selected for illustration (fig. 193, right) shows animal ornament and the human face, with plaited and fret borders, and the violin-shaped tongue of the seventh century. A tinned bronze badge in the form of a fish has been already mentioned (p. 51) ; and there are shoe-shaped rivets as in England, finger-rings, including one of jet with the Christian monogram (Chi-Rho), and several bone combs ; but here as elsewhere the most important items for dating purposes are the brooches.

A circular brooch (fig. 200), found in the north of France, is of interest as an early example of enamel cell-work (*cloisonné*). It is of bronze, with an iron pin at the back, and a cross in front executed in yellow, pale green, bluish white, and red on a blue ground: the partitions forming the cells are of copper, and comparatively thick and clumsy, suggesting an early date. This form of cross was commonest in England in the seventh to the ninth centuries (fig. 123), but enamels here are of the rarest occurrence.

A pair of conical silver brooches ornamented with niello come from the Marne, and are perhaps more Gallo-Roman than the adjoining specimen from Moncetz, Marson (fig. 201), which is a Teutonic form, and probably the ancestor of the equal-armed type connected with Hanover (as fig. 81). Plain and narrow

FIG. 200. Enamelled brooch, with cross, France. (¼)

FIG. 201. Bronze brooch, Moncetz, Marne. (¼)

equal-armed specimens are in Case A 1, with bird-brooches set with garnets, the rosette pattern with cell-work, and later circular or lobed specimens encrusted with stones or glass-pastes in the Merovingian manner of the seventh century.

The S-brooch, the square-headed form with oval foot, and the radiated head with lozenge or blunt foot are all well seen in the series from Amiens and Pontoise in Case A 6: there are also bird and rosette brooches with garnets, and the usual jewelled ear-rings from both sites, but the Amiens find looks more Frankish than Pontoise (90 miles south), which has brooches with the Central European foot, and no encrusted specimens. This method superseded garnet cell-work to a large extent west of the Rhine, and a good example is illustrated (pl. xv, no. 9), but is without locality. The change may have been due to the isolation of France after about 550 (p. 143), and the application of cabochon stones and filigree to the surface of metal continued in France during the seventh and eighth centuries. The older Ostrogothic buckles fluctuate between the two methods: two are in this Case and a larger one in Case B, without locality. Many in South Russia exhibit 'chip-carving' patterns: in Italy drop-shaped stones are encrusted, and in France coarse cell-work was popular among the Ostrogoths and their associates. Two buckle-plates of ordinary Frankish or Merovingian type (fig. 202) show the Christian cross as an ornamental motive.

Several finger-rings of the Merovingian period are exhibited in Case B, but as most of them are without locality it is difficult to decide in what part of the Teutonic area some of them were made. The silver-gilt specimen selected (fig. 203) is interesting not only for its pairs of animals with heads turned back, and eyes set with blue glass, but also for the classical sard intaglio of a horse, which serves as a bezel. Particulars of all can be found in the *Catalogue of Early Christian, Mediaeval and Later Finger-rings*, nos. 146-78.

FIG. 202. Buckle-plates, with cross, France. ($\frac{2}{3}$)

FIG. 203. Silver-gilt finger-ring (developed). ($\frac{2}{3}$)

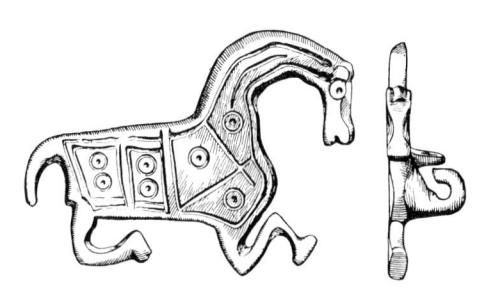

FIG. 204. Brooch in form of horse, with side view, France. ($\frac{1}{1}$)

Other finger-rings and brooches with Frankish cell-work (as pl. xv, nos. 1, 3) or encrusted gems are exhibited in Case A 6, and a series of bronze brooches in the form of a horse (fig. 204) includes one in the naturalistic Scytho-Greek style of South Russia (as on the Chertomlyk vase, third century B.C.) with settings of red enamel: the degeneration of the type in the course of perhaps ten centuries is very striking. A bronze armlet with two small circular matrices for impressing both faces of a wax seal is a rarity, and a bronze sword-pommel from the Seine (fig. 205) has a central panel of gold filigree, and on either side the head of an animal, as frequently seen on pommels (p. 94) and bell-shrines (pl. XIII) of the Viking period, as well as on the earlier Italian pommel (fig. 209).

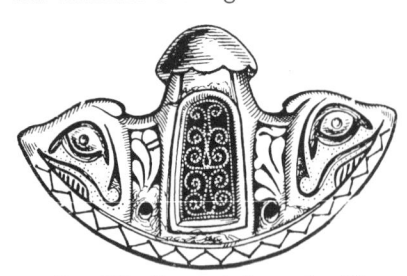

FIG. 205. Pommel of sword, with filigree, Seine. (¾)

Spain is barely represented, but there are two buckle-plates of bronze that may be classed as Visigothic, especially as one of the same kind was included in the Herpes find (Case 59). Several without locality are preserved at Madrid, and may belong to the seventh century. Distinctly earlier is the solid gold buckle with garnets encrusted on the plate, of the same type as one from Tolnau, Hungary, in Case 63 (pl. XV, no. 7), which has part of a classical intaglio mounted in the plate. The type can be traced back to the Crimea, and was evidently distributed over Europe by the Goths when gold was plentiful.

In the middle of the first century the Vandals were settled between the Vistula and Oder, perhaps further west; and after wandering over most of Central Europe raided Italy in 405, and struck through Gaul in the following year from Switzerland to the Pyrenees, to establish themselves in Spain in 409. Twenty years later a combined host of Vandals and Alans left Spain for Carthage, and the series from Bône, Algeria, probably dates before 450. The tongue of the bronze-gilt buckle illustrated (fig. 206) is of the Gothic type just referred to, and the oval plate is engraved in dotted outline with a man fighting a lion, in debased classical

FIG. 206. Bronze-gilt buckle, with engraving, Algeria. (¼)

PLATE XV. FOREIGN JEWELLERY SET WITH GARNETS (NEARLY ⅟₁)
(Cases A 6, B, 61, 63. see pp. 150-2, 155)

style. Primitive cell-work is seen on the circular brooch (fig. 207), which has rounded inlays of amber, and yellow glass on gold foil between, the border being of glass much decayed. With this and other brooches are gold ear-rings with empty polygonal terminals, beads, a spoon with round bowl and toilet articles. A bronze-gilt buckle of this Gothic type, with primitive cell-work of glass, was found at Faversham, Kent (Case D 5). Similar cell-work, including heart-shaped garnets, may be seen in a small series from Beit Jibrin (Bethogabris), Palestine, no doubt due to Teutonic immigrants. A few more specimens from Africa are in Case 60. The Carthage buckles like fig. 66 have been already referred to (p. 60), also one from Akhmim, Upper Egypt. There is another from the same site, and a third from Thebes, on the Nile, with blue, green, and red inlay.

The collection from Italy is small but contains some good examples of garnet cell-work and several gold ornaments. These no doubt date after the Lombard conquest, but some of the ruder work is probably due to the earlier wave of barbarian invaders.

Under Theodoric the Ostrogoths became masters of Italy in 493, but their dominion came to an end in 553. Fifteen years later Italy was invaded by another northern

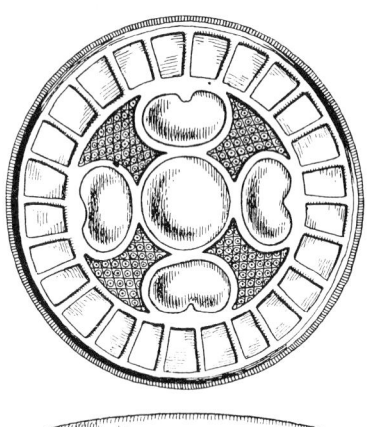

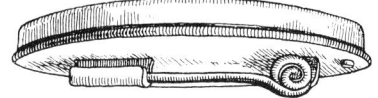

FIG. 207. Jewelled brooch, with side view, Algeria. ($\frac{2}{3}$)

tribe, the Lombards, who after leaving their Baltic home had spent some time in Bohemia and Pannonia, and came into contact with Byzantine culture. To them and their contemporaries in Bavaria was due the blending of ribbon interlacing (like that still surviving in many Byzantine churches) with the animal style of the North; and it is by comparing Lombard productions before and after their descent upon Italy in 568 that a date can be fixed for the abolition of 'chip-carving' technique and appearance of Salin's Style II (p. 10). The interlacing principle was soon applied to the Teutonic animal, and this new treatment of the traditional motive found great favour in Scandinavia, but little response in France or England. In Italy itself, so strong was the classical instinct, in spite of the Ostrogothic occupation, that few examples of Style II survive, as in the minority of gold-foil crosses; but in garnet cell-work, the use of gold and general magnificence the Lombards set an example to their Teutonic kinsmen. In the front rank is the large radiated brooch (fig. 208), with the knobs in two tiers (a special Lombard feature) and a curved band beyond the animal-

FIG. 208. Radiated brooch, probably from Italy. ($\frac{2}{3}$)

head below the oval foot. The four lateral projections take the form of animal heads in Style II with pointed jaws and angular bands behind the eye; the knobs resemble the terminal of the foot, and the cord-pattern of the bow contrasts with the decoration of the head and foot. A less elaborate specimen with garnets belongs to a grave-group dating about 600, but without precise locality. With it were found two glass vases splashed with yellow and red on a green ground, and a curved horn of blue glass with white threads (fig. 192, *f*, *e*) ; a pair of gold ear-rings with filigree and pendant, a brooch with garnet cell-work derived from the S-pattern but almost an oval, and a plain equal-armed cross of gold-foil. Adjoining are several smaller gold crosses from graves near Bergamo, N. Italy, one from Lodi Vecchio being associated with a bronze plate in the chip-carving style, finger-rings and bone buckles. There are also gold coins, heavy buckles of white metal (p. 41), glass beads and squares of gold-foil for sewing to the dress, one engraved with a small cross. The Christian emblem in gold-foil is characteristic of the Lombards in Italy, and those ornamented with embossed animal patterns are generally in Style I, probably dating between 568 and 600. To the same source may be referred the fine gold ear-ring with basket-pattern terminal of garnet cell-work (pl. xv, no. 5), a pair of radiated brooches covered with garnets (pl. xv, no. 2), one without its knobs ; and the pommel of a ring-sword (p. 49) similarly ornamented (fig. 209), the ring having become a fixture and no longer serviceable. A pair of gold clasps has each a cabochon garnet at the centre, but the open-work cells are now empty ; and the incrusted style of jewellery is represented by a gold circular brooch, a small reliquary of quatrefoil pattern, and a few finger-rings.

FIG. 209. Jewelled sword pommel, probably from Italy. (⅔)

All these, however, as well as the fish-shaped brooch (pl. xv, no. 4), are unfortunately without definite localities. A grave-group in Case 61 from Belluno, N. Italy, is all of gold : the brooch (pl. xv, no. 8) has lost many of its garnets ; the foil cross and finger-ring have stamped patterns ; the pin is surmounted by a human hand once holding a pearl, and there are also beads of joined hemispheres.

A small disk with cruciform pattern and blue and green enamel between the arms has been already referred to as a parallel to fig. 200 ; but there is a larger and better example in this Case. The lower brooch on plate x belonged to the Castellani collection, and is said to have come from Canosa in South Italy. It is circular, with three wire loops below for pendants, now missing. In the centre is an enamelled portrait, perhaps of a royal lady ; and though the surface is decayed, blue, green, red, and opaque white are still distinguishable. Of the four concentric zones, two are composed of pearls alternating with gold loops for threading; the third is cell-work of formal design, and the fourth a plain gold frame for the portrait. The three pendants point to the Eastern Empire, but it is difficult to believe that the extremely crude enamel figure is the work of a Byzantine goldsmith. The setting closely resembles that of a jewel in the Italo-barbaric cross of the Lombard king Agilulf (died 615), preserved in the treasury of Monza cathedral, and Byzantine models may have been copied in both cases. The craft of enamelling existed at Constantinople as early as Justinian's time (527-66), and the Castellani brooch may be dated about 600.

The silver trefoil ornament found at Rome with coins of Offa (reigned 757-96) may have been sent to the Holy See by the Mercian king after the Council of Chelsea in 787—perhaps the first instance of 'Peter's Pence'. An iron shield-boss with gilt rivets stamped with a triangle containing three dots (p. 161), and a buckle-plate (obtained in Florence) with debased chip-carving pattern and garnet settings, may perhaps belong to the Ostrogothic occupation, like the larger gilt buckle with triangular settings on the plate that are neither incrustations nor cell-work in the ordinary sense (p. 150).

From the neighbourhood of Grüneck castle in the Alpine district of the Grisons comes a money-box or purse made from a deer's antler and engraved with interlacing: it contained coins of the emperor Louis I, Charles the Bald, and Berenger and Lambert, kings of Italy, and therefore dates from about 900.

North of the Alps lay the central corridor utilized by Teuton and Hun alike in their tribal movements towards the West; and discoveries in Hungary (as at Szilágy Somlyó, p. 8) show the degree of civilization reached by those who began to pass this way from the south of Russia about the year 400. The southern stream of influence postulated by Bernhard Salin (p. 8) can be easily traced in Bavaria; and the series from Nordendorf is typical of the sixth century.

In Central Europe Teutonic art underwent certain modifications, which can be recognized also in neighbouring areas with which communication was maintained. The brooch with oval foot, and the animal-head terminal of this and other types, were certainly local and date mainly from the sixth century. The radiated brooch so common in France occurs naturally in the Frankish area east of the Rhine, where the abrupt termination of the foot often gives place to the animal-head (as pl. xiv, no. 8). Brooches with oval foot generally have square (or oblong) heads (as pl. xiv, no. 11) between 500 and 550, and round heads in the following period like that shown from Nordendorf; but the projecting knobs in both forms are often joined together, and deteriorate into a pearled border.

Earlier forms may be looked for in Hungary: a gilt brooch

with three knobs dates from about 500, and a smaller example of the same type comes from Szent Andrea.

The Tolnau gold buckles have been already referred to (p. 152); the larger has part of a classical intaglio in its plate (pl. xv, no. 7), and the smaller has incrusted garnets, both showing the Gothic tongue with abrupt base. The 'chip-carving' buckle from Germany may be compared with fig. 4, and similar examples in quantity are exhibited in the Rhenish museums; at Linz and Salzburg in Upper Austria; at Trieste, Budapest, and Spalato (Dalmatia), showing that this technique was widely spread in Europe in the fourth and fifth centuries.

Swabia and especially the Main and Neckar valleys were occupied by the Alamans (whence Allemagne, the French name of Germany) till about 500, when they were dispossessed by the Franks, who had been in Franconia a generation before. In these parts the bow-brooch gradually gave place to the buckle, which in Switzerland and Burgundy reached enormous proportions and was generally of iron inlaid with silver (sometimes called damascening).

A good example of Frankish incrustation is the brooch from Kreuznach, in the neighbourhood of which were found the two glass drinking-horns from Bingerbrück, the amber and green glass beakers from Selzen, and the girdle-hangers from Sprendlingen. More of these last were found near Mayence, and the series explains the use of such open-work bronzes as those from Kempston (fig. 86) and Amiens (fig. 199). From a grave on the Rhine comes a lobed beaker (fig. 192, *g*) that is obviously connected with English specimens like fig. 54, *d*, and relations between the middle Rhine and Kent (p. 2) are implied in the discovery at Walluf, near Mayence, of a Coptic bronze bowl like fig. 90, and amethyst beads near Kreuznach. From the district round the junction of the Rhine and Moselle comes an interesting series in the Frankish style: ear-rings with polygonal terminals, bird-brooches, small circular brooches inlaid with garnets, and incrusted brooches, some with keystone garnets. The beads are unusually good and include the Roman 'melon' pattern: there is a pair of scales, and long pins with scoops at the end and cubes on the stem engraved with the cross (p. 149); and a circular brooch with bosses and silver damascening is evidently in imitation of a cell-work specimen.

A silver bracelet and elaborate beads in the same metal were found near Leipzig with coins of our Ethelred II, Harthacnut, and Edward the Confessor (eleventh century), and similar beads date from the Viking period in Scandinavia. At Leuna, near Merseburg in Saxony, was found a group of some importance (Case 63), as it combines Roman and Teutonic antiquities of the fourth century. The two black cordoned vases have been already mentioned (p. 21), and there is an open-mouthed urn of rougher ware, three brooches with the head and bow of fig. 231, and the foot of fig. 230; a pair of spurs and a buckle, all of Teutonic origin contrasting with a bowl of Samian ware (form 37), two bronze skillets (one perforated as a strainer), and two clear glass bowls, one engraved with Artemis and Actaeon and the other with cut-glass pattern like fig. 123, c of *Guide to Roman Britain*. The pottery is quite distinct from the Frankish ware of the Rhine, of which a specimen from Mayence is illustrated (fig. 191, e).

In the North German plain antiquities of the Migration period are scarce, and the absence of any in the north-east is accounted for by the Slavonic occupation. In the time of Tacitus (about A. D. 100) the Slavs were settled north-east of the Carpathians, occupying the basins of the Vistula, Pripet, and Upper Dniester under the name of Veneti (hence the Wends of modern Germany). They were at first dominated by the Goths; but when the Huns became masters of Central Europe, the Slavs turned to the west and held the Mark of Brandenburg by 512. Both their languages belonged to the Indo-European (Aryan) group, but there was no other bond between Slav and Teuton, and all Germanic objects between the Baltic and Bohemia date before 350.

Of the Scandinavian countries, Denmark was first in the field with a new variety of brooch, which had a wide circulation and considerable influence on the taste of the Germanic peoples. It has been already noticed in its proper sequence (p. 30), and the illustration (fig. 20) shows the special features of this silver-plated ornament—the square (or rather, oblong) head and the pair of animal heads springing from the base of the bow and turned downwards towards the foot. Some Crimean brooches have a head approaching the rectangular form, and from about 350 a terminal often took the form of an animal's head (as fig. 14); but the earliest combination of the two features seems to have been in fifth-century Denmark, where our forefathers were presumably preparing for the descent on these shores. The practice of attaching thin plates of silver to a brooch was due to Gothic influence, but the geometrical decoration of the early Danish examples was derived from provincial Roman art, the Nydam finds proving influence from this quarter as early as the fourth century.

Norway is fortunate in having had its long and cruciform brooches classified and dated by Dr. Haakon Shetelig, who brings the main series to an end about A. D. 550. A few, distinguished by a plain hinge in place of a spiral coil, were derived from the provincial Roman brooch of crossbow type; but the majority can be traced to the type with returned foot associated with the Goths in South Russia. The head is a square or oblong plate surmounted and flanked by round knobs (less often polygonal, like one from Östergötland, Sweden, about 500); the bow is more arched in Norway than in Denmark and England, and the foot terminates normally in something like a horse's head. At first the knobs were placed astride the edge of the head-plate, but later were cast in one piece, and the change took place earlier in Norway than in England, and not at all in Denmark. Ornamentation with a punch is common on the brooches of eastern Norway, but rarely found on the west coast. In course of evolution the knobs become flat at the back, the catch-plate behind the foot becomes shorter, and the head broader at right angles to the axis of the brooch. East Norway is not so rich in late forms as the coast, but the latest stages of evolution can only be seen in England. The brooches called cruciform in Norway (fig. 210) generally show higher relief than elsewhere, and the stage illustrated marks the close of their local evolution (about 550).

Another type, the tortoise-brooch, is better represented, and its earliest form is included in a group of the seventh century from Tromsö (Case 55). A remarkable specimen, with the grotesque animal still coherent and intelligible below the framework (fig. 211), is executed in Style III, which was the finest period of Teutonic art in Scandinavia. It dates from the second half of the eighth century. The network persists, but after about 800 the 'grasping' animal (derived from the Carolingian lion, p. 14) appears in the spaces. In the late ninth and tenth centuries the type has a double shell, with a gradual exaggeration of the bosses; and decay sets in soon after 1000. Carolingian influence is also traced in the trefoil brooch (fig. 212), the shape being derived from some unknown source in the West, and the ornament generally consisting of the 'grasping' animal or classical (acanthus) foliage in various stages of degeneration. The type dates from the ninth and particularly the tenth century, and reference may be made to an English find of about 850 (fig. 122).

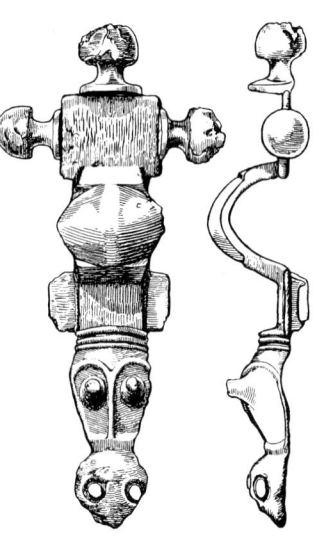

FIG. 210. Cruciform brooch, with side view, Hardanger, Norway. ($\frac{2}{3}$)

The iron weapons are better preserved than usual, and include two swords typical of the early ninth century (according to

Jan Petersen's classification), with bevelled guard and triangular pommel, bevelled below in a straight line. They were both found in Norway, one at Haffer, Aker parish ; and the same hilt is often found on single-edged swords of the ninth century, probably derived from the Frankish scramasax. Another sword from Alleslev, near Roskilde, Zealand, has the under part of the

FIG. 211. Bronze tortoise brooch, with design, Bergen, Norway. ($\frac{2}{3}$)

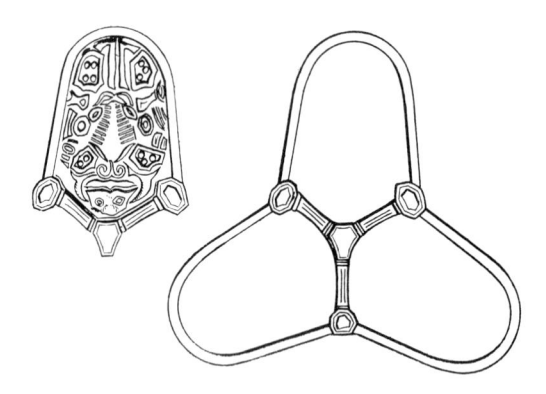

FIG. 212. Trefoil brooch, with detail, Roskilde, Denmark. ($\frac{2}{3}$)

pommel curved. A winged spear-head from Norway belongs to the same class as pl. VI, no. 4, and probably dates from the ninth century, the elaborate iron rattle being a little later. This consists of a loop, shaped like the profile of a dish, to which are attached two large rings and a hook : earlier examples had several rings on an oval loop, which was attached to two poles, and no doubt carried aloft in the eighth century. There is a smaller rattle on a pin, with four loose and two fixed rings. Axe-heads

SCANDINAVIA

with the lower side in a broken line are referred to the ninth century, the others are probably later; and the narrow leaf-shaped lance- or arrow-heads with long tang are characteristic of the Vikings.

Coins afford clear evidence of foreign relations: Gaulish and Byzantine pieces of gold, in addition to abundant ring-money (p. 168) and other forms of the precious metal, show that the golden age covered the fourth and fifth centuries, when coins and medallions were plentiful, owing to the tribute paid by Rome to the barbarians. The importation of gold into Sweden had ceased by 550, owing probably to the conquest of Götaland and the adjacent islands by the Svear of Upland, who were eventually to give their name to Sweden; and the sixth century is characterized by the bracteates, which were at first copied from Roman medallions. One of the commonest types of these Scandinavian pendants (fig. 213) is engraved with a horseman (often with a large head and diminutive body), and perhaps a serpent, bird, or symbol (such as the swastika) in the field. The horseman with bird is supposed to be Odin, and the head above a goat may represent Thor. The bird-and-fish motive that appears here is also seen in Case D 3 and on the Lullingstone bowl.

FIG. 213. Gold bracteate, probably from Denmark. ($\frac{1}{1}$)

Hoards of coins found in Scandinavia have been carefully studied, and it is now established that German pieces range between the years 930 and 1002; Anglo-Saxon (representing the tribute paid to the Vikings) between 950 and 1050; and Cufic (struck at Cufa on the Euphrates for princes east of the Caspian), 800–950, though these only reached Sweden through Russia late in the ninth century.

Silver from the East reached Scandinavia as well as the British Isles in large quantities, probably in the form of ingots (as at Cuerdale, p. 107). These were apparently worked locally into bracelets and other ornaments, and generally decorated with the punch, the commonest stamp being a triangle with one to three dots within; and the technique was probably borrowed from the same source as the bullion. The triangle with three dots is regarded by Dr. A. W. Brøgger as the symbol for a weight of 3 classical scruples (2·9 grammes or 45 grains), a triskele indicating the øre, a weight of 26·8 grammes or 413 grains; and the pair of scales (fig. 214), which can be packed into a small bronze case, was used for weighing the precious metals, the old Norse weight-system being 1 mark = 8 ører = 24 ertogar = 240 penninger.

A few local objects of special interest must be noticed, as their use is not obvious. The flat pointed oval stones (quartz or quartzite) with a channel all round and generally slight grooves on the two faces (fig. 215), have been more than once found

FIG. 214. Folding scales and case, Gotland. ($\frac{1}{2}$)

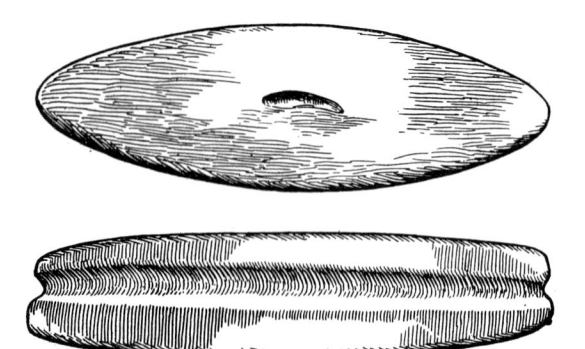

FIG. 215. Tracked stone (quartz) with side view, Upland, Sweden. ($\frac{2}{3}$)

SCANDINAVIA 163

inserted in a belt, and it is clear that they were used with iron strike-a-lights for producing fire. They belong to the period A. D. 300–500. Whale's bone was often made into plates, with confronted horses' heads carved at the top (fig. 216); and the lower plain portion is thought to have served as a board for pressing seams of linen with a bone tool like those used for smoothing the seams of sails. This specimen was found in a barrow 107 ft. long at Lilleberre, Namdalen, with the objects mounted

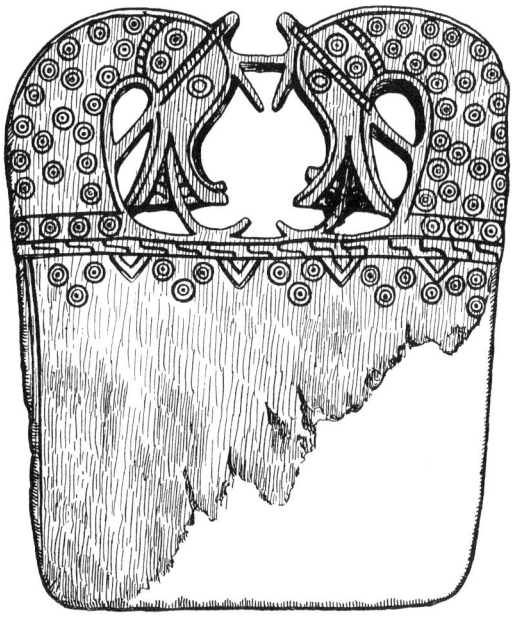

FIG. 216. Whale's bone plaque with horses' heads, Namdalen, Norway. ($\frac{1}{3}$)

on the adjoining board—glass beads and a pair of tortoise-brooches dating 800–50, like fig. 211. Bucket-shaped vessels of pottery, with a handle originally attached to an iron collar (fig. 217), seem to have been made on a large scale in certain parts of Norway and distributed over the country between the late fourth century and about 600. The paste often includes asbestos or mica, and the profile and decoration vary according to date, the true bucket-form being of the fifth century. Keys of the Viking period for displacing the internal springs of a barrel padlock are frequent in Scandinavia (fig. 218), and a specimen from Icklingham, Suffolk, is shown in Case 52. The mechanism is explained in *Guide to Roman Britain*, fig. 45, this type of padlock having been known in classical times.

It has been pointed out by Dr. Sophus Müller that the oldest runic stones east of the North Sea are in Norway, which had been in communication with the British Isles from an early date,

FIG. 217. Iron-mounted pottery bucket, near Bergen, Norway. ($\frac{1}{2}$)

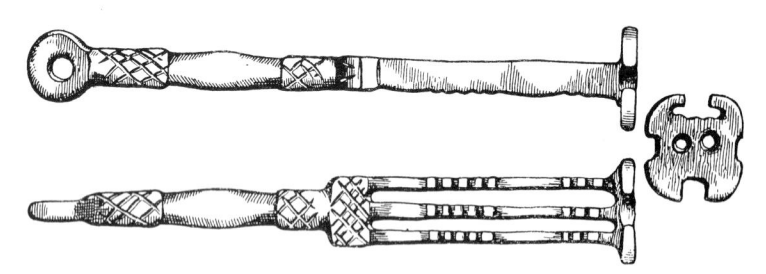

FIG 218. Bronze key of padlock, Denmark. ($\frac{2}{3}$)

and borrowed the *futhorc* (p. 96). Early runes are also found engraved on stone in Sweden, but in Denmark such inscriptions are not found before the ninth century, and most of them date from the tenth, the spread of Christianity soon putting an end to the custom. But runic gravestones are, on the whole, later in Norway and Sweden, and those of Bornholm are not earlier than the year 1000. The Gothic system of writing, before the new alphabet furnished by Ulfilas (p. 171), was transmitted to

England, thence to Scandinavia, and later to central Europe by way of Hanover.

The Norse occupation of Ireland lasted about two centuries, and to this connexion may be attributed the exclusive discovery of Irish metalwork in Norway, and perhaps the adoption of the lappet springing from behind the head of the ornamental quadruped (p. 17); but a distinction is observed in the treatment of its eye. In both countries it is drop-shaped, but the pointed end is in front on Scandinavian work, and behind on Irish examples.

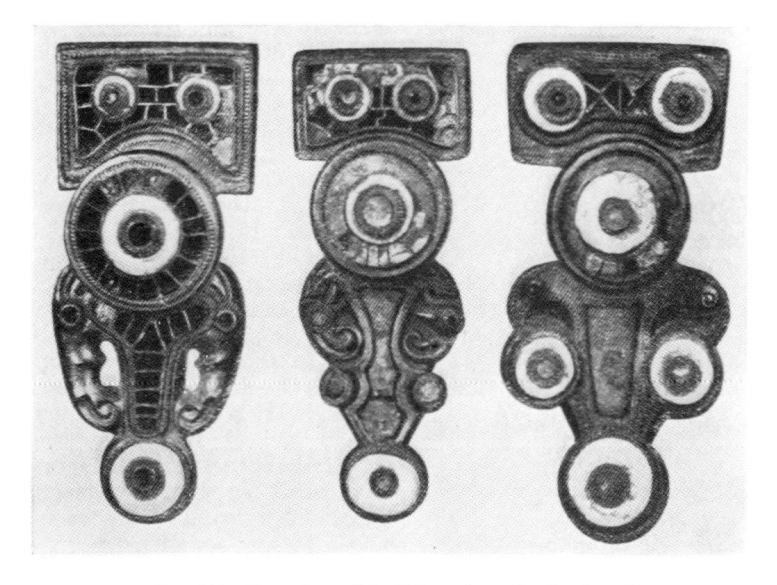

Fig. 219. Brooches with disk on bow, Gotland. ($\frac{3}{4}$)

Gotland stands apart from the rest of Sweden, though it was at certain periods associated with the Baltic islands of Öland and Bornholm (which has been regarded as its colony); and the local antiquities, collected by Mr. James Curle, F.S.A., and recently acquired by the Museum with the assistance of the National Art-Collections Fund, illustrate about eight centuries of its history. Roman influence was felt before 400, and various bronzes including the mounts of a drinking-horn belong to that period; but in spite of the island's importance as a commercial entrepôt and its share in the imperial gold that came from Hungary between about 300 and 550, the best and most characteristic products of Gotland date from the seventh century, when the bow-brooch with disk on bow (fig. 219) was loaded with ornament, and the disk-brooch assumed a bevelled edge and began its transformation into the box-type. The bow-brooch has two animal heads in Style II (with pointed jaws) flanking the foot and a disk at the end, generally adjoining these heads (the true island type), but occasionally separated from them by two small circular settings (fig. 219). These brooches sometimes attain large proportions, and while the head and foot are decorated with garnet cell-work and bosses of white material, the bow and side-edges in some cases bear animal ornament in Style III (eighth century). The use of cell-work was due to continued intercourse with Hungary.

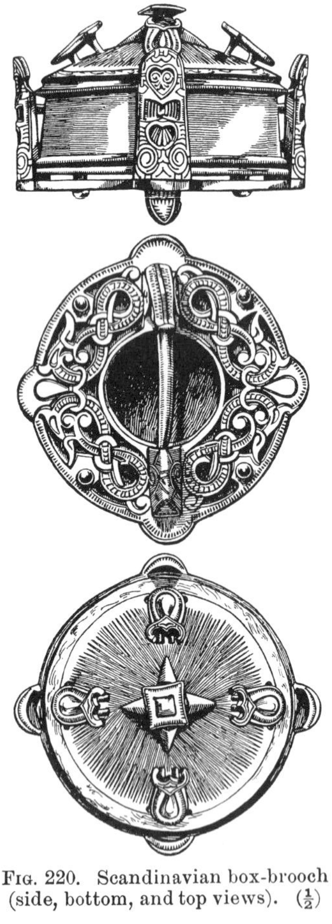

The collection illustrates various stages in the evolution of two other brooch types—the box and boar's head. The former has been traced back to a disk not unlike fig. 32, but smaller: this is given an appearance of solidity by bevelling and deepening the edge, and by the seventh century the depth is about $\frac{1}{3}$ in. (pl. XVI, no. 2). The dimensions increase, and Style III is often represented (nos. 1 and 3), but about the year 800 influence from the West is manifest in the 'grasping' animal often found on the same brooch as the Scandinavian pattern, but in separate panels. An example (no. 4) is illustrated to show the new style on the face of the brooch (late ninth century); and a still later phase of evolution is exemplified in a bronze and silver specimen of unknown locality (fig. 220), with beetle-like additions to the upper disk, and debased animal interlacing on the base with two examples of the union-knot (p. 113), probably about the year 1000.

FIG. 220. Scandinavian box-brooch (side, bottom, and top views). ($\frac{1}{2}$)

The boar's head type (called animal-head, *djurhuvud*, in Swedish) is also abundantly represented in Gotland, and can be traced back to the brooch with returned foot (fig. 13), its evolution occupying about eight centuries (fig. 221). All the stages may be seen in

PLATE XVI. BOX-BROOCHES OF BRONZE FROM GOTLAND ($\frac{1}{1}$)
(Case 56, see p. 166)

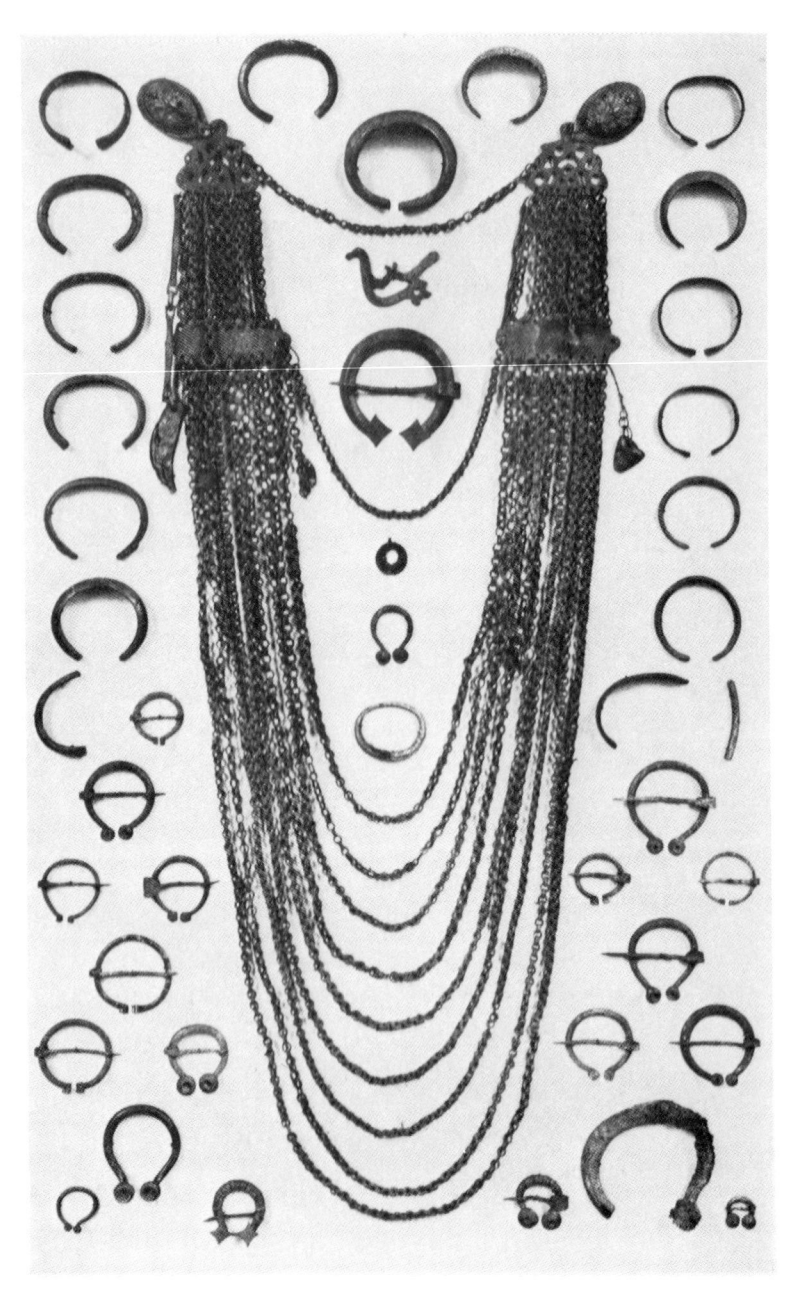

PLATE XVII. GROUP OF LIVONIAN ORNAMENTS ($\frac{0}{11}$)
(Case 64, *see* p. 174)

the Curle collection (Case 56), and the first (*a*) dates from the third century. The next stage (*b*) shows an enlargement of the chord below the bow, and the absorption of the returned foot (fifth century); there is a general thickening in the next century (*c*), the spiral spring being merely represented by moulding, and the chord being now in one piece with the bow; and a by-form (*d*) of the seventh century has the bow elongated and the openings closed on either side of the head. By the eighth century the brooch had become a complete shell, the lateral openings of *c* being retained only as sunk panels; and it is at this stage that some resemblance is seen to an animal's head, but its snout is the foot

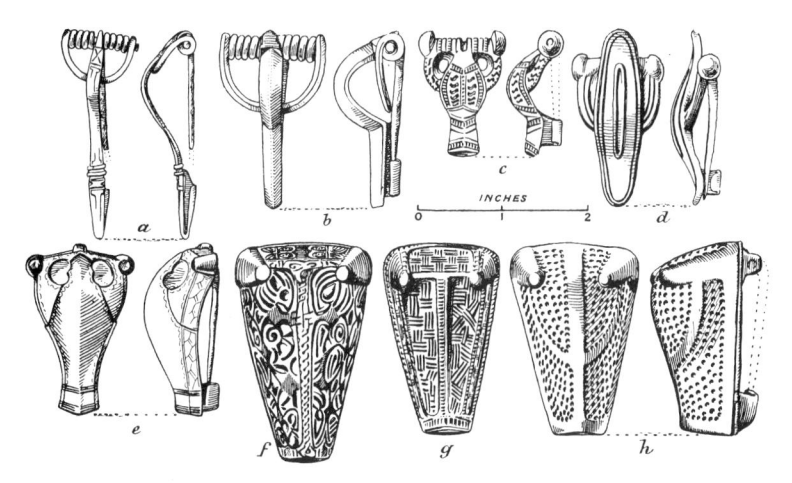

Fig. 221. Evolution of boar's head brooch. (½)

of the brooch. In the next hundred years the type reaches its maximum, both in size and decoration (*f*); and the tenth (*g*) and eleventh (*h*) centuries see a marked degeneration, the decoration becoming a meaningless network of lines or panels of dots. The curved line dividing the panels on the last figure recalls the chord of stages *b* and *d*.

Among the rarities from the island may be mentioned an openwork terret or a saddle-bow dating about 950: probably contemporary is an openwork bronze chape (fig. 222) to protect the lower end of the sword-scabbard, but the mould was evidently much worn. Three dice (as fig. 197) and fourteen bone draughtsmen were found with an openwork box-brooch of gilt bronze (about 900); and a green glass beaker, 8 in. high, with threads below the mouth and ribs on the body, is a cross between *c* and *e* of fig. 54. The glass beads are particularly brilliant, but the series probably represents several centuries: a clue to the millefiori pattern is given by the Tromsö grave-find of the seventh century.

A few pieces of ring-money belong to the period before 550, when gold was plentiful (p. 161), and finger-rings of the Viking period include two made of alternate thin and thick gold strands (p. 117). The Gotland series of bracteates evidently came down to the Viking period: in the centre is a disintegrated pattern, many having elaborate loops with filigree; and some are of silver, of larger size than the earlier specimens of gold (fig. 213). There are several armlets of silver with deeply stamped patterns, and some may be as early as the eighth century. A hoard of silver from Dalhem includes a long torc of three strands and several armlets; and there are many penannular brooches either with polygonal or stud-like terminals, which east of the Baltic are associated with debased tortoise-brooches, a type that is very rarely found in Gotland though common on the Scandinavian mainland.

Southern Russia is now recognized as the original home of two elements in Teutonic art—the animal motive, and the application of coloured stones or glass to the surface of metal (polychromy); and it is agreed that the Goths and their associates owed their taste and efficiency in the arts to the mature civilization which they found on the northern shore of the Black Sea and on the rivers that flowed into it. They arrived as emigrants from the Baltic region (East Prussia) in the third century of our era, but were destined to turn westward owing to pressure from the advancing Huns (375), and to spread their decorative art and runic system of writing throughout the barbarian world of Europe.

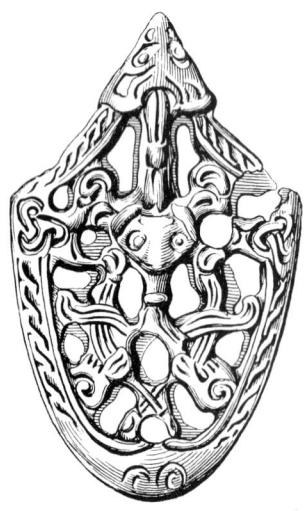

FIG. 222. Bronze chape of scabbard, Gotland. (¼)

The ethnographical sequence of this area, which was known to the ancients (for example, Herodotus) through the numerous Greek colonies on the coast, has been recently elucidated by Professor Rostovtzeff, who goes further than Dr. Minns (to whom we owe a survey of local Greek and Scythian art), and attributes the culture in question to the Sarmatians, hitherto little more than a name in ancient history.

Early in the Iron Age this productive area had been occupied by the Cimmerians, who are thought to have been of Thracian origin and gave their name to the Bosporus or straits between the Crimea and the Tamán peninsula. A port on the western side was Panticapaeum (the modern Kerch), founded by Greek colonists from Miletus about 540 B.C.; and Olbia, further west on the mainland near the mouths of the Bug and Dnieper, had a similar origin. These and other flourishing settlements of Greeks did much to civilize the native population, but the political situation was complicated by the foundation of the Scythian kingdom about the same time between the Don and the Dnieper.

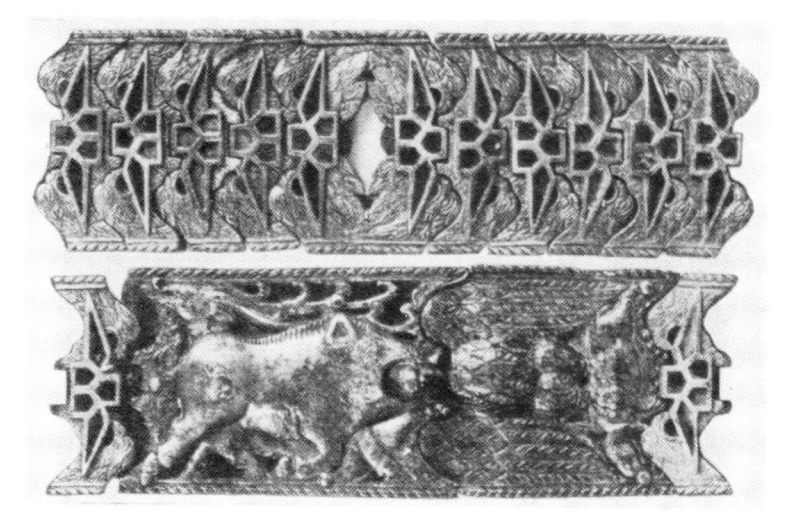

FIG. 223. Silver-gilt belt with garnet cell-work, Sofia. ($\frac{3}{5}$)

The Scythians were an Iranian people, and their art was oriental, including, above all, animal motives distinct from those of their Greek neighbours, but closely connected with Persia and Assyria. The Greeks, however, soon began to consult the wants and preferences of the nomads, who showed some inclination for town life; and the tombs of South Russia have proved immensely rich in precious metals and works of art. The Sarmatian tribes were also Iranian, chief among them being the Alans; and, according to Polybius, they were established between the Dnieper and Don by 179 B.C., following in the track of the Scythians, who concentrated in the Crimea and the Dobrudja, and did not disappear till the arrival of the Goths in the third century A.D. The Sarmatians had for centuries been located between the Caspian and Sea of Aral, and preferred geometrical patterns, but adopted the animal style from the Scythians during their occupation of the Kuban district (between the Western Caucasus and the Don) in the last three centuries B. C., and seem to have been the first to introduce the stirrup and spurs into Europe. Sarmatian writing has been traced back to the second century B. C., when a taste for polychromy was also developed; so that most of the elements of what is generally called Gothic culture had been long in existence locally when the Germanic horde arrived. Their part was to disseminate it in the West; and in this task they were perhaps assisted by Sarmatians and kindred peoples who had once inhabited the Steppes of Russia and Siberia.

In Case 60 are shown a few antiquities from Bulgaria that may be assigned to the Scythian occupation before the arrival of the Goths. The silver-gilt belt, of which portions are illustrated (fig. 223), has flat garnet cell-work in each link between a pair of eagles' heads, and the fastening takes the form of a boar biting the neck of an eagle. It is said to have been found at Sofia with the two pottery vessels adjoining, buckles including two like fig. 66 (right), and a number of arrow-heads, with short socket and three blades, of a type common in the East for centuries.

A bronze-gilt swastika composed of animal-heads with a rosette of garnet cell-work in the centre is also labelled Sofia, and probably was once attached to a bridle. It has a curious resemblance to a well-known specimen from the Heremesse group of grave-mounds, Krasnokutsk, Kharkov; and seems to be related to a silver-plated type of brooch dating from the fifth century in Denmark.

The Kerch finds, of which specimens are exhibited in Cases 65, 66, include some dating from early in the third century, and probably pre-Gothic. Three ancestral forms of the brooch have been illustrated (figs. 23-25), and one of a pair found (probably with three buckles and a glass bead) at Kerch is given in three views (fig. 224), as it seems to contain the germ of the square-headed brooch (fig. 20). The contents of another grave at Kerch consist of an iron axe-head, finger-ring of gold wire, arrowheads, a large pair of boar's tusks, and an iron bridle-bit (fig. 225), which has 'bridle-spurs' threaded on it: this last contrivance may explain the so-called 'bow-pullers' of bronze commonly found in Italy. Other noticeable specimens from Kerch are the beads in the form of ribbed cylinders made of gold-foil; a gold bracelet with swelling ends, like that of silver from the Charente (p. 147); two bronze buckles with split acanthus pattern, like fig. 66 (right); several with abrupt end to the tongue (like pl. xv, no. 7), and others with the hoop almost filled with scroll-work (as *Guide to Roman Britain*, fig. 105 e).

CRIMEA

Several grave-groups from the Caucasus and the Taman peninsula are also exhibited, including daggers, beads, buckles, toilet implements, brooches of early type, gold finger-rings, and a large

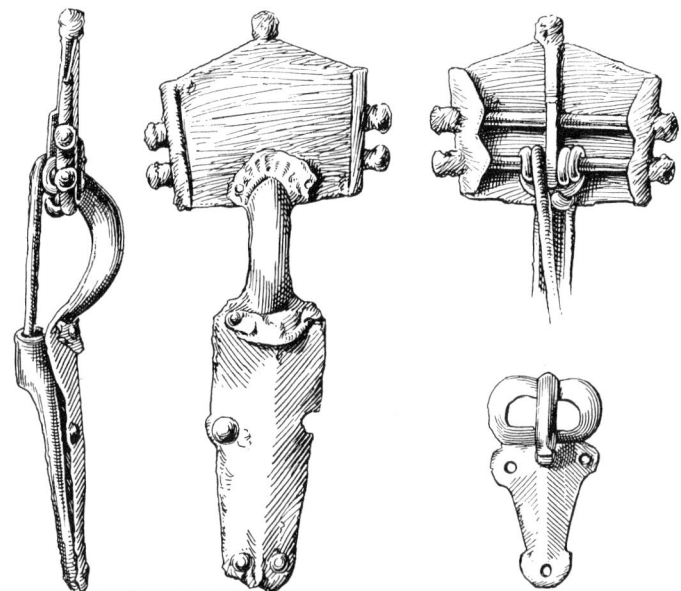

FIG. 224. Brooch with side and back views, and buckle, Kerch. ($\frac{2}{3}$)

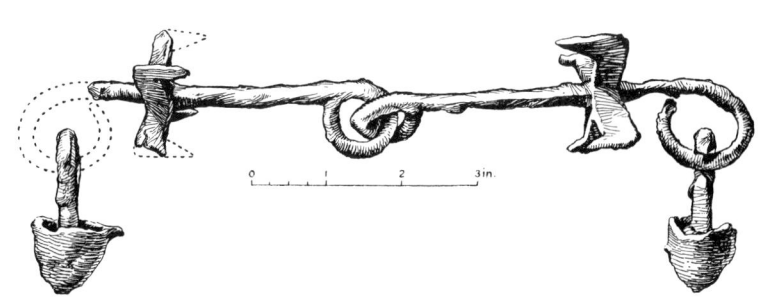

FIG. 225. Iron bridle-bit with bridle-spurs, Kerch.

bronze cross like one in the adjoining Early Christian Room, Case A, which may be of the seventh century, but the Goths had been Arian Christians from the end of the fourth century, when their bishop Ulfilas (died 383) translated the Bible for them.

172   DESCRIPTION OF CASES 65, 64

Near Kanef, on the Dnieper below Kiev, was found an interesting hoard of silver, of which three specimens are illustrated.

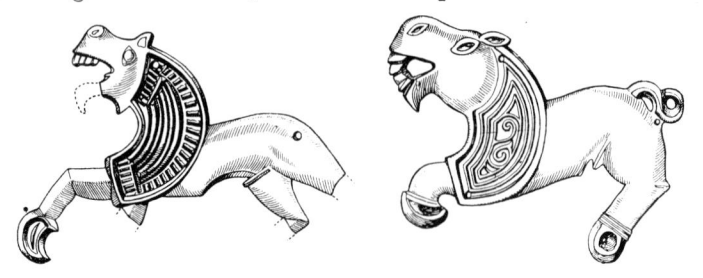

FIG. 226. Silver figures of lions, Kanef, Kiev. ($\frac{1}{2}$)

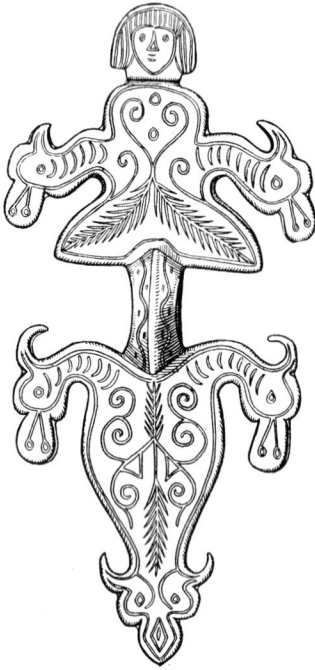

FIG. 227. Engraved silver brooch, near Kanef. ($\frac{2}{3}$)

The animals may be regarded as Gothic lions (fig. 226), and the brooch (fig. 227, one of a pair) is a fanciful production that shows a human head at the top and animal heads not only flanking the foot just below the bow, but also the head of the brooch. There are also an embossed buckle (fig. 228) and bracelets of the usual type with thickened terminals. The date is probably fifth century.

From the Government of Kiev come another bracelet of the same kind, a second with disk terminals, two mirrors of Siberian origin, and a pendant once filled with red enamel (fig. 229); also a small and simple radiated brooch (fig. 230), with ring-and-dot pattern and angular foot, and a still earlier form (fig. 231) with returned foot and long spiral spring with semicircular chord, probably contemporary with the Gotland specimen (fig. 221, *a*). In the same district was found a group of silver ingots and ornaments with niello (p. 100) dating from the eleventh or twelfth century, in the form of ear-rings, finger-rings, and a hinged bracelet (fig. 232), of which the six engraved panels are illustrated. The eagle-and-fish device is of frequent occurrence

(p. 161), and it is possible to see in the two outside panels a travesty of acanthus foliage.

Mounted on large boards in these Cases are many bronze objects from Livonia, as described by Bähr in his *Gräber der Liven*. A representative series is given as pl. XVII, the principal ornament consisting of chain festoons held at either end by a small and debased tortoise-brooch of Viking type (cf. fig. 211). Other chains form tassels; and fragments, dating from the 'Chud' period (9th–13th century) may be seen in the collection recently purchased from Baron de Baye, and temporarily exhibited all together in Cases 3, 4 of the Prehistoric Room (cf. fig. 2).

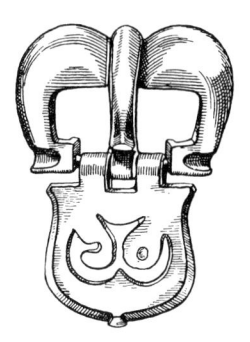

FIG. 228. Buckle with openwork plate, Kanef. ($\frac{2}{3}$)

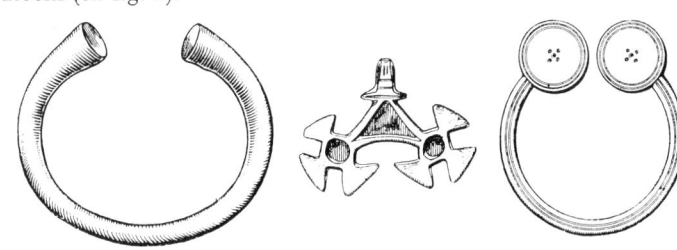

FIG. 229. Ornaments from Govt. Kiev. ($\frac{1}{2}$)

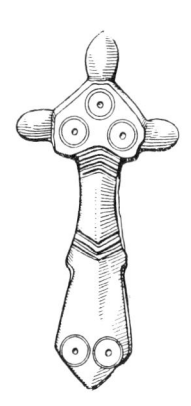

FIG. 230. Radiated brooch, Govt. Kiev. ($\frac{3}{4}$)

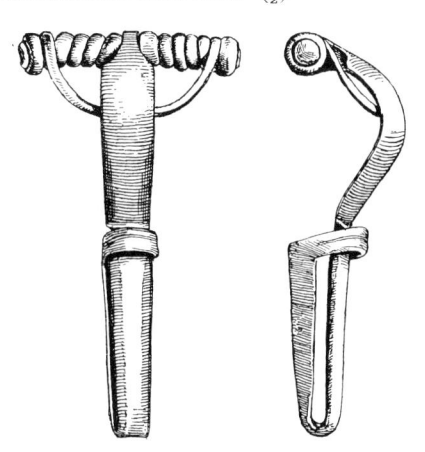

FIG. 231. Brooch with returned foot, Kiev. ($\frac{1}{1}$)

From Livonia come also the iron heads of spears and axes, knives, spurs, armlets, and bears' teeth mounted as pendants. A sword with lobed pommel, and a spear-head with 'damascened' socket are labelled Segewold (Case 64); and with bronze necklets decorated with spangles (p. 75) from Ascheraden (Cases 65, 66) are several spirals of wire that may have served to bind tresses of hair in a wooden casing, like those exhibited from Efaefsk tumulus, near Krasnoslobedsk, Government of Penza, half way between Kiev and the Urals. From Bielovodsk in the Government of Perm (which includes part of the Ural range) comes a fine series of silver ornaments, with stirrups, bridle-bit, and axe-head with open blade (Case 64).

Fig. 232. Silver bracelet with engraved panels, Govt. Kiev. ($\frac{1}{2}$)

Siberia is represented by a series (Case 66) found near Minussinsk (about half way between the Black Sea and Japan), all being of iron—a dagger, bridle-bits, buckles, knives, sickles, and various lance- or arrow-heads that recall specimens from the Far East. Further excavation is necessary before the exact dates of such antiquities can be determined, but it may be mentioned in conclusion that Iranian influence has already been detected in Chinese culture of the Han dynasty (206 B. C.–A. D. 220), and Professor Rostovtzeff thinks that the indebtedness of China to the Sarmatians, especially in military matters, is fully proved. But research in the last thirty years has left much unexplained in the prehistoric relations between the eastern and western extremities of Asia; and one of the problems is to decide when the Bronze Age ended and the Early Iron Age began.

INDEX

Åberg, Nils, 143.
Abingdon, 38, 55, 60, 133.
Acanthus, 17, 102, 110, 159, 170, 173.
Acklam Wold, 62
Addington, Great, 21.
Aelfric, 110.
Aella (Deira), 4.
— (Sussex), 6.
Aethelberht, 4.
Aethred, 115.
Aghabulloge, 121.
Aidan, 7, 14.
Airy, Mr. W., 60.
Akhmîm, 60, 153.
Alans, 143, 152, 169.
Alcester, 17.
Alemans, 80, 157.
Algeria, 152, 153.
Alhstan, 101.
Alpha and Omega, 69, 116, 123.
Amber, 47, 66, 70, 73, 134, 135, 137, 148, 153.
Ambrosius Aurelianus, 6.
Amethyst, 47, 59, 157.
Amiens, 149, 150, 157.
Anán'ino, 8.
Andrew, Mr. W. J., 107.
Angles, 1, 2, 4, 12.
Anglo-Saxon art, 19.
Anglo-Saxon Chronicle, 6, 114.
Angons, 65, 80, 148.
Animal ornament, 9, 16, 42, 43, 54, 55, 57, 61, 85, 87, 144, 168, 172.
Antrim, 133.
Ardagh chalice, 14, 139.
Ardvonrig, 128.
Armlets, 45, 75, 108, 128, 147, 152.
Armstrong, Mr. E. C. R., 137.
Arrow-heads, 66, 161, 170, 174.
Arthur, King, 6.
Asgarby, 89.
Ash, 57.
Auvergne, 149.
Axe-heads, 66, 90, 148, 160, 170, 174.

Bacton, 61.
Ballycottin bog, 142.
Barlaston, 78, 79.
Barn Elms, 61.
Barrows (grave-mounds), 39, 48, 58, 63, 86.
Barton Seagrave, 22, 83.
Basingstoke, 79.
Beads, 47, 56, 57, 66, 70, 73, 84, 88, 137, 148, 149, 153, 155, 157, 163, 168, 170.
Beakers, 51, 64, 69, 157, 167.
Bede, 1, 2, 6.
Bedford, 5.
Belgium, 40, 79.
Bell-shrines, 141, 142.
Belluno, 155.
Belt, 169.
Benedict Biscop, 14.
Bensington, 12.
Beowulf, 4, 48.
Bergamo, 155.
Bergen, 160, 164.
Berkshire, 18.
Bernicia, 4, 89.
Bewcastle cross, 13.
Bibury, 126, 127.
Bifrons, 49, 81, 85, 90.
Billingham, 123.
Bingerbrück, 157.
Birds, 55, 57, 90, 135, 169, 174.
Bird's head pattern, 32, 43, 57, 62, 133, 144.
Blythburgh, 112.
Bône, 41, 152.
Bone objects, 65, 81, 111–115.
Bonsall, 136.
Book-clasps, 104.
Borre, 104.
Bosses of white material, 37, 45, 55, 166.
Bow, 66.
Bowls, bronze, 7, 49, 63–65, 68, 76–81, 145, 157.
Bracelets, 82, 85, 142, 148, 157, 170, 172–174.
Bracteates, 10, 54, 57, 85, 86, 161, 168.
Breach Downs, 44.
Breadalbane brooch, 135.

Bréban, 148.
Bretwalda, 4.
Bridle-bits, 170, 171, 174.
Bridle-spurs, 170, 171.
Britons, 1, 7, 86.
Brøgger, Dr. A. W., 161.
Brooches, 23–38.
— Applied, 33, 36, 70, 73.
— Bird, 57, 150, 157.
— Boar's head, 166, 167.
— Box, 166, 167.
— Button, 48, 57, 66, 67, 73, 81.
— Crossbow, 23.
— Cruciform, 23, 28, 83, 85, 88, 158, 159.
— Disk, 37, 70, 71, 75.
— Disk on bow, 53, 83, 165.
— Enamelled, 101, 150, 155.
— Equal-armed, 72, 81, 150.
— Gothic, 24.
— Horned, 84, 89.
— Horse, 151, 152.
— Incrusted, 150, 155, 157.
— Jewelled, 39, 40, 55–57, 60, 153, 157.
— Keystone, 37, 38, 66, 157.
— Long, 23, 24, 26, 27, 47, 83, 88, 89.
— Oval foot, 156.
— Penannular, 47, 48, 100, 109, 132–137, 168.
— Radiated, 31, 47, 88, 89, 144, 148, 154–156, 172, 173.
— Returned foot, 23, 24, 172, 173.
— Ring (quoit), 48, 54, 55, 89.
— Roman, 67, 70, 71, 81.
— Rosette, 53, 148, 150.
— Round-headed, 31, 32.
— S-shaped, 54, 62, 150, 155.
— Saucer, 33–35, 48, 70, 72, 73, 85.
— Square-headed, 29, 53, 65, 67, 70, 71, 73, 83, 158.
— Thistle, 104, 109.
— Tortoise, 128, 129, 159, 160, 163, 173.
— Trefoil, 14, 102, 159, 160.
— Trefoil-headed, 84, 89.

INDEX

Brooches, Various, 71-73, 88, 89, 101, 103, 155, 171, 172.
Brooke, 83.
Broomfield, 45, 63.
Brown, Prof. Baldwin, 11, 15, 19, 84, 87.
Browne, Bishop, 119, 120.
Buchan, 4.
Buckets, 57, 63, 64, 67, 68, 85, 88, 105.
Bucket pendants, 67, 75, 88.
Buckles, 9, 40, 44, 53, 59, 60, 64, 67, 70, 90, 146-149, 152, 157, 170-173.
— Bone, 81, 155.
— Plates, 41, 43, 57, 60, 61, 151, 156.
— Tongues, 41, 53, 59, 149.
Buredruth, 116.
Burghead, 126, 127.
Burgundy, 11, 143.
Bury, Prof., 3.

Cabochon, 8, 144.
Caenby, 86, 87.
Cambois, 101.
Cambridgeshire, 84.
Canosa, 155.
Canterbury, 15, 17.
Carthage, 60, 153.
Castellani, 155.
Caucasus, 171.
Ceawlin, 6.
Cerdic, 6.
Chadwick, Prof., 2.
Chains, 146.
Chalice, 99.
Champlevé, 101.
Chape, 167, 168.
Charlemagne, 8, 13, 143.
Châtelaines, see Girdle-hangers.
Chessel Down, 30, 31, 45, 56, 65-67.
Childeric, 40, 143, 144, 148.
China, 174.
'Chip-carving', 9, 10, 34, 72, 144, 151, 153, 157.
Chi-Rho, 13, 49, 69, 149.
Christianity, 3, 6, 12, 14, 18, 20.
Clasps, 76, 83-85, 88, 89, 148, 155.
Clogher, 131.
Cloisonné, 8, 150.
Cloneen, 104.
Clontarf, 16.
Clovis, 143.
Codex Amiatinus, 15.
Codex aureus, 15.
Coenwulf, 111, 112.
Coffins, 5, 39, 63.

Coins, 55, 56, 61, 71, 88, 95, 99, 102, 104, 106, 107, 110, 145, 156, 157, 161.
Collingwood, Mr. W. G., 124.
Combs, 22, 81, 82, 112, 117, 128, 129, 148, 149.
Cong, cross of, 18, 141.
Contour lines, 17, 87.
Conway, Sir Martin, 77.
Copts, 76, 157.
Craigywarren bog, 131.
Cremation, 4, 20, 23, 68, 70, 72, 82, 87.
Crimea, 30, 31, 169.
Croft stone, 99.
Cross, Christian, 38, 50, 61, 76, 89, 103, 151, 155.
Crosses in metal, 50, 58, 76, 80, 103, 142, 150, 151, 153, 155, 157, 171.
— stone, 13, 14, 122, 124.
Croydon, 21, 80.
Croziers, 142.
Crundale, 11, 51, 59.
Crystal, 46, 53, 66, 73, 75, 145, 148, 149.
Cuerdale, 107, 108.
Cumberland, 92, 104.
Cups, 44, 51, 63, 65, 76, 109.
Curle, Mr. James, 165.
Cuxton, 103.

Dale, Mr. W., 68.
Damascening, 94, 149, 157.
Daniel and lions, 149.
Danish conquest, 13, 16.
De Baye, Baron, 173.
Deira, 4, 89.
Denmark, 17, 25, 26, 29, 30, 158.
Deorham, 6, 35.
Derbyshire, 118.
Desborough, 75, 76.
Dewsbury, 124.
Dice, 82, 148, 167.
Dickins, Mr. B., 97, 118.
Donegal, 135.
Dorchester-on-Thames, 90.
Douglas, Rev. J., 39.
Dover, 35, 59.
Dowgate Hill, 101.
Dowris, 133.
Dragon, 18, 98, 126.
Draughtsmen, 48, 65, 79, 82, 167.
Drinking-cups, 44, 51, 65, 109.
Droxford, 67, 148.
Dumbarton, 7.
Durrow, Book of, 14, 86, 130.

Ear-rings, 45, 57, 59, 70, 89, 145, 148, 149, 153, 155.
East Shefford, 48, 71.
Edwin, 4.
Egypt, 153.
Enamel, 7, 31, 35, 48, 50, 78-80, 101, 133, 150, 155, 172.
English, 2.
Escutcheons of bowls, 49, 50, 77-80.
Essex, 3, 4, 63.
Ethelswith, 114, 115.
Ethelwulf, 114, 115.
Ethilwald, 110.
Ewelme, 77, 78.
Ewer, 79, 80.
Exeter, 95.
Eye, 22, 82, 110.

Fairford, 33, 34.
Fardel, 121.
Farndish, 84.
Faussett, Rev. B., 39.
Faversham, 35, 38-52, 63, 65, 77, 80, 116, 153.
Fetter Lane, 15, 93.
Filigree, 38, 59, 61, 64, 102, 108, 152.
Finger-rings, 45, 101, 114-117, 149, 151, 168, 170.
Fish-pattern, 43, 44, 51, 59, 74, 75, 80, 85, 128, 149, 155.
Foliage, 13, 17, 93, 96, 98.
Forks, 81, 106, 107.
Forsbrook, 62.
Francisca, 66, 81, 145, 149.
Franks, 2, 142-152.
Franks, Sir Wollaston, 20, 97, 114.
Franks casket, 13, 96-98, 104.
Frilford, 5.
Frisians, 2, 12.
Futhorc, 96, 164.

Garnets, cabochon, 38, 40, 144, 155.
— Cell-work, 38, 39, 42, 169, 170.
— Keystone, 37, 157.
— T-shaped, 38.
Garrick St., 116.
Germany, 20, 21, 70, 76, 80, 157, 158.
Gibbs, Mr. William, 39.
Gildas, 3, 5, 6.
Girdle-hangers, 46, 84, 88, 89, 145, 149, 157.

INDEX

Glass, 51, 63, 64, 74, 80, 146, 154, 157, 158, 167.
Godgytha, 112.
Godwin, 111, 112.
Gold braid, 44, 64, 145.
Gold foil, 38, 153, 155.
Goldsborough, 104, 108.
Goths, 9, 168, 169, 171.
Gotland, 5, 13, 48, 117, 162, 165–168.
Gourgançon, 148.
'Grasping' animal, 14, 128, 159, 166.
Gravesend, 103.
Gravestones, 119–127.
Griffith, Mr. A. F., 80.
Grove Ferry, 59.
Grüneck Castle, 156.

Halton Moor, 108, 109.
Hamilton or Towneley brooch, 101, 128.
Hammersmith, 113, 114.
Hamsey, 117.
Hand-pins, 130, 131.
Hanover, 31, 37, 72.
Harnham Hill, 75, 81, 82.
Hartlepool, 121, 122, 141.
Harwich, 142.
Haslingfield, 89.
Hatfield, 7.
Hawnby, 78.
Hengist and Horsa, 3.
Herpes, 41, 56, 66, 144–148.
Hexham, 105, 106.
Hii (Hy), *see* Iona.
Hoards, 99, 104, 106–108, 161, 168, 172.
Horns, 10, 64, 65.
Hornton, 72.
Horse-trappings, 45.
Howletts, 47, 53, 54.
Howorth, Sir Henry, 3.
Hübner, E., 122, 123.
Hungary, 156, 165.
Huns, 168.
Hunterston brooch, 14.
Hurbuck, 90.
Hwiccas, 12, 35.

Ickham, 57.
Icklingham, 163.
Iffley, 62.
Inhumation, 6, 20.
Intaglios, 71, 116, 151, 152, 157.
Interlacing, 10, 11, 17, 45, 87, 113, 153.
Iona, 6.
Iranian art, 10, 169.
Ivory, 17, 75, 88, 111, 112.

Ireland, 2, 13, 14, 16, 18, 78, 119, 121, 129–142, 165.
Italy, 153–156.

Jarrow, 14, 15.
Jellinge style, 17, 104, 113, 141.
Jutes, 1, 2, 37, 52, 63, 65, 67.
Jutland, 2.

Kanef, 172, 173.
Keady mountain, 130.
Keilschnitt, 9, *see* Chip-carving.
Kells, Book of, 14, 15, 130.
Kemble, J. R., 20.
Kempston, 21, 22, 36, 46, 47, 63, 72–75, 157.
Kenninghall, 27, 29, 30, 83, 84.
Kent, 1, 3, 20, 39–60.
Kerch, 24, 32, 60, 169–171.
Keys, 163, 164.
Kiev, 172, 173.
Killaloe, 140.
Killucan, 136.
Kingmoor, 116.
Kirby Underdale, 74.
Kirkoswald, 91, 102.
Knives, 22, 57, 70, 84, 148.
Kreuznach, 157.

Lancashire, 115.
Lancaster, 123, 124.
Lapis lazuli, 38, 64.
Lappets, 17, 86, 139, 165.
Latchets, 132, 133.
Latin, 7, 13.
Laverstock, 114.
Leagrave, 67, 75.
Leather, 106.
Leeds, Mr. E. T., 2, 34, 36, 52.
Leighton Buzzard, 34.
Leipzig, 157.
Leofric, 95.
Leuna, 157.
Liber Pontificalis, 15.
Lincoln, 104, 117.
Lindisfarne Gospels, 14, 15.
Linen, 74, 85.
Little Hampton, 44.
Livonia, 88, 173, 174.
Llywel, 120, 121.
Lodi Vecchio, 155.
Lombards, 10, 11, 153.
Londesborough brooch, 14, 134.
London, City of, 103, 125, 126.
Longbridge, 35, 85.
Long Wittenham, 7, 37, 45, 68–71.

Lucas, Mr. Seymour, 112.
Lyminge, 47.

Malton, Cambs., 23, 26, 85, 86.
Manuscripts, 14, 15, 17.
Marne, 147, 148, 150.
Marson, 73.
Mayence, 157, 158.
Meerschaum, 74, 75.
Mellifont Abbey, 142.
Meonwaras, 67.
Mercia, 12.
Migration period, 5, 7, 9.
Milton-next-Sittingbourne, 53, 104.
Minns, Dr. Ellis, 168.
Mirrors, 172.
Mitcham, 6, 35, 56.
Moncetz, 150.
Money, Mr. W., 71.
Monkwearmouth, 14, 123.
Montreuil, 149.
Morel, M. Léon, 148.
Moresby, 89.
Mount Badon, 5, 6.
Müller, Dr. S., 164.

Namdalen, 163.
Napier, Prof., 97.
Necklaces, 75, 85, 88, 148.
Nennius, 6.
Newry, 132.
Niello, 31, 38, 100, 115, 172.
Nordendorf, 156.
Northumbria, 1.
Northumbrian art, 11, 13, 96.
Norway, 16, 18, 25–27, 80, 137, 158–160, 163.
Nydam, 158.

Odin, 161.
Offa, 4, 12, 156.
Ogham, 119–121, 137.
Orientation, 12, 39, 64, 68, 71, 82, 145.
Ormside cup, 13.
Oseberg, 14, 16.
Ostrogoths, 144, 148, 150, 151, 153, 156.
Ozingell, 56, 59.

Palestine, 153.
Palladius, 6.
Pallium, 105.
Pearled borders, 125.
Pearls, 155.
Penda, 7.
Pendants, 55, 57–59, 61, 62, 74, 89, 172–174.
Pensthorpe, 82.
Peterborough, 104, 116.

178 INDEX

Phoenix Park, 140.
Picts, 1, 2, 7, 127.
Pillow-stones, 121, 122, 145.
Pins, 43, 57, 75, 82, 88, 89, 98, 100, 113, 128, 130, 131, 137, 138, 148, 149, 155, 157.
Polychromy, 8, 168, 170.
Pommels, 11, 48, 85.
Pontoise, 150.
Porth Dafarch, 133.
Portsoy, 128.
Pottery, 20, 22, 23, 52, 63, 70, 71, 73, 145, 146, 148, 149, 157, 163, 164, 170.
Pouan, 40.
Ptolemy, 2.
Purse, 156.
Purse-guards, 66, 146, 147.
Pyramids of bronze, 44, 45, 63.

Rædwald, 4.
Rattles, 160.
Read, Sir Hercules, 17, 63, 80.
Rigby, Mr. T , 80.
Ringerike, 18, 113, 126.
Ring-money, 161, 168.
Ring-swords, 48.
Ringwould, 148.
Rivets, shoe-shaped, 40, 41, 53, 57, 66, 67, 84, 149.
Rogers, Mr. J. J., 99.
Romanizing style, 34, 42.
Rome, 156.
Romulus and Remus, 11, 97.
Roovesmore, 121.
Roskilde, 160.
Rostovtzeff, Prof., 168, 174.
Runes, 66, 96–98, 116–119, 122, 124, 164.
Russia, South, 8, 9, 168–174.
Ruthwell cross, 13.

St. Aethelwold, 15.
St. Columba, 6, 14.
St. Columban, 130.
St. Cuthbert, 44.
St. Gall, 130.
St. Germanus, 7.
St. Hilda, 121.
St. John's, Walbrook, 126.
St. Patrick, 6.
St. Paul's Churchyard, 17, 18, 96, 114, 125.
Saints, Irish, 141, 142.
Salin, Dr. Bernhard, 8, 156.
Sarmatians, 8, 168–170, 174.
Sarre, 45, 52, 55–57, 61, 77.
Saxons, 1, 2.

Saxons, East, 3.
— West, 3, 5, 35, 68, 71.
Saxon Shore, 2.
Saxony, 21.
Scales, 70, 76, 157, 162.
Scandinavia, 10, 15.
Sceattas, 11.
Scotland, 4, 119, 127–129.
Scots, 1, 2, 6.
Scourge, 99, 100.
Scramasaxes, 61, 70, 90, 95, 96, 148.
Scroll-work, 9, 34, 38, 93, 96, 100, 124.
Scythians, 8, 169.
Seals, 110–112.
Seamer, 62.
Searby, 75, 88, 89.
Seine, 152.
Selzen, 157.
Sevington, 106.
Shears, 22.
Shetelig, Dr. H., 25, 73, 158.
Shields, 86, 92, 98, 148.
Shield-bosses, 22, 49, 62–64, 68, 70, 92, 148, 156.
Shropham, 21, 22.
Siberia, 174.
Silchester, 119.
Silver, see Hoards.
Silver-plating, 31, 41, 83, 92, 149.
Sittingbourne, 95, 115.
Skillets, 76, 158.
Skulls, 70, 71.
Slavs, 158.
Sleaford, 28, 78, 79, 87.
Smith, C. Roach, 39.
Soberton, 117.
Sofia, 60, 169, 170.
Soham, 84, 89.
Spain, 143, 152.
Spearheads, 65, 68, 82, 91, 92, 149, 160.
Spindle-whorls, 47, 71, 89, 145, 148.
Spoons, 46, 47, 57, 66, 76, 106, 107, 153.
Sprendlingen, 157.
Spurs, 80, 158, 174.
Stade-on-Elbe, 20, 21.
Stamped patterns, 21, 29, 59, 155, 156, 159, 161, 168.
Star-pattern, 9, 34, 45.
Stature, 70.
Staunton, Mr. J., 85.
Steeple Bumpstead, 14, 137–139.
Step-pattern, 38, 39, 144.
Stirrups, 80, 90, 91, 174.
Stodmarsh, 57

Stone, Bucks., 35.
Strap-ends, 40, 57, 106, 107.
Strathclyde, 7.
Stratton, 106.
Strike-a-lights, 81, 162.
Stycas, 12, 104.
Style I, 8, 10, 43, 61, 155.
— II, 10, 11, 15, 29, 43, 48, 87, 153, 154, 166.
— III, 13, 14, 15, 17, 159, 166.
Stylus, 75, 112.
Sussex, 6.
Swastika, 21, 28, 88, 89, 106, 161, 170.
Sweden, 23, 24, 161–168.
Swords, 15, 16, 48, 66, 68, 70, 71, 85, 90, 92–94, 98, 148, 159.
Sword-guards, 48, 95.
Sword-pommels, 11, 48, 93, 152, 155, 160.
Szilágy Somlyó, 8, 144, 156.

Taplow, 10, 44, 48, 63–65.
Tara brooch, 14.
Terrets, 67, 167.
Teutonic art, 8.
Thames, 91, 94, 96, 113, 118.
Thaxted, 117.
Theodore, 13, 14.
Thor, 161.
Thor's hammer, 128.
Thorfast, 96.
Tidfirth, 123.
Tinning, 37.
Tissington, 63.
Toilet implements, 46, 71, 73, 81, 89, 137, 146, 147, 153.
Tolnau, 157.
Torcs, 107, 108, 168.
Trewhiddle, 15, 96, 99–101, 136.
Trial-pieces, 114, 115, 128, 140, 141.
Triskele, 81, 88.
Tromsö, 159, 168.
Tumblers, 51, 76, 146.
Tweezers, 22, 46, 79, 84, 145.
Twickenham, 23, 62, 63.
Typology, 38.

Ulfilas, 164, 171.
Union-knot, 113, 126, 166.
Union-pins, 43, 58.
Urnes, 18.
Urns, cinerary, 20.

Vandals, 143, 152.
Vendel, 10, 13, 14.
Vermand, 9, 144.
Vikings, 16, 128, 161, 163.

Vine-scroll, 11, 13, 16, 91, 124.
Virginia, 142.
Visigoths, 143.
Von Grienberger, 119.

Wales, 119.
Wallingford, 112.
Walluf, 80, 157.
Walthamstow, 57.
Wansdyke, 3.
Waterford, 142.

Wayland, 97.
Weaving iron, 56, 67, 148.
Weights, 59, 161.
Welsh, 1.
Wendover, 117.
West Bergholt, 117.
Westmeath, 136.
Whale's bone, 96, 163.
Wheathampstead, 79, 80.
White-metal, 41.
Wigberlow, 89.
Wight, Isle of, 1, 6, 11, 53, 67, 144.

Winchester, 6, 15, 17, 110.
Wingham, 57, 77.
Witham, river, 91, 98.
Woodstone, 83, 89.
Work-boxes, 74.
Writing-tablet, 112.
Wulfhere, 6, 12.
Wye, 59.

York, 16, 124.
Yorkshire, 45, 48, 62, 89, 114, 115.